Yoka Daishi's
Realizing the Way

Published by The Buddhist Society
Patron: His Holiness the Dalai Lama
Registered Charity No. 1113705

Published by The Buddhist Society, 2017
© The Buddhist Society, 2017
Text © The Zen Trust

This publication has been generously supported
by The Hokun Trust and The Zen Centre, London

ISBN: 978-0-901032-45-4 (The Buddhist Society)

A catalogue record for this book is available from the British Library

Text by Yoka Daishi
Translation and Commentary by the Venerable Myokyo-ni
Transcription, text and editing by Michelle Bromley
Edited by Sarah Auld
Designed by Avni Patel

Printed in Padstow, Cornwall by TJ International

The Buddhist Society
58 Eccleston Square
London
SW1V 1PH
T: 020 7834 5858
E: info@thebuddhistsociety.org
thebuddhistsociety.org

Yoka Daishi's
Realizing the Way

Translation and Commentary by the

Venerable Myokyo-ni

Abridged from Yoka Daishi's
Song on Realization of the Way

Fragrance
of the Dharma
Hōkun Trust

CONTENTS

The Buddhist Society is privileged to publish this commentary by Venerable Myokyo-ni (Irmgard Schloegl 1921–2007) on Yoka Daishi's *Realizing the Way*.

Nine years ago Ven Myokyo-ni died in the Rinzai Zen training monastery that she had founded eleven years before, surrounded by some of her senior disciples. Her spirit lives on, not just in the tangible bricks and mortar of the two training monasteries that she set up, but also in her teachings, some recorded, some published and more importantly in the hearts of all those who were her disciples. Her spirit still speaks to a much wider circle of friends and acquaintances, including those who had perhaps heard her speak, or who had picked up one of her books or listened to a recording.

I had the extraordinary good fortune to meet her in the early seventies when she had recently returned from Japan and was working as the Librarian at The Buddhist Society. I was at that time undertaking a training as a Jungian Analyst and had for years been interested in Buddhism, partly through the writings of CG Jung and from my own reading and study going back to my school days and time as a medical student. I wanted to learn something of Buddhism and particularly Zen, and was directed to The Buddhist Society, the foremost Buddhist institution of the time and the most open, as it taught all schools of Buddhism. I had heard it was possible to study Zen Buddhism there. When I called the Society I was invited to 'Come to the Library.' 'Our Librarian

Dr. Irmgard Schloegl has just come back from Japan, you might like to talk to her', said a voice.

On our first meeting I was instantly struck by her natural warmth and vitality, and her wide interest in science and psychology. As I was training as a Jungian Analyst I could hardly believe my good fortune, as here was a person that not only had an interest in Jung but had also spent twelve years in Japan at a leading Rinzai monastery in Kyoto and had returned to teach Zen. There was a great sense of immediacy in her company. Her smoking at that time was continuous, and her enjoyment of conversation was equally great. She loved horses and nature of all kinds, and had as well an appreciation of good whisky. There was nothing otherworldly about her. On the contrary she seemed rooted in the present, and yet there was something indefinable about her that I could not put my finger on. This indefinable quality that I was barely conscious of grew much greater as I progressed in my practice, and remains an enduring aspect of my memory of her. One thing that I did realize immediately was that I had found a teacher, more importantly my teacher. Many who met her at the time and since had a similar response.

That started a relationship that lasted until her death as Venerable Mykyo-ni, Anjusan in March 2007.

I really understood nothing about Buddhism other than the teachings at a purely intellectual level. Ideas of transformation, and 'individuation' were just concepts that I paid lip service to. I reluctantly had to admit this to myself, but I knew that and really wanted to immerse myself in this process of learning, though I had no idea how.

On the other hand, here was someone who had read the teachings, was immersed in the teachings, who lived and breathed the teachings, and ultimately became the teachings. So it was with her, but I did not, could not, fully appreciate that, nor see it at the time. What I did realize was that she was unlike anyone I had met before.

On one occasion as I was beginning to have some idea of Zen and Zen Practice, I was asked to accompany her to see the Lipizzaner horses – a great love of hers – from the famous Vienna Riding School at White City in London, performing a form of dressage originating from the time of Xenophon, an ancient Greek General from around the time of the Buddha. We watched as the horses performed with their grooms, the spirited dressage based only on their natural movements, 'half passes', 'counter-canters', 'pirouettes' and 'piaffes', as well as the 'airs above the ground'. She mentioned that Lipizzaners only begin their training at around four years old, the age that some thoroughbreds are retiring from racing. In the interval she told me that they work with the same groom for up to eight years to master the complex movements required of them. It is a relationship based on trust, and one that rewards man and horse equally. She leant over and said with special emphasis, 'their training requires only three things: perfection of form, strength, and a willingness to learn'. She was also referring to Zen Training, as well as anything that is truly learnt in the body regardless of whether one is a horse or a man. In this case it was 'man and horse', and a mirror of the training which uses the 'Bull and his Herdsman' as an important theme in Zen, as well as 'teacher and disciple'. These two opposites, which at first seem so far apart – the unconscious instinctual and untamed sides of our nature with the rational conscious side – grow closer and closer until they fuse together and the two seeming opposites, become one.

Needless to say I felt quite deficient in all three qualities. As I persevered I discovered that these qualities are not really 'mine'. They grow through practice, and, I discovered that 'perfection of form' has a very profound meaning that does not refer at all to physique, but is a capacity to go with the situation. Far from being anything to do with my willpower, 'strength' is something inherent in all of us. It is far greater than anything I can muster up, and grows throughout the training. 'Willingness to learn', is an ability given to all of us mammals, and is crucial to our adaptation to our environment, as well as our spiritual development. It is to do with the thrill of learning something new. We see it first in babies learning to walk. It has been called the 'beginner's mind' in Zen and has a very special place throughout any spiritual life, not just at the beginning, and needs continuous renewing and deepening as time goes by. Anjusan's own life was an example of a deepening experience of what a human life is and can be, and all those who were associated with her, particularly during her final illness in 2007, could not have failed to be transformed in some way by her spirit.

Venerable Myokyo-ni's association with Rinzai Zen began in 1950 when she joined Christmas Humphreys' Zen Class at The Buddhist Society while engaged in postdoctoral work as a mineralogist at Imperial College in South Kensington, London. Humphreys' conversion to Rinzai Zen began on his first meeting with DT Suzuki at the World Congress of Faiths, an event founded by Francis Younghusband, which was held in London in 1936. Humphreys continued as a Zen student, pioneer and teacher for the rest of his life, contributing hugely to the dissemination of Buddhism and in particular Zen, and became the founder of both The Buddhist Society and The Zen Centre, as well as publishing a series of widely-read books, articles and broadcasts.

Irmgard (Schloegl), as she was known at that time, developed a close association with Humphreys and the major figures in Buddhism, including people like Alan Watts and Edward Conze. All the great teachers from Asia, Europe and America visited The Buddhist Society and gave talks there. A time came however in 1960 when she was invited to Japan to study Zen formally, with the aid of a small grant. It was doubtless there, during her Rinzai Zen training at Daitoku-ji monastery in Kyoto, under two gifted masters, Oda Sesso Roshi and his successor, Sojun Kannon Roshi that she would have first read the text republished here. Irmgard Schloegl returned to England permanently in 1972 and developed the small zazen (meditation) group that she had established at The Buddhist Society at Eccleston Square during a brief visit following the death of Oda Sesso Roshi, and before his successor had been appointed. It had been kept going by Tom Harris, who had been a council member of The Buddhist Society and was later a founding Trustee of The Zen Centre.)

From this humble beginning the classes increased in number and size. Many people of all ages and backgrounds were attracted to Zen, and particularly the opportunity to be able to undertake a genuine formal Zen Training in the Rinzai tradition.

Christmas Humphreys died in 1982. Dr. Irmgard Schloegl was ordained and became Venerable Myokyo-ni on 22nd July 1984 at a ceremony at Chithurst Forest Monastery ordination ground, along with a formal retinue of monastics from Japan, at the invitation of the Abbot Ajahn Sumedho (now Luang Por Sumedho), who was a seminal figure in the transmission of the forest tradition of Theravada Buddhism to the West and abbot of Amaravati from 1984 until his retirement in 2010. The tonsure was performed by Soko Morinaga Roshi who had been head monk at Daitokuji during her training, and was at that time master of Daishu-in monastery in Kyoto. Humphreys' former home was inaugurated as The Hermitage of the True Dharma, Shobo-an, at a ceremony following the ordination, and has become the first Rinzai Zen training monastery in England, and one of the few in the West. Following her death in 2007 in Fairlight Zen Monastery, which she had founded in 1996 and where she had lived for the last years of her life, Daiyu (Great Oak) was added to her name, so she is now formally known as Daiyu Myokyo Zenji. We have retained her more familiar name throughout this volume.

This Commentary on *Yoka Daishi's Realizing the Way* is aptly named because it is a manual and guide to help the student 'make real' the teachings and insight of Shakymuni Buddha. Although couched in the framework of the Great Way, the Mahayana, it brings Myokyo-ni's teaching style vividly alive as technical philosophical terms are rendered in simple, everyday, down-to-earth language, with her effortless ability to use just the right word or phrase or nuance, and sometimes include a story to develop a particular teaching point.

This book is compiled from talks given at both The Zen Centre and The Buddhist Society Summer School between 1994 and 2002. Many have been involved in the transcription and editing, particular thanks go to Michelle Bromley, and of course The Zen Centre for their support financially and practically in bringing this work to the attention of the greater public.

Other books include *The Zen Teachings of Rinzai: The Record of Rinzai, from the Chinese of Lin-Chi Lu*, *Wisdom of the Zen Masters* (1976), *The Zen Way* (1977), *Gentling the Bull: The Ten Bull Pictures, a Spiritual Journey* (1980), *The Daily Devotional Chants of The Zen Centre* (2008), as well as translations such as *The Discourse of the Inexhaustible Lamp of the Zen School with Yoko Okuda* (1996).

Desmond Biddulph
President, The Buddhist Society
London, 2016

INTRODUCTION

In China the Tang Dynasty (618–907 CE) became known as the Golden Age of Buddhism, for it signalled the period of independent growth and the flourishing of indigenous Chinese schools. For many centuries scholars and teachers carefully translated, studied and interpreted the Indian Buddhist texts that had been arriving in China via the Asian continent. Slowly sifting through and absorbing the overwhelming diversity of ideas and practices, a deeper understanding of these teachings began to emerge. Adapting and responding to the Chinese mentality and natural disposition, these ideas were now harmoniously incorporated into the native culture. This gave rise to new expressions of the Buddha-dharma and schools with specific teaching lines under the guidance of individual masters began to appear. The development of these schools, including the Zen School, was now based to a large extent on texts composed in China. Zen (Chinese: chan) developed as a reaction against the intellectual and discursive formulations of Indian Buddhism. Instead it advocated that the practice of Buddhism was not confined to the study of texts, nor to just meditation, but that it could be applied to all activities of everyday life. And its foremost concern was to encourage its practitioners to awaken to the Buddha-nature inherent within themselves.

Yoka Daishi, or Yongjia as he is known in Chinese, belongs to this early period of the Zen School. He was born in 665 CE in Yongjia in Zhejiang Province, from where he derived his name. He left home at an early age to become a monk and began his study and practice of Buddhism in the Tiantai School, receiving instruction there from various learned masters. Just as the Sixth Patriarch, Huineng, is said to have awakened on hearing the Diamond Sutra being recited, so for Yoka Daishi it was the Vimalakirti Sutra which led to his deepest insight.

He was encouraged to have his realization verified by an enlightened master, and this prompted him to visit the Sixth Patriarch at Baolin Monastery in Caoqi. His meeting with Huineng is well documented, both in the Platform Sutra of Huineng as well as in The Record of the Transmission of the Lamp. In this hossen (an encounter between two enlightened people) Yoka Daishi's insight was quickly confirmed. This is why he is considered both Dharma-heir and disciple of the Sixth Patriarch, even though he attained his insight independently. Shortly after this meeting Yoka Daishi was eager to leave again, but Huineng persuaded him to stay at least overnight. Thus he became known as the 'overnight enlightened one.'

He returned to his temple in Longxiong and continued to teach for the remaining eight years of his short life. There he wrote the *Song on the Realization of the Way*; his remaining works are compiled in Yongjia's Chan Collection. He died in 713 CE aged thirty-eight, the same year as the Sixth Patriarch.

The title of this poem, *Song on the Realization of the Way*, is variously translated, but is most commonly known as the *Song of Enlightenment*. Venerable Myokyo-ni emphasizes the fact that the Chinese character which Yoka Daishi uses in the title for realization or enlightenment also has the meaning of evidence or proof, of giving testimony or bearing witness. Thus it implies both a verification or authenticity of this experience, as well as the practical application of being able to live out of it or by it. *The Song*, then, is a hymn or eulogy to the Buddha's teachings as well as a guide to realizing them and putting them into practice.

With vivid imagery and striking turns of phrase, the 67 verses weave in and out of the various Mahayana doctrines. Yoka Daishi tells us that the teaching he adheres to is 'the power of the Mahaprajnaparamita/ Which surpasses ordinary human understanding,/ And not even the vault of heaven can encompass it.' Nonetheless with compassion and skilful means he tries to guide us through the innumerable dualities that characterize our human experience. Steering us beyond good and bad, gain and loss, praise and blame and birth and death, he points towards the 'Mani Jewel snugly contained in the womb of the Tathagata.' This gem lies at the heart of Mahayana thought and symbolizes the germ of the Buddha-nature inherent in all sentient beings – hidden and dormant, but containing the potential and promise of liberation. So, discovering that this 'jewel of the Buddha-nature is inalien-ably imprinted on our heart ground,' we may be inspired to try and walk this Path ourselves.

In this endeavour Yoka Daishi, the 'Man of the Way', who embodies all the Buddhist teachings, acts as our guide. He addresses both the beginner just starting out on the Path as well as those well-established in their practice. He points out how to practice even in the face of adversity and warns of the pitfalls that lie along the way. We are reminded not to let ourselves get carried away by sense objects, for it is our heart that gives rise to all our actions and the body must suffer the unfortunate consequences. It is, therefore, pointless to complain or blame others. Repeatedly he stresses the importance of the lineage, and of passing the teachings on correctly. But most of all he emphasizes that the practice pervades the whole of our daily life: 'Walking is Zen, sitting is Zen,/ Talking or silent, moving or still.' And above all it should be done in 'joyful service to benefit all beings.'

The Song on the Realization of the Way is still studied in Zen temples in Japan today and is one of the four classics in the *Record of Four Sections*, which includes *Faith in the Heart*, the *Bull-herding Pictures* and the *Principles of Zen Meditation*. Yoka Daishi's works also influenced the development of Korean Son (Zen) during the Koryo and Choson periods, when his texts were studied and frequently cited.

Venerable Myokyo-ni (1921–2007) studied this text during her training at Daitoku-ji in Japan and in turn used it herself in giving teisho (formal talks in which a text is presented and commented on). These talks covered a period of eight years (1994–2002) and were given at the Zen Centre and the Buddhist Society Summer School. The present translation and commentary dates from this period.

Myokyo-ni's talks were always very down-to-earth, using a variety of teaching stories from many traditions as well as familiar fairy tales and practical examples from everyday life. This teisho was a great inspiration to all those who heard it then. May it continue to encourage others on the Way.

Michelle Bromley, 2010

1 *Do you not know the Man of the Way who has nothing*
   further to seek?
   He neither shuns fanciful thoughts nor seeks for the Truth,
   For in Truth, delusion and Buddha-nature are one,
   And this illusory body is the Body of the Dharma.

2 *Truly awakened to the Dharmakaya, not one thing remains.*
   The source of one's own nature is the essence of the
   Buddha-nature.
   The Five Skandhas float hither and thither like clouds
   in the empty sky,
   The Three Poisons come and go like foam blown on water.

3 *If the Truth is realized, there is neither self nor other.*
   At that all Karma is instantly wiped out, even that of the
   Avici Hell,
   But those who regale sentient beings with false teachings
   Will suffer their tongues being pulled out for innumerable
   Kalpas.

4 *When suddenly awakened to the Dhyana of the Tathagatas,*
   The Six Paramitas and the 10,000 Practices are already
   completed.
   Although to the dreamer the Six Realms are vividly real,
   After Awakening even the Great Chiliocosm is void
   and empty.

5 *There are neither faults nor benefits, neither gain nor loss;*
In that deep, calm state nothing is lacking.
Till now the mirror had never been polished,
But now it shines brilliantly clear.

6 *Who is without thought, who not born?*
If truly not born, no-birth is gone too.
Ask a wooden puppet whether and when seeking
  the Buddha
And engaging in training can open Enlightenment.

7 *Let go of the Four Great Elements, do not hold on to them.*
In accord with the deep, calm state, eat and drink
  as you like.
Impermanent are all forms, and so all are void –
This is the complete, unexcelled insight of the Buddha.

8 *The true monk shows firm determination.*
If there is one who will not let the Passions ride him, show!
Root and origin being truly cut off is the Seal of the Buddha;
Collecting leaves and searching for branches stifles
  attainment!

9 *People do not know the Mani Jewel*
Nor that it is snugly contained in the Tathagata's Womb.
The Sixfold Wondrous Function is void and again not void.
In full light, the One Way is form and is not form.

10 *Once the Five Modes of Seeing are purified and the Five*
  Powers attained,

They are confirmed and known; no need to measure
 or speculate.
Although all kinds of reflections may be seen in the mirror,
How could one take hold of the moon's reflection in
 the water?

11 *Always on his own, step for step by himself,*
 So the liberated one playfully walks the one road to Nirvana,
 Humming a classical tune. Heart empty and manners
 naturally courteous,
 Lean of form and firm of bone, nothing can deflect him.

12 *All the sons of Buddha are poor,*
 But their poverty is material, not of the spirit.
 While the body is clothed in coarse threadbare robes,
 The heart contains peerless spiritual treasure.

13 *This treasure, however much used, is never exhausted*
 In the joyful service to benefit all beings as suits their needs.
 The Three Bodies and Four Wisdoms mature in the body,
 The Eight Types of Deliverance and Six Supernormal
  Powers imprint the heart.

14 *The superior man settles it once and for all,*
 The middling and inferior learns much but believes little.
 Just cast off the dirty old clothes you treasure
 And don't boast of your pure living to others.

15 *Endure being slandered and spited by others;*
 Those bent to set heaven on fire will soon tire of it.

When listening to their detractions is like drinking nectar,
All melts away and suddenly the Unthinkable is entered.

16 *If being talked ill of is seen as acquiring merit,*
The scoffers become truly good friends and teachers.
If being reviled without cause sparks neither hatred
     nor liking,
There arise compassion and patience, the powers of
     the Unborn.

17 *In such a one, well-versed in both doctrine and exposition,*
Dhyana and Prajna are whole and complete, unobstructed
     by Sunyata.
But not he alone comes by it, for this is the essence
Of all the Buddhas, as many as the grains of sand
     by the Ganges.

18 *Hearing the lion's roar of fearlessness*
Shatters the brains of hundreds of animals;
Even the scent-bearing elephant gets excited and loses
     his dignity.
Only the heavenly dragon listens cheerfully and rejoices.

19 *I crossed rivers, climbed mountains and forded freshets*
To ask Masters for the Way and trained under them.
But since I managed to find the Way of Sokei (Huineng)
I also find that I need not trouble about birth and death.

20 *Walking is Zen, sitting is Zen,*
Talking or silent, moving or still, the essence is ever at ease.

Even on encountering spears and swords it remains whole
    and perfect,
And poisons, too, fail to disturb its serenity.

21 *Our teacher trained under Dipankara Buddha,*
    And for many Kalpas patiently underwent austerities
        as a hermit.
    I, too, went through many births and deaths –
    Births and deaths endlessly without stopping.

22 *On suddenly realizing the non-originated,*
    Neither praise nor blame cause joy or grief.
    I live in a ramshackle hut in remote mountains –
    Wide and steep they range as I sit under the old pine.

23 *In the wilderness my hut is perfumed with the calmness*
        of Zazen,
    And it is tranquil and peaceful all round.
    Once awakened, there is nothing further to do,
    But phenomena, ever changing, are not of that nature.

24 *Giving, if practised with attachment, may bring good*
        fortune,
    But even rebirth in the heavenly realm is like shooting
        an arrow into the sky.
    Once its momentum is spent, it plunges down again and,
    Contrary to intention, only invites unfortunate rebirth
        in the next life.

25   *Far better, then, is to ascend to Absolute Truth,*
     And with one step to enter the realm of the Tathagata.
     Just stick to the root and do not trouble about the branches;
     It is like the moon reflected in a lapis lazuli bowl.

26   *Now I know that this wondrous Mani Jewel*
     Inexhaustibly benefits self and others.
     The moon is reflected in the stream, a gentle breeze in
         the old pine tree;
     Deep and quiet night – what is it for?

27   *The jewel of the Buddha-nature is inalienably imprinted*
         on the heart ground.
     Mist, dew and clouds make the enlightened one's robe.
     His bowl gentles dragons, and on his staff that
         subdues tigers
     The golden rings chime, oh, so clear!

28   *These are not just figments of my empty imaginings,*
     For the traces of the Tathagata's precious staff are
         intimately familiar.
     I neither seek for truth nor shun errors,
     And have come to know that the Two Truths are empty,
     without shape or form.

29   *Without form is beyond both, empty and not empty,*
     And just this is the true form of the Tathagata.
     There are no obstructions on the heart mirror;
     Brilliantly clear it illuminates as many worlds as
         the sands of the Ganges.

30 *All ten thousand things are contained in one shining jewel*
   That has neither inside nor outside.
   Mere empty emptiness denies the law of cause and effect,
   And creates muddles which invite calamity and misfortune.

31 *Equally ill-conceived is to deny being and instead*
      cling to emptiness
   Like jumping into fire to save oneself from drowning.
   Let go of delusions and take hold of the truth.
   However, both letting go and taking hold are still sham
      and deception.

32 *If a trainee mistakes discipline as his aim rather than*
      a means,
   He in fact takes in the robber mistaking him for his
      own son.
   At that, the good fortune of the Dharma is lost,
      accumulated merit wasted,
   And all that because of the picking and choosing
      of the heart.

33 *This is why the Zen school insists on thorough insight*
      into the heart.
   By the power of this wisdom the deathless is suddenly
      entered.
   The enlightened one takes up the wisdom-sword,
   The banner of Prajna, the flaming Vajra-diamond.

34 *He not only crushes the clever capers of those of Other Ways,*
   But vanquishes even the greatest demons.

He lets the Dharma-thunder roll and sounds the
    Dharma-drum.
Clouds of compassion rise and rain down sweet dew.

35   *Majestic like an elephant or dragon, of boundless benefit to all,*
    Those of the Three Vehicles and Five Natures are made to
    awake.
    Hini, the luscious grass is found only on the highest
    Himalayan slopes;
    From these pastures comes the rich milk that is my delight.

36   *One Nature pervades all natures.*
    The One Dharma contains all dharmas;
    Just as the one moon is fully reflected in all the waters,
    And all the moons of all the waters are of the one moon.

37   *The Dharma-body of all the Buddhas pervades my own nature,*
    And my own nature is also the same as that of all the Buddhas.
    One realm fully encompasses all realms,
    Neither shape nor heart nor Karma are there.

38   *At the snap of a finger, the eighty thousand teachings*
    are perfected
    And all the bad Karma of three Asamkya-kalpas is
    instantly extinguished.
    Words and phrases from outside are but shadows
    That cannot reflect the light of my deepest insight.

39   *Beyond blame or praise,*
    And limitless like space,

It is right here, always calm and serene –
But when you look for it, it cannot be found.

40 *It cannot be grasped nor thrown off*
And, while you can do neither, it is as it is.
When (you are) silent it speaks and when (you are)
    speaking it remains silent.
This bliss-bestowing gate stands wide open without bar or bolt.

41 *If asked what teaching I adhere to,*
I reply that it is the power of the Mahaprajnaparamita
Which surpasses ordinary human understanding,
And not even the vault of heaven can encompass it.

42 *For many Kalpas have I persevered in training,*
And do not want to beguile you with idle words.
I hoist the Dharma-banner of Sakyamuni's teaching
To which I too have become heir.

43 *Kasyapa was the first to whom the Lamp was transmitted,*
And for twenty-eight generations it was handed on in India.
Then Bodhidharma himself brought it across the sea
To our own country, and is its first patriarch here.

44 *As is well known, his robe was transmitted for six generations*
And many came to listen and entered the Way.
Truth has no need to be established, and as for the false,
    it is originally empty.
If both, being and non-being, are put aside, the not-empty
    is voided.

45   *The twenty teachings on emptiness are not revealed*
       to begin with;
   The (True) Nature is the same as Tathagatahood.
   If the heart is swayed by the dust of the sense objects,
   Then heart and things are like traces dulling the surface
       of a mirror.

46   *If the traces are wiped off, the brilliance emerges;*
   Heart and things forgotten, the True Nature shines forth.
   Oh this sorry world of the Decline of the Dharma,
   When sentient beings are poorly endowed and find
       control difficult!

47   *Erroneous views increase as the distance from the*
       Buddha increases.
   As the Dharma declines, Mara's strength grows,
       and with it hatred.
   Even though they hear the Tathagata's sudden
       teachings expounded,
   It would not shake them out of decline, as a brick
       is smashed at one stroke.

48   *The heart instigates all actions and the body suffers*
       all the consequent misfortunes.
   So do not complain about or blame others.
   If you do not wish to incur unlimited bad Karma
   Do not slander the Tathagata's Wheel of the True Dharma.

49   *Only sandalwood trees grow in a sandalwood grove.*
   Only lions inhabit the primeval jungle,

And they alone play about in that vast wilderness.
No other animals live there and no birds fly.

50 *Only the lion cubs follow at the foot of their parents;*
When three years old, they roar full-throated.
How could jackals pursue the Lord of the Dharma?
Thousands of shape-shifting imps gape open-mouthed.

51 *The complete and sudden teachings have nothing to do*
*   with human sentiments;*
If there is doubt, nothing is settled and quarrels are sure
*   to arise.*
This is not just the babbling of an old mountain monk,
My fear is that your learning might land you in the cave
*   of either eternalism or nihilism.*

52 *No is not No, nor is yes Yes;*
Even a hair's breadth difference and it goes a thousand
*   miles apart.*
When 'Yes', a Naga girl suddenly becomes a Buddha,
When 'No', Zensho Bhikku falls living into hell.

53 *From when I was young I have enjoyed scholarly pursuits.*
I studied the Sutras, Sastras and Commentaries,
Quibbling about names and form and forgetting the body.
All is like diving into the ocean to count the grains of
*   sand there!*

54 *The Tathagata strongly condemned such pursuits,*
For what is the use of counting up the treasures of others?

My former achievements and efforts now seem useless,
But for years I was blown about like dust in the wind.

55 *If the seed-nature (where we come from) is not properly*
   understood,
   The Tathagata's complete and sudden teachings cannot
   be reached.
   Although the Two Vehicles are devout, they lack the Way
   of the Heart,
   And as for those of Other Ways, they are intelligent
   but lack genuine Wisdom.

56 *There are those who, foolish and childish,*
   Mistake the empty fist or pointing finger for Truth.
   But mistaking the pointing finger for the moon
   dissolves all their merit
   And, like phantoms they bob about in the sense fields
   of objectivity.

57 *Seeing the emptiness of all things is becoming Buddha.*
   If a name can be put to it, it is called Kanjizai Bodhisattva
   ('Seeing all Things').
   Truly seen into, the karmic bonds are originally empty.
   If not fully seen into, the karmic debts for all past deeds
   are fully exacted.

58 *If the starving refuse to eat of the banquet spread before them,*
   Or the sick spurn the help of the doctor, how can they be helped?
   Practising Zen while in the realm of desire becomes the
   power of Prajna.

The lotus blooms unblemished amid the flames.

59 *Yuse (Bhikku) had committed a heinous crime, but with*
   genuine insight into No-birth,
   He at once became Buddha (awakened), and now still exists.
   The lion's roar proclaims fearlessness.
   Alas, foolish and stubborn like old leather, people do
   not know it.

60 *All they know is that grave offences obstruct the*
   attainment of enlightenment,
   And so they do not see the door of the Tathagata's
   secret teachings.
   As to the monk who had committed a murder, and the
   other guilty of a carnal offence,
   Upali's understanding of their offence is shallow, only
   further tightening their bonds.

61 *But Vimalakirti instantly dissolved their doubts*
   Like frost and snow vanish in the radiance of the hot
   midday sun.
   The power of enlightenment is utterly incomprehensible,
   The wondrous functioning is as incalculable as the
   sands of the Ganges.

62 *Then the Four Necessities are gladly offered;*
   Ten thousand pieces of yellow gold are not enough,
   Even bones crushed and body broken do not pay
   For one phrase that obliterates the Karma of millions
   of Kalpas.

63   *Tathagatas as innumerable as the sands of the Ganges*
    confirm
That the Dharma King is of unsurpassed splendour.
Now that I truly understand this Mani Jewel, I know
That all true believers are in accord with it.

64   *Clearly seen, not a single thing exists,*
And there is neither human being nor Buddha.
A Great Chiliocosm is like spray blown on the ocean,
And sages and saints are but flashes of lightning.

65   *Even though an iron wheel was turning on one's head,*
Though the sun may turn cold and the moon red-hot,
The clear radiance of Dhyana and Prajna can never be lost.
Not even all the Maras combined can destroy the true
    Teachings.

66   *The elephant steadfastly pulls the carriage uphill;*
How could the grasshopper in the rut ward it off?
A big elephant does not play about in a hare's track.
Great Satori is not hemmed in by little rules.

67   *So do not try to measure with your narrow views*
The vast expanse of heaven.
If you have not yet understood,
I'll sort it out for you.

1   *Do you not know the Man of the Way who has nothing*
        further to seek?
    He neither shuns fanciful thoughts nor seeks for the Truth,
    For in Truth, delusion and Buddha-nature are one,
    And this illusory body is the Body of the Dharma.

2   *Truly awakened to the Dharmakaya, not one thing remains.*
    The source of one's own nature is the essence of the
        Buddha-nature.
    The Five Skandhas float hither and thither like clouds
        in the empty sky,
    The Three Poisons come and go like foam blown on water.

Commentary

Yoka Daishi is considered both a contemporary and a Dharma heir of the Sixth Patriarch, Huineng (638–713 CE). His *Song on the Realization of the Way* has always been a favourite text. It is particularly relevant for us because it is a very early text, and deals much more with the Mahayana teachings than the later Zen texts do, which consist mainly of questions and answers between master and seeker.

The title already indicates the main theme. The Chinese term, here translated as 'realization', could be considered the logos of the Zen school. It begins with Bodhidharma's 'a special transmission outside the scriptures', which demands more than just knowledge of the scriptures – not just the understanding of them intellectually, but the realization of them in the sense of 'realizing one's assets', to come into the use of them, being free to make use of them. Thus, learnedly quoting scriptures is spurned by the Zen school, not because it denies the scriptures, but because it considers mere knowledge pitifully inadequate. We all know, Christians and Buddhists alike, that we should love one another, but do we, can we? To come into the inheritance of the spiritual teachings, to be able to put them into effect – in short, to live them rather than to talk about them – that is true 'realization'.

The Chinese character can also mean to manifest or appear, and is a standard term for enlightenment. But this same character also has another meaning that frequently goes together with the context of 'realization': that is the connotation of proof or evidence – giving evidence of having come into, having realized, and now being able to use and handle, the insight.

In its development within the Chinese cultural framework and social climate, and to render Buddhist concepts more readily acceptable, Zen adopted some of the Daoist terminology. The term that comes to mind at once is Dao, the Way, a synonym for the Buddha's Way, for the Dharma, for the way all things really are. Indeed, Verse 25 of Laozi's Daodejing ends with, 'Man obeys the laws of Earth; Earth obeys the laws of Heaven; Heaven obeys the laws of Dao and Dao obeys the laws of its own inherent nature.' Zen texts equate a 'Man of the Way' with a fully-realized person. And so Yoka Daishi opens his *Song on the Realization of the Way* with the rhetorical question 'Do you not know the Man of the Way who has nothing further to seek?' This 'nothing further to seek', which became a favourite phrase of Master Rinzai three centuries later, refers to the Mahayana teaching of the Three Stages of Training: of studying, pondering or meditating, and nothing further to learn or seek. This 'Man of the Way' is, so to speak, the role model we want to follow; we want to become like him.

So let us look in more detail. The Dao or Dharma is the principle that is inherent in all of us. As the Buddha said, 'How wonderful, how miraculous! All sentient beings are fully endowed with the wisdom and power of the Tathagata. But sadly because of their attachments, human beings are not aware of it.' They do not realize it as long as they have those attachments. My immediate reaction is likely to be 'But surely I have no attachments. I am, after all, going the Buddha's Way. I have no attachments whatsoever!'

This view is just as much an attachment as anything else, and somehow I hang on it. As long as I am there, as long as there is the feeling of an 'I', there is attachment. Without attachments there can be no 'I'. It is quite wonderful how all the Buddha's teachings, however variously expressed, always link back to two or three of the basic insights. If we look carefully, what do we see? It is not that I have attachments; it is not even that the attachments have me. Rather, I am the attachments, and so it is no good for me to try to get rid of my attachments because I cannot do that anyway, I cannot pull myself up by my own bootstraps. The purpose of training, therefore, is to little by little whittle away a tiny attachment here, a bit of 'I' there. What am I really most attached to? Myself, my convictions, my opinions, my rights, my this and that. Look around, look at the newspapers. We will see how very much we are under the sway of attachments.

A 'Man of the Way', by contrast, has realized the Way. There are no more attachments. Master Rinzai also says of this 'Man of the Way' that he has nothing further to do. However, we must not mistake 'nothing further to do' for inactivity, for sitting comfortably without stirring. Actually, a 'Man of the Way' has many things to do – in essence, to help others – but he himself has nothing further to seek. He has realized his training; has attained full insight, and so no longer needs to look for anything. We always chase after something new, something more, something bigger, something better, something faster. But the True Man has nothing further to seek. He has realized his assets and now, as a 'Man of the Way', lives his life – not for himself because that feeling has gone, but open-endedly, for others. And as such, 'He neither shuns fanciful thoughts nor seeks for the Truth.'

We feel that once the Way is truly realized, fanciful thoughts will not come up anymore. We could not be more mistaken! A superb example of not shunning them is given in the story of the Japanese Samurai who, after years of loyal service to his liege lord, began to feel a tremendous draw towards Buddhism and Zen training. He fought it because to leave his liege lord and enter a monastery would be the most despicable thing, unthinkable for a Samurai. After grappling with it for five years, he could bear it no longer (we are reminded here of the Buddha, who also could no longer bear his problem, and left palace, wife and child). One night, with his heart at breaking point, the Samurai crept out and joined a Zen monastery. After twelve years of formal training and having 'nothing further to seek', he left the monastery to go on pilgrimage, as was customary. And as the Dharma and the karmic connections usually arrange it, hardly had he left the mountain monastery and walked along the valley, when towards him on horseback came a Samurai. They recognized each other, having served the same liege lord. The mounted Samurai looked at the beggarly figure. 'Unbelievable! Despicable! How could a Samurai leave his liege lord?' He drew his sword to lop off his head, but thought, 'No! The sword of a Samurai is noble and honourable, not to be sullied with the blood of such a creature!' He sheathed his sword and, on riding past, spat full into the monk's face. In the act of wiping off the spittle, the monk had a fanciful thought, a memory of what would have happened and how he would have responded, emotionally as well as physically, if that had happened twelve years ago. At that moment he realized what a tremendous change had taken place. He turned round and made three full prostrations towards the mountain monastery and composed a little poem: 'The mountain is the mountain, and the Way is the same as of old. Verily, what has changed is my own heart.' It is this change of heart which is the important thing. Fanciful thoughts come up quite naturally with memory, but now they have no more power, so 'He neither shuns fanciful thoughts, nor seeks for the Truth.' He 'has nothing further to seek.'

Nor does the 'Man of the Way' 'seek for the Truth': it is no good to seek the Truth abstractly. We have to do the training. In Zen practice there is much emphasis on training with the body – it is the basis of Daily Life Practice and of Zen practice. We have a lot of trouble with this training with the body because, from of old, we believe in mind over body. We may pamper the body nowadays, as some do but, by and large, we do not trust the flesh, for surely it is our 'understanding' that is more important? If only I understand it, I'll know it. But my understanding is only in the head, it cuts no ice at all, and fails at the moment it really comes down to the nitty-gritty.

'For in Truth, delusion and Buddha-nature are one.' That same nature is in all of us. In Truth, there is no difference, but subjectively there seems all the difference in the world. I may spend my life chasing this, that, or the other, and be unhappy because I cannot have it, and suffer because I will not accept facts. There is a Zen saying: 'Every day is a good day.' Every day is a good day? I have just cut half my finger off! I have an abscess on my gum! I have had the worst possible news about my job! Every day is a good day? Well, on the surface it does not look like it. However, if there is really that full feeling of being rooted in what is and not just in 'I' only, then the abscess and the hurt finger, etc. need to be taken care of, but it is still a good day. That is what is meant when the Buddha, says 'Suffering I teach, and the Way out of suffering.' He does not say that it does not hurt if we lose a leg or sprain an ankle or get old and disabled. Of course it hurts, but how we react to that pain is what counts.

So, 'in Truth, delusion and Buddha-nature are one.' In a way, we know it. In a way, we also know that inside us there are really two inhabitants. There is one who inevitably knows and may quietly whisper. But mostly we do not like to hear that whispering, we do not like the message that comes through because we have got other ideas. I want to go out for the day, even though I know I shouldn't. There is a quiet voice that says, 'Don't!' Either I refuse to listen to it, or, more often, I make all kinds of fanciful excuses in order to be able to do with good conscience what I want to do, what I know I should not do. And so I deceive myself. Are we aware of that, really and truly?

It is useful, therefore, to listen to this voice of Truth, this information which is in all of us and informs all forms – just as the snowdrop knows when it is time to come up and as the leaves know when it is their time to fall in autumn. They obey, they do it. This inborn information is the Buddha's wisdom and power. Those soft crocus spears of green, what gives them the strength to pierce through semi-frozen ground? That is the wisdom and power of the Buddha-nature; not the brute aggression with which we quarrel and fight with each other, but that enormous power which we also call 'life force' by which we live.

Think of a little child. When it is born, it is incapable of doing anything. How long does it wriggle its arms and legs about before it begins to crawl? Once it has learnt to do that, it is time – and it knows it – to try and get up on its legs. These, of course, will not yet carry it. So it grapples to pull itself up on whatever it can get hold of, and it tries to stand up. Then it falls down, and howls, but it does not think 'No, I can't do this!' It just tries again, falls down again and howls. It never thinks 'I give up!' What is it that makes it persevere?

That strength is in all of us, only we do not respond to its promptings, or we misunderstand them, and this is what delusion is all about. Fundamentally, in Truth, the two are one. In the Mahayana view, 'The Passions are the Buddha-nature, and the Buddha-nature is the Passions.' We know the power of the passions when they really ride us, when we really want or are convinced of something, when we are in a real rage, or when we think that we really know and would bet our life on it. It is the same energy, force or power that wildly flares in the passions, and as such deludes us, even though it is the universal current, the full strength or power of the Buddha-nature. The one is the other: not on the surface, not in the functioning, but in essence.

And so, therefore, 'in Truth, delusion and Buddha-nature are one, / And this illusory body is the Body of the Dharma.' Here we come back to the word 'Dharma'. We said in the beginning that Dharma and Dao are used interchangeably. The Chinese concept of Dao, the Way, and Dharma in the Indian Buddhist sense of the 'way all things really are', readily express the same meaning. The Dharma has no form. Speaking of the 'Body of the Dharma', 'body' is used not in the sense of a form, but as the essence of the Dharma, perhaps like the 'body' of a wine, which is not something physical, but a quality that is nonetheless clearly perceptible. However, one can only talk about it, one cannot touch it, cannot see it. One can taste it, but strictly speaking it is not a taste either. It is a quality that comes over in drinking the wine, but one cannot put one's finger on it, and one cannot put one's mouth to it. So in that sense the 'Dharma Body', the 'Body of Information', informs us of the way all things really are. And this, our physical body, made up of the four great elements, is impermanent and ever-changing – coming to be, existing for a span and then ceasing to be again. Yet it is accurately informed and fully endowed with the wisdom and power of the Tathagatha. Whilst it lives, it too is the 'Body of the Dharma'. So we need to listen to this inherent wisdom which he pointed out and, in so doing, not mistake the pointing finger for the moon, for it is within, it is not something to be got from outside.

'Truly awakened to the Dharmakaya, not one thing remains. / The source of one's own nature is the essence of the Buddha-nature.' Bodhidharma brought Zen Buddhism from India to China. Tradition tells of his meeting with Emperor Wu, a devout Buddhist who, rather pleased with himself, told the Indian monk of his good works and piously asked what merit he had thereby gained. Bodhidharma said, 'None whatsoever!' Startled, Emperor Wu asked, 'What then is the essence of Buddhism?' And Bodhidharma replied, 'Vast emptiness. Nothing holy.'

So, 'Truly awakened to the Dharmakaya, not one thing remains', not one thing remains in that vast realm of emptiness. I would like to make a little addendum to that 'Vast emptiness. Nothing holy.' Before we get too pleased with such a radical answer that sweeps everything away, we would do well to consider that this was not just said for the fun of it. In front of a sixth century Chinese emperor, the 'Son of Heaven', governing the Middle Kingdom, one lies trembling with one's face down and obeys. The slightest twitch and 'Off with his head!' Bodhidharma was fully aware that his answer might meet with just that response. But he nonetheless maintained, 'Vast emptiness. Nothing holy.' That reply really roused the Emperor who, glaring at the Indian monk, now asked, 'Who is he who stands before Us?' 'Not known!', came the reply; no 'I', no fear, no death – no-thing. There he stood, a form that incorporated the principle, and as that, not afraid. The Emperor let him go.

'The Five Skandhas float hither and thither like clouds in the empty sky.' The Five Skandhas are: body/matter; feelings and sensations; perception/thoughts; volitional/mental formations; and consciousness. In Buddhist teaching that is what comprises an individual person. Nowhere is there any trace of an 'I' to be found. The usual analogy for it is a cart – you can pull it or ride in it, it is useful while it exists, but if it is taken apart and broken down into wheels, axle, body, etc., where then is the cart? Is there a cart at all? Yet without a doubt it was rolling along quite happily just now. So these Five Skandhas help us to realize that this is what makes up a human being, and they themselves also constantly change, they 'float hither and thither like clouds in an empty sky.'

And 'The Three Poisons come and go like foam blown on water.' The Three Poisons are also called the Three Fires, which are apt to flare up as long as 'I' am there. They are desire, hatred and delusion. The Fires? At this moment, I cannot see them, nor do I feel anything. But the next time I feel, 'I must have, cannot do without, will die unless...', then I no longer have any time to consider whether this might be a Fire that is flaring up, because it has already carried me away. The same thing happens when 'I cannot bear it anymore', or 'He/she/it is outrageous, more than flesh and blood can stand!' This occurs when somehow, almost unbeknown to ourselves, our neighbour across the garden fence or our colleague in the office suddenly takes on the features of a devil. 'I cannot bear it any longer!' This is the bane of my life, isn't it? Something must be done to get rid of it. From personal infatuation or enmity to wars – deluded and inflamed by the Fires, we all suffer the consequences. This is what the training is really for – long and painstaking, but in the end the Fires are transformed and will no longer carry away.

3   *If the Truth is realized, there is neither self nor other.*
    At that all Karma is instantly wiped out, even that of the
        Avici Hell,
    But those who regale sentient beings with false teachings
    Will suffer their tongues being pulled out for innumerable
        Kalpas.

4   *When suddenly awakened to the Dhyana of the Tathagatas,*
    The Six Paramitas and the 10,000 Practices are already
        completed.
    Although to the dreamer the Six Realms are vividly real,
    After Awakening even the Great Chiliocosm is void
        and empty.

Commentary

'If the Truth is realized there is neither self nor other.' Then the seeing has become Buddha-seeing, seeing all things the way they really are. This insight of 'neither self nor other' is common to all religions. Mahayana or Northern Buddhism puts a lot of emphasis on the Bodhisattva (literally, 'enlightened being'), whose state of realization leads to Buddhahood. All Mahayana training is along the Mahasattva-Bodhisattva Way. The Bodhisattva has lost the sense of 'I', has come to the Truth of the Buddha-seeing where there is 'neither self nor other', so he can be freely available to whatever is needed within the situation. Hence his other aspect is that of compassion, the mark or condition of which is 'I'-lessness.

'If the Truth is realized', if the sight is really cleared, 'there is neither self nor other.' That realization has ramifications. This is reflected in the Zen saying, 'I look at the flower and the flower looks at me!' Now, a flower is lovely. Therefore, it is not too difficult to imagine that the flower looks at me, but in that we deceive ourselves. Only when it can also be extended to, 'The floorboard looks at me – I look at the floorboard' is it genuine. If everything I look at looks at me, then there is a full relationship with everything, and then there are no longer any 'dead' things. We also discover this when we really practice giving ourselves into what at this moment is being done. We have to be very careful with language here. It is not what I am doing at this moment, but what at this moment is being done or is happening. Then things suddenly come alive, even things that I do not particularly care about or just consider unimportant come to life in a most remarkable way.

'If the Truth is realized, there is neither self nor other. / At that all Karma is instantly wiped out, even that of the Avici Hell.' Karma, roughly speaking, is the consequence of what we do. By good actions we can steer clear of tenure in the three lower or unhappy realms, but not from bondage on the Wheel. Only when there is no more self or other and actions are no longer intentional is Karma worn out too. Meanwhile, intentional actions have results: if I overeat, I get a stomachache; if I eat rotten food, I get food poisoning. We very easily get carried away by activity, either overdoing or underdoing things. In the duality of 'I' and other, I can drown in water and can also die of thirst. As long as there is the split, I am out of harmony with the scheme of things, and so the results of what I do willy-nilly create Karma.

Buddhism conceives of life as a Wheel with six states of being, and also of tiered 'worlds' with the Buddha and Bodhisattvas on top, descending through to the divine states and the human realm, and finally down to the miserable states and hells below, Avici being the deepest, the most unhappy and painful hell. So you can look at existence as being both an ever-turning wheel and as states in elevation, going up and down. All of these states are lovingly described by various Buddhist scholar devotees, but for us it is useful only to realize that these are not states out there, but that we have our existence in them, shunting from one to the other, up and down, umpteen times a day. This becomes clear in meditation.

We must not mistake descriptions of inner states for outward localities. We now know that there is no concrete Paradise somewhere on top of a pear-shaped world, nor heavenly host in the stratosphere. Likewise, hell below might be experienced as a volcano, but is not a place. It is, however, important to realize – and that is why we find them in all religions – that these descriptions are accurate psychological maps and, as such, are most useful. In order to actually walk the Buddha's Way, of which we know very little, we need a map in order not to go astray. Being deluded by the feeling of 'I', as separated from all else, makes me prone to going astray, so to have and to follow a map is essential.

Of all the Buddhist hells the Avici is the deepest, and is reserved for those who deceive others, 'regaling sentient beings with false teachings', and so misleading them. This is considered the worst harm, and this is why they have their tongues pulled out. But Yoka Daishi assures us that even the worst and most terrible Karma is wiped out once the Truth is realized.

The delusion of 'I' is our basic delusion. For us, for every 'I', the great wish is for immortality, because the other side of 'I' is fear – which is, in short, fear of oblivion. Fear has many faces – of losing control, of vanishing, of dying, of pain, of fear itself. And so I look to the East or the West for immortality. The alchemists looked for the philosopher's stone, or gold, the elixir that bestows immortality. In Hinduism it is called Amrita or soma juice, and the Chinese Daoists experimented with red cinnabar as the element for immortality. It goes right through human history and cultures – always looking and longing. But sadly I fashioned the wrong picture: 'I' wanting to become immortal, which is not possible, instead of becoming aware of the Buddha-nature, which is within and has never been lacking. Nothing can be said about it; it neither is nor is not. Conceived as an essence, it is inherent and always prevails but, because of this 'looking for something', we seek it elsewhere. Such looking is not necessary and, therefore, 'those who regale sentient beings with false teachings / Will suffer their tongues being pulled out for innumerable Kalpas.' Fear and suffering prevails in all the miserable states on the Wheel. Only when there is no more fear, and thus No-I, is there then just a smooth flowing with what is. At that, 'Karma is instantly wiped out.'

Why are we misled? Why do we look so desperately for something, for our own immortality? Is it not because all forms, being fully informed by the virtue, strength and wisdom of the Tathagata, have an inherent knowledge that we are not all that exists, and that there is something more, something 'other'? Ever since becoming self-conscious, we have somehow become aware of it and are looking for its realization, but also, being deluded, we make false pictures of it. Ever since we climbed down from the trees and became at least semi-human we have felt compelled to picture and to render perceptible what is ineffable. Thus, we tend to project outside what we do not realize is inside, and believe in these pictures. Does the embargo against graven images make sense? The moment we have made a picture for ourselves we believe in it, we see it, but at that moment it misleads us.

The Venerable Ajahn Maha Bowa, a Thai teacher who rarely leaves his jungle Wat, once told of a monk who during meditation suddenly saw a golden ball bouncing up and down in front of him. It almost seemed to invite, as if it wanted to be caught. The monk became distracted, but just as he reached out to grasp it, the ball bounced out of reach. The monk leaned forward to catch it and, not knowing how it happened, he suddenly found himself on his feet chasing the elusive shimmering object. However fast the monk ran to catch it, the ball always kept ahead, turning and spinning all the way and finally it bounced up into a tree. The monk, having by now lost all sense of reality, shinned up after it, following that elusive golden ball from branch to branch. High up in the tree, a branch suddenly began to sway under the monk's weight, and with that he came to himself, and shook with fright at finding himself perilously high up in a tree, unable to get back down. And the golden ball had vanished! In vain he shouted for help and was only found the next morning, shivering and utterly miserable. 'And', finished the Venerable Maha Bowa, 'it served him right! Why did he let his heart jump out and run away from him?'

The heart, our own heart, is that shimmering 'thing'. For that monk it was a golden ball. It will drape itself like a glistening mantle over any object that evokes our liking – or our loathing. And since it is our own heart, there is a feeling of 'I must have it. I cannot be without it!' Whatever 'it' might be, from the most ludicrous to the most elevating, it does not matter. Whatever object it drapes itself over, that object has caught us, even if it is one of dread or fear. In the absence of a material object, it can even manifest as such a 'golden ball'.

What is that power, which is not mine and seems to be in that golden ball, but in fact is in my own heart? It is the power and strength of the Tathagata. What misleads me is my deluded seeing. Mistakenly seeing it as an 'object' outside, I become dazzled and blinded by it. There is a difference between running after that golden ball and just letting it be, not taking issue with it one way or the other. But the moment we pay it any attention, like the monk with the golden ball, we have had it. Thus 'caught', attached to any object, something else takes over. And in Buddhism, thoughts, notions, ideas, etc., are also 'objects', objects of the sixth or mental sense.

But once 'the truth is realized', even the Karma of the Avici Hell is wiped out, because where there is no longer an 'I', Karma has nothing to take hold of. Without 'I', there can be no intention, and no more wrong-seeing either. Without an agent that sets a cause in motion, there is no result and no retribution, because there is nobody to receive it. It is empty, truly empty. And that is why, right from its beginning, the Zen School stresses the Empty Heart. When the heart is truly empty, when there is no 'I' and no other, then there is no-thing left.

'When suddenly awakened to the Dhyana of the Tathagatas', then 'the Six Paramitas and the 10,000 Practices are already completed.' The Six Paramitas are the training way of the Mahayana. Actually, there are ten, but the remaining four are consequent on the six. This is different from the Southern School that works mainly with the Four Noble Truths and the Noble Eightfold Path. The Northern teaching is specifically orientated towards the Bodhisattva Path, hence the Paramitas, 'Going Beyond (beyond 'I')'. The first one is Dana, giving; the second one is Sila, restraint or keeping the Precepts; the third is Ksanti, patient endurance; the fourth is Virya, energy, the fifth Dhyana, meditation and the sixth is Prajna, insight or wisdom.

However, practising them is not a progression from one to the next, but rather, as in a circle, each one contains all the rest. If one considers Dana, or giving: under normal circumstances I am concerned with preserving myself, and so do not fancy giving. As children we are taught to give, and then we start it as a practice. We can at least offer a flower and bring it to the Buddha. I might even get an allotment and start growing flowers. With that a new problem can arise, for now that I have nice flowers I start becoming stingy about picking them. Anyone who has ever had a gardener knows what tyrants they can be – and it is in each of us. So I begin to pick and choose; I may take a flower here and there, but the choicest ones I leave. That is how it starts. Hence giving is the first Paramita, learning to go beyond selfishness.

It is deeply ingrained in us, for at the bottom is the survival instinct, which has, in the presence of the delusion of 'I', gone to excess.

There is a pertinent training story on this theme about Master Joshu. It is said that he came to genuine insight at the age of sixty, and then went on pilgrimages all over China for twenty years, testing himself. Only after that, at the age of eighty, did he start on his teaching career. He lived to be a hundred and twenty, and so spent forty years teaching. It was said that he was so wise that it seemed he had gold on his lips, and he was revered by his monks. One of them, knowing that the Master liked flowers had, in gratitude, raised a couple of bonsai trees for him. These little trees are very difficult to cultivate, and take many years of careful and skilful tending. When they were well matured, the monk took them to Master Joshu and, bowing deeply, presented them as a gift. Master Joshu realized that this monk was 'ripe' and saw the purity of his heart, but he also saw that he was still attached, still caught by shape and form. Therefore, he firmly ordered, 'Drop it!' The monk, being well-trained and responding to the second Paramita (discipline and obedience), did not hesitate, and let go of one pot. The pot broke and with it the little tree, but he could not bear the thought of both being smashed. If you devotedly care for something for many years, you become attached to it, it becomes part of you – we all know that, don't we? So half of his heart was given: the other half still held on. Again Master Joshu ordered, 'Drop it!' and as the second pot shattered, Joshu roared, 'Drop it!' Totally bewildered, and no doubt heartbroken, the monk stuttered, 'But Master, I have nothing more to drop.' Joshu nodded, 'Then take it away.'

If there is nothing more to drop, what remains is the real. As Master Mumon said, 'The heirlooms of the house do not come in by the front door.' They are already inside. When nothing more remains, then it is empty, and all is wide and clear, but it does not come easily. The heart breaks with that final drop. We might usefully remember this the next time something comes along which we do not like, or do not want to lose, or think we cannot do without. 'Drop it!' If the first drop is not complete, then again 'Drop it!' And at that moment something lights up. If we are ready for it, it remains; if not, it goes away again. At moments we have all known this opening, but in a way we also have not really known it, for it has gone away again. 'Suddenly awakened to the Dhyana of the Tathagatas, / The Six Paramitas... are already completed.'

From the giving of the first flower to the complete giving away of 'I' is actually a long, long way. Yet only when I am truly given away is the heart truly empty. That is all that is necessary – the rest takes care of itself. The same applies also to the other Paramitas: each one contains all the others. Therefore, practising the Dana Paramita inevitably entails the practice of the Sila Paramita until the whole self can be laid down. For that, much steady strength is required, and this accrues from Sila, from training in restraint and following the Precepts. Such training is not fashionable today. Moreover, Sila is often translated as 'morality', which in the West gives it a Christian connotation, but this is not implied in the original. Rather, it functions foremost as a training device to produce inner strength, which may also be seen as moral strength, not falling into temptation. 'Virtue' comes close in meaning, and in a way that is really what it is, as when we say, 'By virtue of something, I have been able to do something.' In other words, by virtue of this training there is the strength to act, or the strength to continue when I think I no longer can, so this strength is the opposite of the untrammelled forces of the passions. The Latin root of this word has this meaning, and in the East virtue always implies this cultivated power or strength, like the power of the Way in the Daodejing.

Gradually, with application, as in any training, this strength grows along with it. We also know that when we begin to sit Zazen (meditation practice) our legs hurt, and within a quarter of an hour we want to get up. Legs will always hurt if we sit for a long time, but we learn to endure it, and with practice they do not hurt so much. It is a kind of half-and-half. In every sport skill and strength are cultivated, and so also with the inner training. Fully developed, with no 'I' to throttle it, it is the strength and power of the Tathagata, and that can and does endure, even throughout what is unpleasant. That is why patient endurance, Ksanti, is the third of the Paramitas.

Without this strength, patient endurance soon fizzles out. To patiently endure means to say yes to what I do not particularly fancy, to be able to function nevertheless. It implies the strength to hold together, which is called self-discipline. This is not obedience to what is laid on from the outside, but the inner one that comes from the own heart, that can stand the course even when I do not really want to anymore. So the first three Paramitas of giving, discipline and patient endurance play into and enhance one another, and are an enormous asset to our daily lives. This strength is then further cultivated as spiritual energy, the fourth Paramita. The importance of the Paramita training cannot be stressed enough.

So the Six Paramitas all merge into each other. To help us further, we also have the 10,000 Practices – religious observances of all kinds and types: services, chanting, bowing, prostrations, little extras to tighten things up when they begin to fray. Bowing is found in all religions. In the beginning it might mean very little to us, we might even dislike it, but sooner or later it becomes natural, and then there is a chance of something opening up.

'Although to the dreamer the Six Realms are vividly real, / After Awakening even the Great Chiliocosm is void and empty.' The Six Realms are also the Six Destinies for those who whirl on the Wheel of Change. The Buddha's basic teaching is the Way that leads out from this endless round on the Wheel, Samsara. It thus points to the entrance of deliverance and, seen from this state, the Six Realms are like a dream. Awakening is another term for enlightenment. Since we have various notions about enlightenment, perhaps awakening is a more helpful term – awakening as from a dream.

'Although to the dreamer the Six Realms are vividly real, / After Awakening even the Great Chiliocosm is void and empty.' Basically there is a Great, a Middle one and a Little Chiliocosm. A Little one consists of a thousand worlds, each with its own Mount Sumeru (the mythical centre of the universe), sun, moon, and even its own Buddha. Thousands of these Little Chiliocosms form a Middle one, and thousands of Middle Chiliocosms form a Great Chilocosm. Indian teaching loves to go into multiples of hundreds of thousands only to show how vast things are. And in all this, there is actually nothing. It is no-thing at all!

5 *There are neither faults nor benefits, neither gain nor loss;*
   In that deep, calm state nothing is lacking.
   Till now the mirror had never been polished,
   But now it shines brilliantly clear.

6 *Who is without thought, who not born?*
   If truly not born, no-birth is gone too.
   Ask a wooden puppet whether and when seeking
       the Buddha
   And engaging in training can open Enlightenment.

Commentary

'There are neither faults nor benefits, neither gain nor loss.' The Great Chiliocosm has been found to be void and empty. After awakening there is no duality. In the vast emptiness that has opened up there are neither faults nor benefits, rewards nor punishments, gain nor loss. 'In that deep, calm state', there is neither fear nor longing; in it 'nothing is lacking'. Master Rinzai used to ask his monks, 'At this moment, what is there lacking?' Try it! At this moment, at this infinitesimal short instant – now – what is there lacking? I can't think – and so there is nothing lacking. Just a moment later, and all the things that I think are lacking come flooding in like water through a burst dam, but at this moment nothing is lacking. And so, as long as we are floating in Samsara, 'bobbing up and down in the Sea of

Birth and Death' as the Zen texts like to describe it, naturally there are hopes and fears, faults and benefits, gain and loss, and all 'the ten thousand things'.

The basic Buddhist teachings assert that as long as I exist, there will inevitably be faults and benefits, punishments and reward. There is cause and effect, Karma, gain and loss. But we are told in Verses 3 & 4 that when vast spacious calmness opens up and the awakening from the dream occurs, at that moment all Karma is instantly wiped out. And that is because there is no feeling of 'I' left. When everything has truly turned to no-thing-ness, then every thing is wiped out; in that state there is now nothing lacking. Where there are no things, there can be nothing lacking. If we take 'nothing' as the opposite of 'something' rather than the mystery which it is, then we have firmly put ourselves into the realm of the dreamer, into the Six Realms, where the Wheel churns on and on. But in that 'deep, calm state' which opens with awakening, no Wheel can turn because there is no Wheel. There is nothing, and so nothing lacking.

'Till now', until that awakening has occurred, 'the mirror had never been polished.' The mirror was dull and full of squiggles, and I, the dreamer, looked at the squiggles and took them to be real. Even with our ordinary glass mirrors, unless there is a frame around them, can you actually see the mirror? Have you ever looked carefully? You can see the reflections, not the mirror itself. But when the sun suddenly shines into that mirror you can no longer see reflections – just a blinding radiance; and you quickly close your eyes or you will be blinded. 'Till now the mirror had never been polished', but now, after awakening, 'it shines brilliantly clear.' And so Yoka Daishi asks 'Who is without thought? Who not born?' Thoughts are squiggles on the mirror, such as 'born' and 'unborn', 'form' and 'no-form'. In the Southern scriptures, the Udanas, the Buddha addresses his monks: 'There is, O monks, an Unborn, Uncreated.' Is Yoka Daishi contradicting the Buddha when he asks, 'Who is without thought, who not born?' Master Rinzai used to ask his monks, 'Who, at this moment, stands right before your eyes? Do you know him?' Who is he, this one who is not born, and so is not a 'who' either? Who is without thought? Certainly not 'I', because I myself am thought. I myself, this temporal body as it is, is born and ceases to be. What makes it live? 'There is... an Unborn, an Uncreated.'

The Zen texts stress that all teachings are only medicine to cure specific illnesses; they help the dreamer awake. When the illness is cured, the medicine becomes superfluous. This is shown in the wonderful parable of the raft. The Buddha likens his teaching to a raft, a means for crossing over to the Other Shore. Having arrived there, what is the use of taking that raft on one's shoulders and carrying it over dry land? I cannot imagine what is on the Other Shore, but to make the journey, to cross over on a raft – this is what the Teaching is.

But we need to be careful. The vehicle alone does not carry across; it needs one who rows and steers across. However perfect and unsinkable it may be, the vehicle of itself will not cross over. The river is wide and deep. With nobody steering it, the raft will either be carried downstream, or will very soon come to grief over rapids and on rocks, or it will be stranded on a sandbank, and there sit fast. The vehicle is a means, and must not be mistaken for the end. What is the use of medicine put on the mantelpiece with a big label and there treasured without actually taking it? Or looking at the teachings without being incited to do any training?

This is stressed in the last two lines of Verse 6: 'Ask a wooden puppet whether and when seeking the Buddha / And engaging in training can open Enlightenment?' And again we think of Master Rinzai's, 'Behold the puppets prancing on the stage and look for him behind who pulls the strings.' Forms are such puppets, coming into being, prancing for a while on the stage and then disintegrating again – going into transformation. But who pulls the strings?

We look again at the Wheel as a map that helps us to steer across to that Other Shore. There are the wooden puppets prancing on the stage, bobbing up and down in the sea of birth and death, coming up here, going down there. Who pulls the strings? Look at the centre! There we see that they are driven by the desire for gain and fame, driven by the urge to be some-thing, to be, to exist. And frightened of or resisting not being, ceasing, becoming no-thing. The argument about existence and non-existence is pre-Buddhist, and carries over into Buddhism. 'I' is seen as all our wants and all our fears together, and this 'I' wants to exist; every 'I' does. And in order to do so, to secure my position, the lust for gain and fame arises, and with it the fear of losing. This is also where aggression comes in, and as a result of being in this sorry state of Samsara, whirling on the Wheel, there is not only an increase of our own suffering, pain and unhappiness, but it also extends to the detriment of others. All this, as in a dream, is the urge of 'wanting to be'. This is the root of 'I', the basic delusion. The moment I want to be, I must make myself secure, I cannot help it. All this leads to is thinking, thinking and more thinking, scheming how to manipulate, how to get, how to have my way, my rights, my whatever.

Once we look steadfastly at the base of our intentions, what do we find? Even our deepest, natural intentions, feelings and wishes to do good are definitely 'I'-based. They are to please me, even if they seem altruistic. When it really comes down to it, even if I give my life, and willingly give it, for something, it is still 'I'-based because without that value I cannot or do not want to live. To look at that realistically rather than idealistically will help us to see clearer. Basically we desire to 'become' or to 'be' – whether that is to be good or right, or we want to be rid of a menace (we always have a 'God' or a 'devil' somewhere). This is then extended from 'I' to 'we' to 'our world', which we want to order or coerce according to our liking, forgetting that its nature is night and day. Thus, seen clearly, it may be possible to desist from, rather than being carried away by, one of our many, many false dreams, and to learn to look at the place where our own feet stand.

We tend to shy away into extremes rather than looking at that place where our feet stand. We do so not because some psychologists tell us there might be something ugly or fearful, but because there is a mystery which is impenetrable to 'I'. In our modern times we no longer believe in anything except our own notions. We do not know faith, and think it is just fanciful, a lot of old wives' tales. We have lost the sense of awe and wonder which fills and satisfies the heart, and is where the heart lives. But when the head denies the true spirit which the heart longs for, the heart fashions pictures, sees squiggles in the mirror, and takes them for real.

The head wants to grasp and understand, but you cannot understand a mystery – it is a mystery.

All spiritual traditions warn against attempts to grasp and possess the spirit, the Ineffable Mystery. If we try, the moment we come close it knocks us for six. Fortunately for us, this is rare. More often when we encounter something which is so tremendous that it dwarfs us, we immediately try to denigrate it and make it into 'nothing but'. True, in itself it is nothing, but nothing contains the Tremendous, the potential of Wholeness.

In a Greco-Egyptian mystery play this warning is expressed in the story of a young and ardent acolyte serving in the temple of the great goddess Isis. Every morning and evening he watched the head priest ceremoniously approach the veiled shrine of the goddess, open the curtain to make his offerings and then let the curtain fall again. The young acolyte was inflamed with the desire to see the face of the goddess. He frequently begged and implored the priest to let him have just one glimpse, but the priest always adamantly refused, saying, 'You are not ready for it yet.' But, blinded by his desire, the youngster secretly crept up to the statue one night to lift the veil. Nobody knows what happened, but in one version the priest found him the next morning lying dead in front of the veiled statue. In another it is said that the acolyte went mad – the sudden breaking in of something that is too great cannot be borne.

When 'I', any 'I', comes face to face with it unprepared, it shatters 'I'. A mystery is not to be understood, but to be revered. It speaks to the heart, not to the head. And in bowing to the mystery, the heart opens and can partake of that mystery, is nourished by that partaking.

Until not so long ago, there would be a crucifix in every house, and if there was a study, there would also be a skull with 'Memento Mori' (Remember Death) written underneath it. How morbid we may think, how terrible to live with such negative thoughts all the time! On the contrary, most helpful. They remind us, when the Fires of 'I must' burn, of how it will look before long, in sixty years time, in five years, in five minutes! We do not know. That is helpful to bear in mind.

Zen Master Sokei-an, addressing his students, said, 'When that moment comes, there is nothing more you can do. You fold your hands and go with it to where you have always been.' And if that place is known – which is no 'place', but is where we come from and where we go back to, this spacious expanse in which there is Nothing – then there are no more obstacles and no intentions anymore. But it is not empty. This is the paradox, the mystery. In that emptiness there is complete fulfilment. In that emptiness the forms play. Even at its most horrific, the forms play. But it is essential to be awake in that play, to be aware while partaking; not blindly driven by those elementary forces of gain and fame, of fear and loathing, because that makes us aggressive. It is in blind, careless aggressiveness that we do harm, not only to ourselves but also to others; not only to human beings but to all beings, to the world we live in.

There will be no peace in our world unless we, each one of us, have made peace in our own heart, and there is no more picking and choosing. This is the pivot: with peace in our heart, we at least do not produce any further harm. Without peace, blinded by the Fires, even the best intentions go wrong. We need to be careful. It is not only when we are blindly driven by loathing and hatred: it is even with our best intentions that we mess things up and produce much harm. This is why it is so important to learn to see clearly. Then in a given situation, a course can be adopted which is 'right', in harmony with the long-term situation; clearly seeing, not through the partiality of 'my ideas' and 'my wants', but because the situation demands it.

I, the puppet, have got my ideas, and most of them are irrational and out of touch with reality. However convinced I may be of my sensible, clear understanding and my reasonableness, I am driven from underneath by something quite different. So it is of the utmost importance to look at the place where our own feet stand because there we find those elemental drives, and only then can we begin to work on their transformation. Our first reaction on encountering them is, 'I do not want them!' When forced by our practice to behold them, we become aware of their tremendous strength, so we try to refuse: 'I won't have you!' But the practice admonishes, 'No! Endure. That is what you are to work with. This is what needs to be humanized.'

This is illustrated by the analogy of 'gentling a bull' which is traditionally used in Zen training. The bull symbolizes the tremendous, elemental force of life, which has nothing to do with an individual human being; it is not inhuman, just simply ahuman. The question is how to gentle that tremendous force which is likened to a bull? The analogy shows it to be a lengthy process that demands the strength which accrues from self-discipline, as different from a discipline that is imposed from the outside and blindly obeyed. A real gentling of that tremendous force is the concern of all religions, their formulated teachings set out the way. However varied these formulations are, they proclaim with one voice, 'You yourself must do it.' They set up the rules of the game; we have to get used to them, but above all we ourselves must play. You yourself must do the walking, 'Buddhas only point the Way!'

On this Way that is to awaken me from my sleep I will, however, come across places which do not suit me and occasionally make me fret and kick. But just where the Buddha's Way and 'my way' seem to go apart, that is the place to look where our own feet stand and to decide, 'Am I going to follow the Buddha's Way which leads to Awakening, or am I going to stubbornly stick to my way?' That is what it comes down to. If I think I can follow the Buddha's Way while keeping to my way, I am only going further astray. It would be so much easier if the Buddha's Way and my way were the same, but factually – and as far as I am concerned, unfortunately – this is not so. The Buddha's Way and my way are diametrically opposed, and so at every step the direction I take is my free choice. The question is, am I courageous and disciplined enough to cautiously experiment and find out, or am I just refusing and want to have it my own way?

To find that out, we need a particular Buddhist practice usually translated as 'mindfulness', but since for us Westerners this implies a self-conscious watching, 'I' observing myself as it were, we'd better take it as 'awake awareness'. It is the beginning and the end of Buddhist practice, and what we call Daily Life Practice is merely another word that leads into this awareness. If this then widens out into Zazen, a practitioner is well on the Way.

VERSES 7 AND 8

7   *Let go of the Four Great Elements, do not hold on to them.*
    In accord with the deep, calm state, eat and drink
       as you like.
    Impermanent are all forms, and so all are void –
    This is the complete, unexcelled insight of the Buddha.

8   *The true monk shows firm determination.*
    If there is one who will not let the Passions ride him, show!
    Root and origin being truly cut off is the Seal of the Buddha;
    Collecting leaves and searching for branches stifles
       attainment!

Commentary

'Let go of the Four Great Elements, do not hold on to them.'
The Four Great Elements are earth, water, fire and air
(or wind). They are said to make up everything that is – all
forms. And so to let go of the Four Great Elements is to let go
of form, of attachment to all forms, including the one that
makes up what I am pleased to call 'my body'.

'In accord with the deep, calm state, eat and drink as
you like.' That is the true Zen stance, but we must not forget
that Zen is within the Mahayana Buddhist Way, and so is the
Buddha's Way. Therefore, 'eat and drink as you like' does not
mean to eat and drink as I would like or fancy, but to be free

from attachment to eating and drinking, which is not difficult if the Four Great Elements are not held on to. Otherwise, it becomes my likes and dislikes, and that is precisely what is called 'delusion', because 'I' am always mixed up in it.

To do as I like and as it suits me is being in bondage to attachments rather than real freedom, which can take things or leave them according to the situation, without any kind of prejudgements or presumptions. So 'Let go of the Four Great Elements, do not hold on to them.' And 'In accord with the deep, calm state', where the Four Great Elements are truly let go of and 'I' is blended out, there are no more attachments either. Of that state, Master Torei, the great disciple of Hakuin, says, 'Then begins another Life', which is that deep, calm state where nothing is upset anymore. Yes, that is how I want to be – never to be upset by anything anymore. But such a one would be a monster: he would be without pity, compassion or humanity, and surely the Way of the Buddha does not lead to such monstrousness? Indeed, the Buddha is not only the All-Wise One, he is also the All-Compassionate One. He does have feelings, but is not driven by them, nor is he invaded or carried away by judging and valuing.

'In accord with that deep, calm state, eat and drink as you like.' Eat and drink as the situation demands – that is 'as you like'. Then there is harmony with the situation, at-one-ness. What I like and what the situation demands often differ greatly. If I must give in to what the situation demands, I cannot do what I like. But, miraculously, having let go of the Four Great Elements, what the situation demands is just what I like, and there is accord again between the situation and 'I'. So there is not only peace, but also joy all day long, even if it hurts.

'Impermanent are all forms, and so all are void.' 'Impermanent are all compounded things. Strive on heedfully!' were the last words spoken by the Buddha to his grieving disciples. What is compounded is made up of parts and falls apart again. There is nothing permanent; all forms are void of any permanent entity, are a shadow-play, not real. 'This is the complete, unexcelled insight of the Buddha.'

The Southern Canon contains a volume called *The Questions of King Milinda*. The king was very interested in Buddhism and had read many of the scriptures, but he was of a doubting disposition, and always asked questions and wanted more explanations – we are all familiar with such a tendency. He was very fortunate to have the wise Bhikkhu Nagasena to instruct him and answer his questions with patience and compassion. Having just read about the 'afflicting passions' and how they contribute to our unhappiness and our difficulties, King Milinda asked, 'Surely a life completely without passions is bland, without excitement and not worth living?'

Bhikkhu Nagasena did not simply give a doctrinal answer, but offered an analogy: 'Imagine you have been invited out and have been served an absolutely delicious dish. You want it again, and order your cook to get the recipe and have it on the menu tomorrow. But between now and tomorrow your memory plays up as you look forward with great anticipation to that exquisite dish. The cook puts the dish in front of you, and you are disappointed because it does not taste as it did yesterday. The dish is the same, but you do not just taste the food, you taste your memory and your expectations. You have it cooked again the next day, and again it does not taste how you imagine it should taste. But without passion you taste it truly, as it is, and you find it delicious. Then it is gone because you have eaten it. And when you get the dish again it is equally delicious, because you do not entertain such imaginings, and just taste and savour it afresh, as for the first time. So life without passions is not bland: on the contrary, it makes it possible to savour things exactly as they are each time they come up.'

In that 'deep, calm state, eat and drink as you like. / Impermanent are all forms, and so all are void.' In themselves they are empty, they come and go, contain nothing permanent, like clouds in the sky. If the clouds are in front of the sun, the sun cannot be seen. Yet these impermanent forms are themselves endowed with the 'complete, unexcelled insight of the Buddha'. Without human forms, without conscious awareness, that insight is also void and for this reason the forms are equally important. Moreover, it is in the form that insight and awareness need to be gained – and that is only possible by letting go of the Four Great Elements. Then it appears of itself, I do not have to make it happen.

The Buddha-nature is inherent in all forms and informs all forms. When we let go of the Four Great Elements, of our assumptions, of our picking and choosing, then it shines forth like the sun or the moon when the clouds have dispersed. But for that to happen, much training is necessary, and so, 'The true monk shows firm determination.' Not only the 'true monk', the true trainee, the true follower of the Buddha. We are all liable to say and feel, 'Now I have had enough!' and want to give up. Steadfast determination is needed.

Then Yoka Daishi asks, 'If there is one who will not let the Passions ride him, show!' Come forth and show, demonstrate it – because that is truly the test. As long as there is 'I', there is a place for the afflicting passions. This is why the training has to be so careful and so thorough.

The Chinese character, which has been translated as 'realization' in the title *Song on the Realization of the Way*, actually means this 'showing', this 'proving', this 'confirmation'. All those connotations are connected in that one character, which also means to realize something, as one realizes an asset. How to show the inherent Buddha-nature – that is the question. In the Rinzai Zen School this is dealt with in Koan training. The final working-out of the passions is done in the interview room, where we come and try a hundred times and are told, 'No!' I do not want to appear not to know, so I try to put off going for interview until I do 'know', but of course I never do. That may go on for some time. Then over a Sesshin (a full retreat), I come for an interview again, because I have to, and again it is, 'No!' I do not want to be wrong, do not want to be made a fool of. I refuse, and I smart if I cannot avoid it: 'I have gone to a Sesshin, with an interview each day, and nothing has changed. Isn't it a real waste of time, making all this effort and nothing happens?'

Interviews are important, but not because I can get something out of them or I can see an answer. Interviews are like a grater that scrapes off layers of skin, like peeling an onion. Raw and smarting, I am then dealt either a kick or given a carrot. So between being pulled and kicked, by the grace of the Buddha, by the grace of the Bodhisattva Kannon, and by taking refuge in The Three Jewels, I am beginning to realize that I am nothing but a fool, and that I need the support of the Buddha, the support of the Teaching and the support of the Community. I am now beginning to fade a little. I don't mind quite so much any more. I return from the Sesshin light-hearted. Back at home, the load becomes easier and the 'afflicting passions' cannot carry me away so far because they no longer have quite so much hold over me. Since all genuine insight comes with hindsight only, I may suddenly realize after many years that, 'This little thing which I always told myself was so unimportant, yet nonetheless used to upset me so, now no longer does.' At that a further insight comes rushing in: 'But this wasn't really so little! My goodness me, the whole thing hangs on that one little thing which I tried to ignore!'

Now, why did I try to ignore it? Was it perhaps because another part of me realized its true significance, and that is why I kept steering away from it? That is what we habitually do: find a good excuse for doing or dropping something. Usually it is something that is not very difficult to do or drop, and we feel rather good about it, but the real point is left untouched, so no change occurs.

'If there is one who will not let the Passions ride him [or the delusion which is the root of the Passions], show!' Prove it! 'Root and origin being truly cut off is the Seal of the Buddha.' What is 'root and origin'? Where do all those thoughts come from? From where does delusion arise? That basic delusion from which we human beings suffer, which gives rise to our attachments, what is it? How does it come into being? 'Root and origin being truly cut off ...' But before it can be cut off, I must know what it is. Or must I? True insight, genuine insight, is only possible with hindsight. This is of importance for the training, which is not blind, but closely follows the Buddha's Way, testing every step, until it suddenly becomes clear.

In that 'deep, calm state,' in which the Path has come to an end and there are no more clouds floating about, all is space and clarity. But in the realm of form, there is joy and there is suffering – both caused by delusion. Yet, because of this, there is also compassion; and out of this compassion arises the will to be of service to everything, to all that exists. So, with that, the 'root and origin' has been touched.

Certainly in this our world there is much that is malignant and harmful, but it needs to be cured in our own heart. And in our universe there is night and day. It would be lovely if it would be day only – or would it? However, there is night and day alternating, and that is just how it is. Both are impermanent. And to the extent that we empty our own heart, free it from the bondage to attachments, there is a lightening of the burden of suffering. Herein there is then also the possibility of helping others; not only by what we say, but much more by what we actually are. We cannot all become great Bodhisattva-Mahasattvas, and are even less likely to become Buddhas – there is only one in each world era. We can only diligently walk the Way. Even if we only go a little stretch, if it but brings a bit more joy and a bit more selflessness into our workplace and our family circle, contributing to the happiness of others, isn't that already a great achievement, especially in our time?

As it has now been clearly demonstrated that the 'root and origin' are connected to 'my' and 'mine', 'I' can now also fall off like the eggshell falls off the emerging chick, discarded and unimportant. This is why it is said here that this 'is the Seal of the Buddha' – it falls off by itself; 'cut off' means just that.

'Collecting leaves and searching for branches stifles attainment.' We always want a little bit more of the teaching:

'I do not quite see it, there must be something more.' In trying to find it out, I go here and there and everywhere, to this teacher, to that school, where they will surely know it. Well, I can be told a thousand times how to ride a bicycle, but it will still make no impact unless I get on one myself. To collect head-knowledge – 'collecting leaves and searching for branches' – will only fill the head, which is already full to bursting. If a cup is full to the brim, nothing more will go in; it has to be emptied first. Thus, this emptying of the cup is the emptying of our heart. Instead of stuffing it still further with leaves and branches, clear it out, and again clear it out. When it is completely empty, something else can and will light up.

9   *People do not know the Mani Jewel*
    Nor that it is snugly contained in the Tathagata's Womb.
    The Sixfold Wondrous Function is void and again not void.
    In full light, the One Way is form and is not form.

10 *Once the Five Modes of Seeing are purified and the Five*
        Powers attained,
    They are confirmed and known; no need to measure
        or speculate.
    Although all kinds of reflections may be seen in the mirror,
    How could one take hold of the moon's reflection in the water?

Commentary

'People do not know the Mani Jewel, / Nor that it is snugly contained in the Tathagata's Womb.' What is that Mani Jewel? The Buddhist life begins with the Refuges, The Three Jewels. These Refuges are not places to hide away from daily life, but are a support to help us go through our daily life without too much commotion, without making too many ripples, smoothly, in accord with the Dharma. The Mani Jewel reflects these aspects: the three facets of Buddha, Teaching and Sangha, the religious community. The appellations are manifold – the Wish Fulfilling Gem, the Wonderful Gem, the Gem of Wisdom. As the Jewel of Wisdom, it is often portrayed in the right paw of a soaring dragon.

The Western dragon slayer is young, and soon after the deed tends to come to a sticky end due to his own hubris, but in the East the old sage has undergone and been tested by the training; he does not slay the dragon, rather the dragon carries him. And it is that dragon that holds the wish-fulfilling wondrous gem, the Jewel of Wisdom, the many-faceted Mani Jewel which reflects all that is.

'People do not know the Mani Jewel', but there is an intimation of it. In all traditions, under whatever name, the search is for that Mani Jewel, for the elixir of life, for the philosopher's stone, or gold, or salvation. There is also the feeling that if it could be found and, by extension, could be possessed, it would bring peace and happiness ever after. But having begun the search, it soon appears that the jewel needs to be fashioned by one's own labour. In a way this is true, but in a way is also not true. It is there, but it has to be dug out. So Yoka Daishi says 'People do not know the Mani Jewel, / Nor that it is snugly contained in the Tathagata's Womb.'

With the Tathagata's Womb (in Sanskrit, Tathagata-garba), we come to a profound teaching of the later Mahayana, and one that is particularly important because the Tathagata's Womb is also the mother of the teaching that the Buddha's wisdom and power is inherent in all sentient beings. The Tathagata-garba is the potentiality of the Void from which everything is brought forth. We must here consider that the later developed teachings are not just philosophical speculations, but result from the profound and deep meditation of devoted and ardent monks who then recorded their insights.

Buddhism is a well-travelled religion, and has shown that its roots can grow in every soil, can be carried from one culture to another. In India the concept of the Tathagata-garba had no great impact, but it was very instrumental in Buddhism being taken up in China. Chinese culture at that time, from about 200 CE onwards, was Confucian with a strong sense of order in the universe and in society, with man's duties extending up and down between them. To repudiate this family system was seen as disloyal, and as a disharmonious act that would have disastrous results. The Indian tradition, particularly the Southern branch, considered that deliverance could only be achieved by monks in full training. In China, Buddhism became acceptable through the Tathagata-garba teaching, which stated that the potentiality for enlightenment was in all sentient beings; one did not have to become a monk. The same applies for us today. Although institutions offering teaching and training have invariably been monastic, they were open to monks and laymen alike. The potentiality is inherent – our training realizes it.

In the Mahaparinirvana Sutra it is said that the Buddha's body is the universe. It explains that the lakes are his eyes and his bones are the mountains, etc., and concludes with, 'it reveals itself everywhere and always in a way that is perceptible to the beholder.' Now, 'perceptible to the beholder' is a tremendous statement. Something that is too great, if suddenly perceived, can be shattering, while something that is inconceivable is also not perceptible, and therefore means nothing. But revealing itself as perceptible to the beholder – that is the Jewel! Perhaps to a Stone Age hunter an oddly shaped rock or a piece of driftwood might represent it, whereas we might think, 'A bit of driftwood, goodness me, how simple, how can he possibly see something in it?'

But in his perception it represents the greatness, so what is important for us is to find what in our perception reveals the wholeness and the power of what actually is and works.

When one suddenly comes across the 'tremendous', especially when not quite prepared, one perceives only the power. Although it can also break in of its own accord, or we can break through to it, what concerns us in the training is that if we are not sufficiently prepared, if there has not been enough sincere bowing and not enough sincere abdication and laying down of 'I', then it appears in its horrendous aspect. The Tibetans are very good at depicting their deities or forces as two-faced in their demonic and beatific aspects.

So this is the Mani Jewel. We have to be prepared and it has to be fashioned – the one is the other, and only then does it truly shine. Unless we have fashioned it, we do not know the Mani Jewel itself, only its projections, nor do we know where it is. 'It is snugly contained in the Tathagata's Womb', where everything is contained – everything that is, was, or will be, everything conceivable and everything inconceivable. That is why it is so important to realize change. For in that constant change, new things also come up – things which as yet are not, but will want to be.

We would like to speculate, to grasp and understand, but that is not possible, for it is too deep and profound. Rather than trying to understand, the task is to take part in that wondrous miracle that life actually is. To live life instead of thinking about it, for the latter is unsatisfactory. And we learn to live by partaking in it.

Moreover, when the heart is truly open, then whatever might still be in it spills out and is gone. Only when the heart is truly empty, are all things seen as they really are, for the perception goes straight through the sense-gates. In our deluded state, the six senses are usually called the Six Dusts or the Six Robbers because we do not see clearly and cannot listen properly. It cannot be said often enough that our perceptions are all mixed up with our assumptions, judgements and opinions, but when the heart is empty and open sense perceptions can come straight in. That is usually the first instance that provokes Awakening.

'The Sixfold Wondrous Function is void and again not void.' That 'Sixfold Wondrous Function' is, of course, the six senses, because in Buddhism we have six senses, thinking or mind being the sixth. You may have noticed that the word 'mind' has so far been studiously avoided. Because the Buddhist term for 'heart' (xin in Chinese, shin in Japanese) has so many connotations including heart, mind, spirit, soul, etc., it has been very difficult for us Westerners to get it right. Recent translators are beginning to use the term 'heart', which is better because the heart does have feelings and, if it is misguided, the emotional passions flare up. But in the context of the sense-gates a different term is used for mind or thoughts, which is the sixth sense. 'Mind' stands for reason and consciousness, and lacks any connotations with feelings and emotions. So the sixth sense is thought, but it can become befuddled with all the imagination and picture-making that feelings and emotions usually engage in.

'Picture-making? I don't make pictures! I am a rational being, am I not? I have got my senses, and seeing is believing. I can hear exactly what is said.' But do I really? This needs to be made very clear, not as intellectual understanding, but on a very concrete level. Once 'dust' (see above, the Six Dusts) is cleared from the sense-gates, beguiling or fearsome pictures no longer becloud the heart, colours and squiggles no longer distort the reflections of the heart-mirror. Then the 'Sixfold Wondrous Function' is void and empty and, therefore, there is also nothing wrong with what comes into it. Hence it 'is void and again not void.'

Master Rinzai said, 'In that red lump of flesh there is one who daily goes in and out of the sense-gates. Do you know him?' When the sense-gates are cleared, or even when not cleared, who is the one who goes in and out all the time? When the sense-gates are clear, that is the 'Sixfold Wondrous Function', which at the same time is void and not void – ever-changing shadows. And so, 'In the full light [of clear seeing], the One Way is form and is not form.' The one who goes in and out of the sense-gates and what is seen – that is the form which is not form.

In his *Song of Meditation* Master Hakuin says, 'To take the form of No-Form as form. To take the thought of No-Thought as thought.' Depending on how I feel when reading or hearing such statements, I react in one of two ways. Either I am inclined to babble, 'How wondrous! How profound! I do not understand it, but it sounds good.' Or I may think, 'What utter nonsense! Goodness knows what they are talking about. They are having us on with mysterious words!' But it is neither/nor. This is exactly what it is.

In the Hekiganroku there is a verse by one of the great masters on just this point, and perhaps because of that it is so very difficult to translate. If we think of form as 'being', or if it is translated as 'being', we have already made it a 'thing'. But if we take form or that 'being' as 'essence', then perhaps we can translate it as:

> Essence, perceptible only when wrapped up in
>   swaddling clothes,
> Only lately have I come to accept and truly realize it,
> And now find it intimately familiar, clear and true.

It takes a long time to understand that one cannot 'understand' or 'see' the essence itself; it is only when wrapped in some covers, when 'pictured', that it becomes comprehensible. Similarly, life is perceptible only in living beings. We cannot help it, we must make pictures or concepts to conceive. It is the same with the sense of reverence in the heart. It does not matter whether it is that odd-shaped piece of driftwood or whatever, for the person looking at it, it conveys the essence; and on so beholding it, he bows in worship. It is not the driftwood that he worships, it is the essence. And another bows in front of a Buddha-image. It is not the Buddha-rupa he bows to, it is the essence. It is the same essence whether it is in the driftwood, in the Buddha-image, in Christ, or whatever. It is not a 'thing', not a given 'picture', but the essence, and it is in us too. To that we bow.

If we have realized the essence, then we will not quarrel about our various religions, but will understand them. Once that is seen into, there is no question of serving false gods, but rather reverence and worship is given whatever the form it happens to appear in. If that could be understood, all our religious quarrels would fall apart instantly and there would be mutual understanding, for it is the same essence that we all worship. Even if the head says, 'No, no, no! There is nothing to worship!', the heart knows and longs to realize and behold that essence. And through that recognition the whole of nature has once more become animated, spirited and alive. Everything is of that essence, and everything – all pictures, all forms – are but manifestations of that essence, but we need to be careful here. Although the form shrouds the essence, the essence is not separate from form, and form could not be without the essence. As it said in the *Heart Sutra*, 'Form is emptiness and emptiness is form.' And so, 'In the full light', in clear seeing, 'the One Way is form and is not form.'

'Once the Five Modes of Seeing are purified and the Five Powers attained, / They are confirmed and known; no need to measure or speculate.' 'The Five Modes of Seeing are purified' means having learned to see clearly. As Master Rinzai said, 'In the eyes, not to be deceived by form and colour. In the ear, not to be deceived by sound,' etc. But this kind of 'seeing', especially in the north-eastern Buddhist traditions, is the same as 'understanding'. We also say, 'Oh, yes, I see,' meaning 'I understand.' So seeing or perceiving or 'taking in' is whole and direct: not in the head only, but a total, real understanding.

For example, in the Noble Eightfold Path the first step is often translated as 'Right View' or 'Right Understanding'. In the Chinese it is written with the character for 'seeing'. Thus 'Right Seeing' is non-deluded seeing, which is also non-deluded thinking, because if the sight is correct, if the sense perceptions are clear and direct, then the thinking is unlikely to be clouded.

'Once the Five Modes of Seeing are purified and the Five Powers attained, / They are confirmed and known; no need to measure or speculate.' 'Confirmed' is again the same character as 'realization', which is part of the title of this text. Here we take it in the sense of 'coming into the inheritance', where it can now be put to use. Once it can be put to use and is really ours, and 'known', there is no need to measure it, because it is known. There is also no need to speculate about what it might be, for it has already become one with one's own.

'Although all kinds of reflections may be seen in the mirror, / How could one take hold of the moon's reflection in the water?' We have already had the mirror analogy, and we know that the mirror can only reflect when it is clean and empty, without any squiggles on it – no spots on it, and not blind. For a mirror can be blind, and it is interesting that we have the same word for it. A mirror will reflect exactly what falls into it, sharp and clear. It will not choose what to reflect and what to blend out, as our ordinary seeing does. Nor will it put in what it does not see but believes it sees. The mirror just reflects what is.

This happens when the sense-gates are unobstructed, and is the perception to which the practice of mindfulness is supposed to lead. Awareness is not like a spotlight focused on what I am now doing and everything around is blended out. Awareness is to be fully open to what actually is – and that happens when we are really 'at home' rather than letting our mind roam about all over the universe. Really 'at home', the mirror reflects clearly. Equally, if really 'at home', the slightest sound or touch is perceptible. We should not shut ourselves off, but be aware of the whole room as we are sitting there: aware if somebody over there moves, aware of each other, aware of the body, of the feelings that are there, aware of the thoughts that float through. All this is clearly there; some things clearer, some less so, but thus clearly seen, it is then set free and no longer agitates, because it is no longer 'mine'. What I particularly want is also seen, and is quite all right too. If not suitable, I do not need to give in to it, but the awareness of it is there. That is what Vipassana, the other part of meditation is, or what Koan meditation is all about. But first there must be this clear reflection that shows the background, the foreground and everything down to the last little detail, without blending anything out. Should the mirror or the scene shift, a clear mirror then again reflects what now is. It does not hold to any particular of the previous picture, but lets it go. It reflects what is and it holds on to nothing.

Since all kinds of reflections may be seen in the heart-mirror, you can play with them too, but do not take those reflections for real: they are temporary only and will soon change. So in order to make that quite clear, Yoka Daishi asks, 'How could one take hold of the moon's reflection in the water?' It is but the reflection, it is not the real moon. Do not be deceived.

There is a Japanese ink drawing of a monkey hanging by one hand over a pool with the full moon reflected in the water. His other paw is just about to touch the water. It perfectly portrays us because, like the monkey, we want to grab the shining moon down there, and then are distraught that it eludes our grasp because the reflection vanishes when the water is touched. Our rational mind tells us that we cannot grasp the moon in the water, it is not the real moon. However, it does not prevent us from repeated attempts at grasping something we love, or of trying to understand what is not subject to reason. So we dip our impatient, impious hands into the water, the surface breaks into ripples, and the moon is gone. Then we deny it: 'Well, there wasn't a moon after all. It was all a mistake.' Yes, nothing.

But if we realize it is a reflection, then we can look up and suddenly behold the moon. That is perhaps the deeper meaning of that analogy – of not grasping for the moon in the water, which we know perfectly well we cannot do. But because all forms, even reflections, are part of the essence, each single one will lead us straight to the essence if made skilful use of rather than being either destroyed, disturbed or mistaken.

11   *Always on his own, step for step by himself,*
     So the liberated one playfully walks the one road to Nirvana,
     Humming a classical tune. Heart empty and manners
         naturally courteous,
     Lean of form and firm of bone, nothing can deflect him.

12   *All the sons of Buddha are poor,*
     But their poverty is material, not of the spirit.
     While the body is clothed in coarse threadbare robes,
     The heart contains peerless spiritual treasure.

Commentary

'Always on his own, step for step by himself.' We often moan, 'Always on my own ... so sad with nobody there ... all by myself ... cut off.' But are we ever alone? We are always amongst things, we are not in a vacuum, yet the text says, 'Always on his own.' Although we go for support to the Buddha, to his teachings and his community – indeed, we need to do so – a verse in the *Dhammapada*, one of the oldest Buddhist texts, says, 'You yourself must walk the Way, nobody can do it for you.' Just like nobody can eat for us or go to the loo for us or breathe for us – we have to do it ourselves, by our own effort. Again, 'You yourself must make the effort, Buddhas do but point the way.' So it is going step for step by oneself.

'Step for step by himself, / So the liberated one playfully walks the one road to Nirvana.' The liberated one, who has learnt the skill of the Way and now also has the strength to walk it, need have no doubts about it because he knows it as the one road, and playfully walks along. So the liberated one walks playfully. He does not strut or stomp along, he has got form and strength and swings along in a collected way, neither hurrying nor tarrying.

This 'playfully' is of importance. In the Zen School there are said to be nine states of real 'at-oneness' – nine types of Samadhi – of which the highest one is that of 'playfulness'. We could also say 'sport', but nowadays, totally orientated towards results, we no longer know the true meaning of sport. Either I grimly apply myself with the attitude of 'I must win' or I opt out altogether, deeming it all too demanding. And then there is also the killjoy who feels, 'If I don't have to do it the really hard way, it's not worth doing!' But that's not true: that kind of puritan dourness is taking things far too seriously. Once I saw a party of little children. For one and a half hours they were sliding down a slope – up they went and down they came, eagerly playing. They seemed inexhaustible. Three grown-ups had to look after them in turn because they got tired out – and that was at the end of the day when they had been out and about since morning! If we had to do that we would be drooping by four o'clock, complaining about how hard we are worked. Look at the playfulness of those children – hardly had they sat down for a moment's rest, when they were up again like yo-yos, chasing each other, racing each other. It was fascinating watching them, and the Daoist saying suddenly came to mind: 'When used it is inexhaustible.' But only when used in that playful way. If only we too could do so instead of taking ourselves and our training and our problems so seriously, and getting so exhausted from them that we can hardly keep going. If we could just relax a bit, look at things in a more playful way, and encourage ourselves: 'There, there, you old thing, don't be such a fool!' Then things would begin to look quite different.

In old-fashioned, very polite Japanese language, by means of a special suffix to the verb, it is said of the emperor and high aristocracy that they 'play' at doing. Whereas we, for example, might go to Brighton, the emperor and his family 'play' at going to Brighton. And just as we play chess or tennis, they 'play' going into battle. And they also 'play' fighting in battle, even 'play' dying. It shows that they are not forced, yet do not take it seriously either, they do it 'playingly'. And so, perhaps we could remember in our own thinking processes that we play taking up our daily chores, play cooking dinner, or whatever it might be. If I can play at it, can I chafe at it at the same time? If I play at something, can I get angry about something that easily? Do learn to play!

'Humming a classical tune.' Now, why do we call something 'classical'? Because it is very highbrow? By no means: it is classical because it is understood through all generations, from olden times to the present. It is striking, like all great art is striking, whether it is primitive, medieval or whatever, because it is in harmony with the great laws, and renders perceptible that essence which, in itself, is 'nothing' but informs all forms, and all forms respond to it. This is what speaks immediately and directly to the heart. We can all perceive it and see it as that. Whatever is done on purpose, like most modern music, does not endure. It is not 'classical' and will not speak to the next generation. It is fine enough if you like it, but it is sound engineering, and the heartbeat tom-toms are a cultural regression to the neolithic. The classical, on the other hand, from the simplest tune to primitive religious painting or cave painting, affects one. It conforms to that which is 'nothing' and the heart vibrates to it. This is why it speaks.

'Manners [that are] naturally courteous.' That is another point, especially for us nowadays, when we are only too easily inclined to think that 'anything goes', and that we can do without them. Manners that are naturally courteous come from the heart. If the heart is really empty, it perceives that Buddha-nature is inherent in all things. And if all things are Buddha-things, from a glass of water to Buddha himself, would we then not quite naturally be inclined to treat them with respect? And does not respect naturally evoke courtesy? If we extend that courtesy to ourselves too, then 'good form' would hold, wouldn't it? In such a strong form the transformation can and does take place, just as the chick grows in the egg. Hence the Zen School is particularly careful about manners that are courteous. This is why we cultivate the attitude of care for everything we handle.

'Humming a classical tune. Heart empty and manners naturally courteous.' Now there is complete harmony, not just between oneself and others, but between oneself and all that is 'other'. That is what 'liberation' means. There is now a natural containment in which the heart opens, joy and warmth well up, and with it the reliance of being carried. Concomitant with it is that our usual preoccupation with self has fallen by the wayside.

'Lean of form and firm of bone' we may equate with the Third Patriarch's saying, 'Nothing extraneous, nothing superfluous' – just what is. 'Look at the place where your own feet stand', without additions of great systems of learning from here, and great ideas from there, or seeing everything in the light of my basic assumptions or fears. That is all delusion. 'Lean of form' – there is nothing there but just the form, just as it is.

'Firm of bone' has very much to do with what is known as being reliable. Then we realize that 'lean of form' also denotes that no additions stick to it, no frills and flounces distort it, no brambles catch the foot. It has all become spare, there is not much left. So 'firm of bone' is knowing what to rely on and relying on it. 'Nothing can deflect him' anymore.

The great teacher Nansen used to declare, 'Heart is Buddha. Heart is Buddha.' A young monk gained his insight from just this. Eventually he left Nansen's assembly and spent many years on pilgrimage. The Zen texts, especially the Chinese ones, tell of monks on pilgrimage, but do not think that monks went on pilgrimage, entering one monastery and then after a couple of months, finding it a little bit too much, going on to the next one. On the contrary, they joined a monastery and they stayed perhaps for life. But those who, after many years, had come to real insight, went on pilgrimage, that is, they wandered from monastery to monastery, testing themselves in dialogue with other teachers, to find out whether there was still something lacking. And if so, they stayed with that teacher until settled.

After the monk who had come to insight under Nansen had been on pilgrimage and found that there was nothing lacking, he settled down on a faraway mountain, and a community began to form around him. Years later, news of it reached the old master who, by that time, had found that many imitated his 'Heart is Buddha' without relevant insight, and so he now firmly taught, 'Neither heart nor Buddha.' Nansen sent an experienced monk to find out what his erstwhile disciple taught and to tell him about the old teacher's change of style. The emissary arrived and duly asked about the teaching. Told that it was, 'Heart is Buddha', he delivered his message. 'You know, our Master has of late changed his teaching. He no longer says, "Heart is Buddha." Nowadays he teaches, "Neither heart nor Buddha nor anything."' But Master Daibai, which means 'The Great Plum', firmly replied, 'I don't know what the old man is up to. He can teach what he likes. I got my insight under him, Master Nansen, and I got it from the insight into "Heart is Buddha." This is the insight that I teach and the insight that I show. I know no other.' When the messenger returned and told what had happened, Nansen nodded and said, 'I distrusted The Great Plum, but now I know it is ripe.' This is self-reliance derived from truly knowing. It is the confirmation, the realization, of which Buddhism talks so much. Once realized, one can put it to use. 'Nothing can deflect him', not even a test by his old teacher.

'All the sons of Buddha are poor, / But their poverty is material, not of the spirit.' Needless to say, monks do not have many possessions. What does 'possessions' in that sense really mean? Actually it means 'attachments', because possessions in themselves are not a hindrance. Living in the midst of a fortune, if there is no attachment to it, that is all right, but there is also a poverty that is not material. There is much talk in religion about the 'poverty of the spirit', because one can become quite proud of one's knowledge and attainments. Therefore, doctrinally speaking, the last of the factors to overcome is not only attachment to material property, but pride, and thus to become 'poor in spirit'. True poverty of the spirit is not hypocritical, not personal, hence not attached and so clearly sees all things as they really are. So it also sees the tiny dot that I am in its right proportion as well as in its right 'at-oneness'. With that, there is awareness – not of what I am, but deep reliance on that Essence which informs all forms. With that, one has come into one's inheritance, and the spiritual riches are realized, compared with which material possessions are as nought – just look at the story of the Buddha's life. Thus 'their poverty is material, not of the spirit.' This spirit cannot be possessed in any case – it just is. Having become one with it, and once more come back into that complete Union, the ephemeral material, which includes the material form, becomes irrelevant.

'While the body is clothed in coarse threadbare robes' is wonderfully illustrated by Mahakasyapa, who had become so used to a life of material poverty that it completely suited him and he felt comfortable in it. The Buddha compassionately suggested that he should make his life a little easier in his old age. But Mahakasyapa very humbly replied, 'I have got used to it over fifty years. Please may I carry on with it, because it is the most comfortable for me.' What for a given body is really the most comfortable is a simple way once got used to. However, as long as 'I' go rushing about picking and choosing, we do not know that, so there is always the need to come back to the Buddha's Middle Way, and away from too much of what I must have or get rid of.

However, whether wealth or poverty, material or spiritual, if attached to, they all become hindrances. So from of old the Zen School has stressed the art of making do with what is there, not to make distinctions between what I would like to have and what is there, and not to cling to either. It always comes down to the clinging, to attachment. Only if nothing is 'mine' anymore can the heart open, and is seen to 'contain the peerless spiritual treasure'. For in that Nothingness, where no-thing is owned, and I too am nothing, 'I' has also lost its pull and strength. The 'peerless treasure' that I have looked for outside, that I have chased like a golden ball, is now discovered shining in my own heart, and has become one with me.

13   *This treasure, however much used, is never exhausted*
In the joyful service to benefit all beings as suits their needs.
The Three Bodies and Four Wisdoms mature in the body,
The Eight Types of Deliverance and Six Supernormal
    Powers imprint the heart.

14   *The superior man settles it once and for all,*
The middling and inferior learns much but believes little.
Just cast off the dirty old clothes you treasure
And don't boast of your pure living to others.

Commentary

'This treasure, however much used, is never exhausted / In the joyful service to benefit all beings as suits their needs.' Of this 'treasure' the last line of Verse 12 says, 'The heart contains peerless spiritual treasure.' This is the treasure to which the Buddha 'awakened' and proclaimed, 'How wonderful, how miraculous! All beings are inherently endowed with the Tathagata's wisdom and power. But sadly, because of their attachments, human beings are not aware of it.'

What is that 'wisdom and power'? Is it something supernatural and occult, or perhaps the power to put a jinx or a curse on something? Surely not, because that would not reflect the wisdom of the Buddha, which is something much more total. Have you ever seen a blade of grass when it comes out from under a stone? A soft, little spear of grass cannot penetrate the stone, nor can it deny its urge to grow and unfold, so it shoves and shifts horizontally until it gets out from under the stone and then begins to stand up. It is quite pale when it emerges, for it had no sunlight but, inherently endowed with the whole life force, it had the power to obey its nature and come up. Another good example is the snowdrops pushing up through half-frozen ground which we mentioned earlier. And so it is with all living beings. Why are we the exception? The Buddha tells us that our attachments prevent us – the act of disobedience. How so?

Only we, because we have our own attachments and, therefore, our own opinions, do not work and live in harmony with the universal Law which is the Dharma. So 'I' am in the way and, therefore, in a given situation I habitually either over-react or under-react. Tainted by my predilections, I cannot respond correctly to the situation by an act of will. However, there are also times when I forget myself, am un-self-ish, and this actually happens not infrequently in the course of a day. If this un-self-ishness becomes a permanent attitude, then the 'spiritual treasure', the whole wisdom and power of the Tathagata, begins to manifest naturally, and to work in the ordinary daily life.

This spiritual treasure 'is never exhausted in joyful service.' Joyful service? Nowadays we have forgotten service, disparage it, and so are unaware that it can be, and is, joyful. To wish to be of service means to have a feeling of reverence, which is a quality of the heart. We have lost this in our headlong rush for more knowledge, more gadgets, and more information. With a head thus stuffed, a sense of proportion and common sense are all but obsolete. We have become estranged from our own humanness, and thus from our joint humanity – how we all fit together with each other and with everything that lives on this planet of ours. We do have misgivings about what we are doing to it, but instead of seeing the way all things really are, we get fired up by odd or unrealistic ideas of quick, short-sighted solutions, or opinions of how to help which only raise more problems. And that because all our solutions are not as suits the real needs, but are only momentary or fashionable surface tinkering. So our ideas lead us from bad to worse – we caulk a leak here, and another and bigger one springs up somewhere else. We no longer know what suits our needs, even less how to benefit other beings as suits their needs. For that the wisdom of the Tathagata is needed, that sees all things the way they really are, and the strength or power to act in accord with that wisdom and to put that wisdom into action in joyful service.

'The Three Bodies and Four Wisdoms mature in the body, / The Eight types of Deliverance and the Six Supernormal Powers imprint the heart.' In the Mahayana framework, the Three Bodies are the Dharmakaya, the Samboghakaya and the Nirmanakaya. The Dharmakaya or Dharma Body refers to the Fully Enlightened Seeing, complete awareness. It may be thought of as 'principle' or 'essence', because it is not material. So we best conceive of the Insight/Wisdom or the Dharma Body as the principle of the Dharma, which underlies everything and which is in everything; and that is precisely the 'wisdom and power of the Tathagata'. And so everything acts according to it and to its own nature, except that we, due to our attachments, are not aware of this, our 'birthright'.

The next Body is the Samboghakaya or the Enjoyment Body, the 'joyful service for the benefit of all beings as suits their needs' – not grimly serious, weighed down by loads of sorrow, not assertively demanding, but playfully joyous. And lastly there is the Nirmanakaya or Material Body. If we think in terms of the Buddha, Nirmanakaya Buddha is Shakyamuni Buddha as he was born, lived and died – a human being as we ourselves also are. That gives us the courage and the understanding that it is possible to come to the same awakening as he did, provided that we exert ourselves to become 'full' human beings, completely aware of and at one with the way all things really are. And now living and acting in accordance with that way is no longer our short-sighted way – how I see it, or think I see it, etc.

The Four Wisdoms are first, the combined Six Sense Wisdoms, respectively of the eye, the ear, the nose, the tongue, touch and thought. These are co-ordinated by the second, the Great Observing Wisdom. The third is the Clear Insight Wisdom, which is the opposite of 'I' – the wisdom that clearly sees not only the needs of all things, but the way they really are. And finally there is the Great Mirror Wisdom, in which everything is reflected and which serenely reflects everything just as it is.

In Zen training we are aware of the teachings but, rather than trying to fathom them immediately, we first of all try to realize the fundamental insight, and then from there begin to understand what the teachings are about. So we will not go into great detail on the Eight Types of Deliverance and the Six Supernormal Powers that 'imprint the heart', but rather exert ourselves to realize the Three Bodies and the Four Wisdoms, that is, the full insight with its corresponding strength. These mature in the body by training with the body, much as a physical exercise. Then the Eight Types of Deliverance and the Six Supernormal Powers 'imprint the heart'. With that the sight is cleared and it is possible to live according to it.

'The superior man settles it once and for all, / The middling and inferior learns much but believes little.' This brings up the question about Karma and roots. The texts often mention beings of superior, middling and inferior abilities. Nowadays we do not like such terms, so we had better have a good look at their meaning. Buddhistically speaking, the superior man has worked up good Karma and has for many lives followed the Path, so now he has the strength, the will and the determination to settle it once and for all. 'The middling and inferior learns much, but believes little.' That is still so today. We hear the message and it seems quite interesting, but we don't quite believe it, not really, so we cannot live it. And when it comes to the practice of it, we don't quite believe that either. We are willing to do a little, or to go that far, but not any further. So in the beginning we say yes, not really knowing. And then it comes to that first little bit of bother – 'Well, perhaps not today. I'll have to think a bit more about it', or whatever it might be. And the next time I procrastinate, 'It's not really suitable just now.' Finally, approaching the nitty-gritty, I shy away if I can.

When I went to Japan in 1960 soft beds were still preferred, and sleeping on a futon on a tatami floor took a couple of days to get used to. Ruth Sasaki always consoled us: 'Don't worry, it is good for the back and good for the practice. Something must give – and it's not the floor.'

What gives? We are actually very adaptable provided there are no options. But we believe that we have options and despair if it looks like our life, as it is, has no more options. Do we not feel, in our innermost being, that we must be free, all options open, and that we are in full control of our lives and of everything that happens in our daily lives? And strive to realize that? When we then come into Zen training we find it to be very difficult – such things as making a timetable for ourselves and keeping to it. It requires us to get up at a specific time, to have meals at a certain time, and a few other fixed points during the day. The moment it is suggested to keep to it, I don't want it. I want to get out of it, feel I am imprisoned.

What is it inside us that will not settle into a particular framework? That is where Zen training truly begins. What is it that I must exert my will, have my way, by hook or by crook? If I cannot have this my way, then I will have it that way, but it is still my choice. Do we remember that grass stalk that worked itself out from under the stone? It does so obeying its own nature and the principle of growth – it is in accord with the Dharma. But 'I must have' is the selfish warping of that same strength which vainly exhausts itself when actually it 'is never exhausted / In the joyful service to benefit all beings as suits their needs.'

According to a Mahayana saying, 'The passions are the Buddha-nature and the Buddha-nature is the passions.' It is the same energy. In the presence of the delusion of 'I' – as in 'I must have it', or, 'I can't bear it', or, 'I will' – energy roars up like raging flames, and is aptly called the Three Fires, or sometimes the Poisons. These are desire, dislike/aggression/

fear, and that basic delusion that 'I' exist and that 'I' am right. It could be called, in varying degrees, a 'God Almighty complex'.

But in the absence of this delusion of 'I' as a separate entity, unconnected, unrelated and alone, the Fires have no fuel, do not flare, and so revert back to their own nature called the Buddha-nature, which is ever at one with the way things really are. So when you read about the Fires roaring, they are kindled by 'my' reaction to circumstances. And we react either to what we do not like or to what we like more or less strongly. In both cases it is 'I' who reacts. This is the misapplication of that precious energy. Without 'I' choosing, it would actually completely inform about and accommodate the way all things really are, but because of my reaction, I cannot see. My reaction flaring up drowns out that quiet voice that gives the full information which is always there in a given situation. And so my response does not fit, is either exaggerated or inadequate.

Two of the Fires, desire and dislike/aggression, are both 'hot'. But if we look closely at what makes them hot, desire is basically what I want and aggression is what I dislike, hate and fear. Why does a reaction come up? Because I want or I dislike an object, situation, etc. Why do I dislike it? It is fear. Everything that threatens me and mine or threatens my opinions, which are like my own children, I hate and fear. Everything that threatens my life, my property, everything that diminishes me, that makes me feel small – all these threaten me and, therefore, there is worry, anxiety and fear. To that I react, and the energy roars up. Two types of reaction are possible and both are in all of us, one being the more habitual outside one, and the other one more inner.

If you do something to me which I intensely dislike – you may even do it quite unwittingly, you may stumble and tread on my bad foot while trying, with all good intentions, to help me out of my chair – the moment you do it, the Fire flares. I may not hit out physically, but it is the first instinct. We have learned to hold in the reaction, but there it is. Next comes self-pity – poor me. It thus goes either into aggression or into depression. 'That's just my luck. Everything is always going from bad to worse. Now I've been injured, and on my bad foot. It really hurts and look, they couldn't care less!' By the time this gets into a replay – well, everything back to my earliest childhood is liable to come up! I have to go and see a psychologist, who is at least paid to listen to my grievances.

Yoka Daishi says, 'Just cast off the dirty old clothes you treasure.' What are those dirty old clothes we treasure? They are my needs, my opinions, my convictions, my understanding, my this, my that. These are the dirty clothes we hold on to as precious. 'Cast them off and don't boast of your pure living.' What does 'pure living' mean, not just for monks? Do we think of 'pure' too much in a moral sense? Yet clinging to 'right' or 'good' again leads to opinions, views and convictions. How quickly we then disagree with each other, and how quickly we are willing to take up the cudgel. So we are ready to go on a demo or march for or against something. These are the things we had better cast off as quickly as possible and open up to the way all things really are. So 'cast them off and don't boast of your pure living to others.' Perhaps most of all, don't boast of a better understanding and of knowing how this world is to be righted. This is one of our worst delusions.

Although we think we know ourselves very well, we don't really. It is surprising how little we are acquainted with ourselves and with our own emotional household, but to become familiar with that and learn to understand it is the beginning of the training. Like charity, the Way also begins at home, right under our feet. Only from our own understanding of ourselves, and our willingness to work from that, does the ripening unfold of itself.

15 *Endure being slandered and spited by others;*
Those bent to set heaven on fire will soon tire of it.
When listening to their detractions is like drinking nectar,
All melts away and suddenly the Unthinkable is entered.

16 *If being talked ill of is seen as acquiring merit,*
The scoffers become truly good friends and teachers.
If being reviled without cause sparks neither hatred
*   nor liking,*
There arise compassion and patience, the powers
*   of the Unborn.*

Commentary

These are extremely helpful lines: 'Endure being slandered and spited by others; / Those bent to set heaven on fire will soon tire of it.' We are not very good at enduring slander and spite from others, are we? We do not like it. It causes strong reactions because inherently we want to be something, ideally something good, something great, and if that is in any way diminished or is not recognized, it feels like a small death. Actually, it is a small death of 'I', of what I think I am and have, and that is why I am so touchy.

As we have already mentioned, all Mahayana schools stress the practice of the Paramitas. The lessons we learn and the strength we gain from practising them enables us to begin to 'endure being slandered and spited by others'. The third of these Paramitas is patience, often called 'patient endurance', and that is ideal for grinding down the excessive self-conscious touchiness of 'I'. If I do not like this, or cannot do without that, it is patiently endured, particularly what seems to diminish me, such as being slandered and spited by others. It is not easy, is it? We want to defend ourselves. How quickly we react if somebody corrects our mistake, and yet the willingness to be corrected is the basis of learning and changing. Without being willing to be corrected and learning from that, how can I ever learn anything? It is impossible. That is where the training comes in. Many years ago Soko Morinaga Roshi told me, 'All Zen training does is to make a fool of one. Only a fool can take everything just as it happens and still smile.' There was real wisdom in that, and I have never forgotten it.

Yoka Daishi continues: 'When listening to their detractions is like drinking nectar, / All melts away and suddenly the Unthinkable is entered.' Master Hakuin said, 'If you want to go that way, then be prepared to sweat white beads, for it means bearing the unbearable and enduring what is unendurable.' Everything has to fall away. 'I' clings on to the last bitter moment, and so there is no peace, there is no opening. The Unthinkable opens up a new Life, a new wisdom in which there is no more 'I' ghosting about, and so there are no more problems. There is now a willingness to go with things as they are. This willingness, this 'at-oneness' with things as they are, without harming or any kind of intentional interference, is what the rather enigmatic Chinese term 'wu wei' tries to express.

'If being talked ill of is seen as acquiring merit.' At first we react when we are corrected – 'But I have always done it this way!' Then we concede – 'Oh, alright, I'll do it that way' – but with ill grace. And next comes, 'I'm getting used to it', to being corrected. When being corrected is no longer difficult, there is a willingness and eagerness to learn. In my childhood, children played together. There were games for toddlers and for the older ones, and the peer group had still other games. I remember how keen we were to be upgraded into the next stage, how we wanted to learn the rules of that game in order to be able to play with the older ones. And have you ever heard or known of a game that has no rules? We did not mind being corrected or scolded, and really applied ourselves because we wanted to play with the older ones. And playing was fun, it was a joy. No bad-tempered, 'Now, I've got to learn those rules', but keen to play, for our mutual enjoyment, not just for 'me' or 'us', not just to win. And the one wanting it all 'my' way was dubbed a spoilsport. Perhaps next time I want it all 'my' way, I might remember that, if I offend against the enjoyment of all, I am a spoilsport.

Now, do we want to be such spoilsports in life or do we want to participate in the Game of Life? That means learning to play according to the rules of this our Earth on which we live, for we have not yet gone to Mars, nor even inhabit the moon. There may be other rules to the game there, but whilst we are here, the game is played according to the laws of Earth, the Dharma.

Yoka Daishi's, 'If being talked ill of is seen as acquiring merit', indicates that we are well on the Way. What is more, 'The scoffers become truly good friends and teachers.' If we no longer react when our weaknesses are touched and it hurts – 'If being reviled without cause sparks neither hatred nor liking' – then instead, 'There arise[s] compassion and patience, the powers of the Unborn.' Just because of that, being talked ill of is seen as acquiring merit, whereas, 'Those bent to set heaven on fire will soon tire of it.' And because we learn not to react to them, 'The scoffers become truly good friends and teachers.' Leave them to their problem and ill will; untouched by it, go forward.

Before we get too serious, here is a story about an old couple, Isaac and Becky. They live in a small house in a narrow street. One night, Becky is already in bed but Isaac restlessly walks up and down the bedroom. Becky calls, 'Isaac, come to bed, I want to sleep.' 'Yes', says Isaac, but continues pacing up and down. Becky gets a bit annoyed: 'Isaac, come to bed now!' 'I can't sleep! I'm worried', says Isaac without stopping. Becky asks, 'What are you worried about?' And Isaac says 'Well you know Solly across the road?' 'Of course', says Becky, 'a good friend he is.' 'Yes', says Isaac, 'but the trouble is I owe him £100.' 'Well then, you owe him £100, now come to bed and go to sleep!' Isaac, still walking up and down, says 'But I am to repay him tomorrow morning.' 'Then do so tomorrow morning, but come to bed now!' 'But I haven't got it!' says Isaac. Becky thinks for a moment then jumps out of bed, runs to the window and calls across the road, 'Solly! Solly!' Solly appears at his window: 'What's wrong Becky?' Becky calls over, 'Isaac says he owes you £100.' 'Yes', says Solly. 'To be paid back tomorrow morning?' 'Yes', says Solly gleefully. 'Well, he hasn't got it', states Becky, slams the window shut and hops back into bed. 'Isaac, come to bed. Now it's his problem!'

In the training, our reaction mechanism is tested from time to time to see how quickly we can still be 'touched'.

Do we still react? Do we not react? In our school, Sanzen (private interviews with the master) are ideal training for not reacting. 'I don't know!' 'I can't do it!' 'I don't understand!' 'I am never right!' So some people will not come for interviews. They think, 'I'll wait until I know', or, 'I'll sit it out until I know', or, 'I won't go, because I'm always being faulted.' What we fail to understand is that we go for interviews just because we do not know. We do not want to be exposed, yet this is part of the purpose. Again we are rung off by the Sanzen bell – 'Once more I haven't got it!' And, having done my utmost over a Sesshin, 'I still have not got it, so what's the use?' Just go back again. And just because you go every time, you do much more work on it, and something will come up – it may be wrong, but it is not for us to judge. As long as we have really worked on the Koan, done our utmost, showing, 'This is as far as I got', it is for the teacher to judge and point. As long as I am deliberating, I am still driven round and round the old track, and nothing will come out of that. Only when I no longer react can things be seen just as they are.

But there is still a final test. 'If being reviled without cause sparks neither hatred not liking.' We usually react when corrected, but when scolded for something which we have not done, well, then we are truly up in arms, defend ourselves hotly, sue in the courts, demand compensation – 'I want justice! This is not right!' It is so important, this being really willing to take it without any kind of reaction. After all, that is how we have to take the weather, isn't it? Sometimes there is nothing but cold and rain, but it has to be accepted. It is no good saying, 'Oh, I wish it wouldn't rain and that the sun would come out.' We can't change the weather, and have to take it as it comes. So, 'If being reviled without cause sparks neither hatred nor liking, / There arise compassion and patience, the powers of the Unborn.' And perhaps there is a first glimmer of understanding that such reviling and slandering does not come from a happy person, but rather from a very unhappy one. To understand this is to have compassion for such a person, and to help by not reacting. That is the point. Do not say that such non-response is of no consequence for the one who is doing the reviling or gossiping or whatever, because my 'hot' reaction, my own Fire fans the flames of the other's Fire, too. If there is no fuel, the Fire will go out soon enough.

17   *In such a one, well-versed in both doctrine and exposition,*
     Dhyana and Prajna are whole and complete, unobstructed
         by Sunyata.
     But not he alone comes by it, for this is the essence
     Of all the Buddhas, as many as the grains of sand
         by the Ganges.

18   *Hearing the lion's roar of fearlessness*
     Shatters the brains of hundreds of animals;
     Even the scent-bearing elephant gets excited and loses
         his dignity.
     Only the heavenly dragon listens cheerfully and rejoices.

Commentary

In Verse 16 there was one in whom 'arise[s] compassion and patience, the powers of the Unborn'. Now follows, 'In such a one, well-versed in both doctrine and exposition, / Dhyana and Prajna are whole and complete.' What we are talking about here is that the Precepts, study and training all need to come together. When study and training combine and begin to mature, they bear fruit 'in such a one', who then also has to be 'well-versed in both doctrine and exposition.'

If we think of Daily Life Practice and meditation without the framework of the Teachings, we are likely to get carried away by our own opinions of how things are. The Teachings alone are of no use, even if we know them by heart. And practice alone, without the Teachings, becomes self-centred. Only when the Teachings have been learned and the practice has brought them to life is it possible to live them fully. But although they may now be lived, they cannot yet be transmitted to others. For that, exposition is needed. 'Such a one' needs to be 'well-versed in both doctrine and exposition,' and to be completely matured.

'In such a one, well-versed in both doctrine and exposition, / Dhyana and Prajna are whole and complete, unobstructed by Sunyata.' Dhyana is the religious discipline of meditation. There are many schools of Buddhism, each with different meditation practices, and there are many misleading notions about meditation. Basically, there is Samatha, or calming meditation, and Vipasyana, insight meditation, which we Westerners usually misunderstand. Calming meditation is what we do when we give ourselves over into the breath or the count until 'I' is forgotten. That takes daily practice over a long period. Such a quiet state cannot be forced or speeded up. It comes about of itself, and a short meditation course is unlikely to produce it.

Dhyana, then, is twofold – Samatha, the inner calm, the quiet, in which the voice of the Buddha-nature can be heard, and listening to that voice and seeing things the way they are, which is Vipasyana. It cannot be stressed too much that Vipasyana is not 'I' thinking, but implies the absence of 'I', 'hearing with the eyes and seeing with the ears.'

In Zen training, especially Rinzai training, we are expected to be well-grounded in this inner quiet. Slowly we learn that in such quietness there is clear perception of the slightest pinch, of the weight of the body, the soles of the feet on the floor. All these perceptions come of themselves, we do not need to actively observe them. Thus there is full awareness of the situation, here and now, as it is. There is no expectation, no dislike, no wanting to prolong it, etc. – just the information as it is coming through the six sense-gates.

Buddhism lists six senses, with thought as one of them. In the Zen texts they are called the 'robbers'. For example, I see something, and immediately want to know what it is, want to have it. Or I dislike it, or get captured by it, as by a phrase or a tune going round and round in my head – ever-repeating thought streams. Thus dragged away and pursuing objects, I do not know what is happening 'at home'. I may not hear someone knocking at the door, or the phone ringing. But if I am 'at home', what is happening comes in through the sense-gates and arises in 'awareness'. This 'awareness' is often called 'mindfulness', which can be misleading, for it has nothing to do with thinking. Krishnamurti calls it 'choiceless awareness'. In that state even the slightest sound or change of light is registered, and so are thoughts. Thus when calmness has settled in, the Four Foundations of Awareness can be practised: of body, of feelings, of thoughts, of mental objects.

Prajna, then, is the quiet voice of the Buddha-nature, its wisdom, which is uncovered by Daily Life Practice and by meditation. 'In such a one, well-versed in both doctrine and exposition, / Dhyana and Prajna are whole and complete.' That voice is with us not only when we sit motionless, but also in movement. It is always with us. It is the voice of the Teachings, and expounds them as suits the needs of the hearer.

Dhyana and Prajna are said here to be 'whole and complete, unobstructed by Sunyata.' Sunyata (emptiness) is devoid of anything. What does that mean? Have you heard it said that 'nothing really exists', or, 'it is all in the imagination, all in the mind'? We can mouth such sentences, almost hypnotize ourselves with them, but then something unpleasant happens, and suddenly everything exists after all.

We live in a world of opposites. In Chinese the term 'the ten thousand things' is used to stand for everything. Everything has its opposite, and so where there is emptiness, there must also be fullness. It is useless to try and capture emptiness through working with concepts; it cannot be 'caught' by thinking. To go into that emptiness, we have to be weaned off our misconception of 'I', and then we do not need to go into it, because there is no 'I' left to go anywhere. That is being fully and properly 'open'.

A well-known Zen text is called *Mumonkan, The Gateless Gate*. Those who go through the gate discover that it was never there. I throw myself against the gate or barrier, but it will not give way. If I really want to go through, I will throw myself against it again and again (that is what it is there for) until 'I' becomes less and less, until much of me wears away. Now it can be seen that there never was a barrier, that I myself am the heavy gate through which I cannot pass.

So in one in whom have arisen the 'powers of the Unborn' (Verse 16), 'In such a one, well-versed in both doctrine and exposition, / Dhyana and Prajna are whole and complete, unobstructed by Sunyata. / But not he alone comes by it, for this is the essence / Of all the Buddhas, as many as the grains of sand in the Ganges.' He incorporates the Great Wisdom, so meditation and insight, Dhyana and Prajna, are complete and whole and unobstructed by emptiness. In the Mahayana view, all beings are inherently endowed with Buddha-nature. There are also innumerable Buddhas, not only in the three worlds of past, present and future and in the three worlds of desire, form and formlessness, but even the innumerable worlds and universes each have their own Buddhas. Moreover, there is Buddha in everybody because of the inherent Buddha-nature. Such awareness evokes reverence and devotion because when all things are Buddha-things we are constantly surrounded by and touching Buddha. Obviously such an outlook differs profoundly from our usual 'I'- centred one. You would not carelessly lift up a Buddha-glass, or heedlessly put it down. You would reverently take up this Buddha-broom. You would reverently sit down on a Buddha-chair, look after it and care for it, wouldn't you?

With the awareness that all things are Buddha-things, life is lived in unity as well as in reverence, and things that otherwise are rather difficult become easy and natural. Real reverence is a quality of the heart, and arises from my being willing to allow myself to be ground away – with every step in the practice 'I' becomes a little bit less. To that extent the heart can open and the inherent qualities of the heart emerge. These are not accessible to 'I', but are natural to the heart. They start with the feeling of gratitude; from that comes compassion, and from compassion comes real joy and reverence. When these really begin to flow, life takes on a quite different aspect. Then personal difficulties, dislikes and misfortunes are certainly there in the way that, for example, a decayed tooth will hurt, but they do not interfere with the general perception of the miracle and shine of things.

The condition for getting at least a glimmer of this is that I lay myself down, so we come again to the bowing. Please experiment with the bowing as much, as frequently and as wholeheartedly as you can. The head may not understand and may query the purpose of it, but the heart knows – not only because of the millions of years behind that gesture in all cultures, but innately because in the act of bowing, of laying head and body low, something happens. Try it! When you do not want to do something or are sad or upset, go quietly where nobody sees you and bow. Still better, prostrate yourself. Does it then still feel so terrible? But by the time we have done some three thousand physical prostrations by ourselves, either when in trouble or religiously mornings and evenings, we are softened up to a remarkable extent, and insistence on having 'my way' has shrunk.

'But not he alone comes by it, for it is the essence.' When 'I' is gone, so are the Fires. But 'I-only' cannot live this essence, cannot be conscious of it, 'for this is the essence / Of all the Buddhas.' When there is nothing left – No-I – then all things are Buddha-things. Suddenly there are good friends and companions all around, and they all teach me.

Training in Japan, I often found myself in difficulties from which I could not see a way out, so I used to go for long walks. One took me through a large wood to the confluence of two shallow little brooks, with a beam across for the woodcutters. I would sit on it and look down at the waters and listen. These streams, literally, told me things. They scolded me, told me what a fool I was, that I had better put my nose to the grindstone, or do more prostrations, and not to make such a commotion. But however much scolded, there was consolation in it too because, being dressed down, I could see I was making a mountain out of a molehill. I felt purged and better. I often had recourse to those waters, and still feel grateful. I have learned to listen.

If only we would listen. We do not need to have a brook. We can listen to a tree, or to the wind blowing through the branches or over the grass – all say the same thing: obey the circumstances, because that is the natural way in which life exists. When it is spring, buds and shoots sprout, flowers and leaves open. It is no good wanting a situation other than it is, or wanting to escape, for here and now is where we are. In the Buddhist view, we are karmically always in the right place. It is not our personal misfortune that we are born under these circumstances and have to face dreadful afflictions and fearful situations. We are exactly where, in our karmic linkage, we belong. And this is not only so as to wear out our previous misdeeds, but also to learn the necessary lesson, and so to grow further. We need to be aware of the all-important continuation: that what was has resulted in what is now, and that what is now is the stage from which the future unfolds, and so is just the right place to shape it. So we say yes, and respond to the demands of this given situation; not blindly or carelessly but as the Buddha enjoined us, 'heedfully'. Then we will really learn the lesson. But if we only think that we have learned the lesson, it will repeat itself again and again until eventually we are willing to listen, and to respond correctly.

'Hearing the lion's roar of fearlessness / Shatters the brains of hundreds of animals.' Zen texts often use the simile of the lion's roar shattering the brains of animals. The Buddha's teaching is compared to the roar of the lion. The lion is king of all the animals: he is fearless, and has no equal among animals. In the human realm, this true fearlessness results from 'I' having become so little that there is nothing to fear. Carefully pondered, it is only 'I' who can fear. I can be heroic, but I cannot be fearless; it is not possible.

When 'I' is shed, going along with things becomes natural. Just think of that wonderful Buddhist image of the ocean and the waves. One wave, 'I', thrown up by the swell, jostled by other waves in a raging ocean, itself shoved forward, willy-nilly trampling on what is in front and terrified of plunging down as it reaches the crest. But if that wave were aware that, whether up or down, it is nothing but ocean, and that all the waves around are also nothing but ocean, would that not be totally different? To learn to live by that ocean-nature rather than being confined by the fear and the wanting of 'I-only', that is the purpose of our training. The Buddha's message, the lion's roar, is that there is an end to suffering – if you are willing to go that way.

So the Buddha's teaching is called the lion's roar because it points the way out of suffering, and thus out of fear. Hence also the teaching of No-I, which is a declaration of fearlessness. I cannot imagine a state of No-I, it is totally other, and yet we can have an inkling about what fearlessness is. A Bodhisattva, doctrinally, has gone beyond 'I', and is now there to assist and help all sentient beings. He is the representation of compassion, and his emblem is that of fearlessness.

Real compassion is not possible for 'I'. I can feel pity, I can be highly sentimental, more often than not too much so, or be the opposite, callous. I can be partisan, rebel, take up the cudgels in defence of someone or something, or may be frightened of the consequences, but 'I' always intrudes. Real compassion has none of that – hence the fearlessness of the Bodhisattva. This fearlessness is necessary, because in trying to help someone, a robust 'get going' is sometimes called for instead of maudlin sentimentality, and that cannot be done freely in the presence of 'I'/fear.

The 'lion's roar of fearlessness' expresses that compassion; it is fearless because 'I'-less, and 'it shatters the brains of hundreds of animals.' Little 'I' whines, 'How can he be so cruel? I just don't understand it.' Shattering the brains of hundreds of animals means just that – they cannot understand. We in our human world are in the world of relative truth in which 'I' lives. In this world there is bad and good; in it, the good has to be cultivated and the bad or the harmful avoided as far as possible. But there is another understanding, which is that of No-I, and this is informed by the concatenations and connections which are 'underneath' and which, although unseen, pervade or perfume our world. This is very difficult for us to realize. It is agony to just let things be, to resist the urge to manipulate and interfere, so it 'shatters the brains of hundreds of animals.' Perhaps, once their brains are shattered, and 'I' with it, they also awake to the underlying truth.

'Hearing the lion's roar of fearlessness / … Even the scent-bearing elephant gets excited and loses his dignity.' The scent-bearing elephant carries the amphora with the perfume of the Buddha-nature. It needs an elephant as carrier: big, majestic, slow and completely impassive to cheering crowds or howling foes – every single step majestically unperturbed. Yet even the magnificent, scent-bearing elephant, when he hears that 'lion's roar of fearlessness... gets excited and loses his dignity.' There is a call from 'beyond': up goes his trunk, and he has lost his majestic balance. Something has been scented – and since an elephant is not easily frightened, the scent he is bearing wafts him on to where he wants to go, inspires him, but it rushes to his head, and he gets carried away by the prospect. There is still a remnant left.

'Only the heavenly dragon listens cheerfully and rejoices.' The dragon in Far Eastern mythology is a joyous symbol. He lives in rivers and the sea and brings life-giving rain. The heavenly dragon holds the Pearl of Wisdom in his front paw. He soars up from the depths, rides the clouds and bestows the jewel on the wise old sage with whom he has an affinity, but he can also be capricious. We also have dragons in the West, but whereas the Eastern dragon soars as an aspect of the 'Wisdom Gone Beyond', the Western dragon hides in caves, hoards treasure. He is always fierce, and imprisons virgins. And it needs a young innocent hero to come along to do battle with the dragon, slay him, win the treasure and liberate the damsel. But strangely enough, soon afterwards the young hero comes to a sticky end, because of his own hubris – almost as if he had somehow become the killed dragon and was slain. And the lesson? The young hero kills the dragon and comes to a sticky end: on the heavenly dragon the wise old sage freely rides.

19   *I crossed rivers, climbed mountains and forded freshets*
     To ask Masters for the Way and trained under them.
     But since I managed to find the Way of Sokei (Huineng)
     I also find that I need not trouble about birth and death.

20   *Walking is Zen, sitting is Zen,*
     Talking or silent, moving or still, the essence is ever at ease.
     Even on encountering spears and swords it remains whole
          and perfect,
     And poisons, too, fail to disturb its serenity.

Commentary

Yoka Daishi describes the Way towards genuine insight. He had been training for a long time and tells us what it entailed. He wandered about and 'ask[ed] Masters for the Way and trained under them.' Only well-attained monks with great aspiration might go on a pilgrimage to test themselves, to find out whether there was still something lacking. By the time Yoka Daishi set out on his pilgrimage he too was a well-settled monk. He went 'To ask Masters for the Way, and trained under them.' He must have been on the Way for quite some time already, 'But', he says, 'since I managed to find the Way of Sokei / I also find that I need not trouble about birth and death.' Sokei we know as Huineng, the Sixth Patriarch – it was under him that Yoka Daishi's enlightenment opened.

In the Platform Sutra, which is attributed to him, we are told that as a young man Huineng happened to hear the Diamond Sutra expounded in the marketplace. Insight opened and, being deeply moved, he wanted to find a place where such things were taught. Told of the Fifth Patriarch, he made the long journey to his monastery. Since he was still very young, not a monk, illiterate, and from the deep South where only uncultivated barbarians lived, he was put to work in the rice-hulling shed. Because of his slight build, he used to tie a heavy stone to his waist in order to have enough weight to work the treadle. This is the diligence necessary for the training and giving ourselves into it, wholeheartedly doing as best we can in a given situation. That is where the inner strength and fortitude is cultivated, and that is what staying power really means.

He did not run about asking a lot of questions, but just diligently kept working. A year went by, and then the Fifth Patriarch, who was old and felt his death drawing near, wanted to make sure about his succession. So he let it be known that all the monks were to compose a poem that expressed their insight. The succession would then go to the one whose understanding was the most profound. None of the monks troubled very much about it, because they were sure that the wise old head monk would receive the transmission. The head monk, though aware of this, was not quite sure of himself, and did not want to commit himself publicly. So in the dark of night he secretly wrote a verse on the wall of the corridor. It was found there in the morning and admired. The Master himself came and nodded his approval.

The body is the Tree of Enlightenment,
The heart is like a bright mirror on a stand.
Carefully clean that mirror all the time
So that no dust can settle on it.

Literally, the text says 'polish' because glass mirrors were not known at that time. If we realize that the references are to metal mirrors, we will understand the frequent mirror analogies in Buddhist texts better. The polishing of a metal surface until it shines is quite a different proposition from cleaning a glass surface. Also, if you polish a dull metal mirror which has no reflection, the shine does not come out bit by bit. Still almost blind, it shines up suddenly. Metal mirrors also easily get scratched, and a mirror that is dusty or scratched cannot reflect clearly. If clean, it will reflect naturally, and will do so to the finest detail, so that poem advises to polish the mirror all the time so no dust can settle.

The news about the poem and the Master's approval spread like wildfire throughout the monastery, and soon reached the rice-hulling shed. When the young man there heard of the verse on the wall he immediately composed another, but unable to write himself, he asked a monk to write his comment next to it.

From the beginning there is no Tree of Enlightenment.
The bright mirror has no stand.
Originally all is void;
Where could dust settle?

When there is nothing, what dust can settle where? There was even greater commotion in the monastery. Whose was that second verse? Nobody knew. Now, regarding these two verses: the first one bids to carefully go on polishing all the time, so that no dust can settle; and the second one asks if there is nothing, where can dust settle? We can take our pick. We know that it was Huineng (in Japanese, Eno) who became the Sixth Patriarch, and that it was his 'sudden' school, from which the Zen line arose, while the 'gradual' or 'Northern' line died out quite soon. So being biased in any case, and also liking to side with the one who wins, we might feel, 'That's my line. Look, no nonsense about it. No study, no training, none of those boring old things. You sweep it all away, and hey presto!' But another one cautions, 'Well, I am not quite certain. I am for the slow but sure, with rules to be kept. Don't be hasty, it should be just gradual preparation, step by step.'

Both would be wrong. With slow preparation, the means often become the end before we know where we are. It goes on and on and on, and becomes dead in the process. But the other one is likely to throw out the baby with the bathwater. I may 'show my freedom', but it is only blind foolishness, if not worse. So neither alone is effective, and what these two matched verses actually show us is that both are necessary. The one is not possible without the other, and the other is not possible without the one. They need to come together, become one, be at one. Similarly, there is no mind without a body, nor a body without a mind: the latter is a corpse and the former a ghost.

We have to get used to seeing things in the round. While picking and choosing, which is our habit, we cannot help but take sides, but calling it a habit is wrong. A habit I can get rid of, but not so picking and choosing. Factually, 'I' am the picking and choosing – as the Buddha told us – because of my attachments. That is the primary delusion, one of the Three Signs of Being and the first link in the Chain of Causation. There is no need to get rid of the delusion that there is such a picker and chooser, only to awaken from it as from a dream.

And so Yoka Daishi says, 'But since I managed to find the Way of Sokei (Huineng) / I also find that I need not trouble about birth and death.' If that Way is really found, which is also the Buddha's Way, the Great Way, and the Great Matter of Life and Death, it is seen as a natural occurrence – 'coming to be and ceasing to be'. We die many times each day, though we do not realize it. Now we are reading. Then we die to the reading as we go out for a walk and are born to the walking. We die to the walking and are reborn in making the tea, then die to that, and so it goes on. If we really go with this, as it happens all day long, just dying to one state and being reborn into the next, then it begins to flow easily and we just adapt to what is. If the body feels uncomfortable within the given possibilities, it naturally chooses what is more comfortable – which is quite different from 'I must have'. So we learn to flow with things. When reborn into the picking and choosing of our food, we are not going to choose what we do not like, we choose what we like within what is there. I might prefer coffee to tea, but if there is no coffee, then I drink tea gratefully because I am thirsty. That's all. If I really do not like tea I do not have to drink it, but neither do I need to make a fuss about it.

'I also find that I need not trouble about birth and death.' If one is really used to going with the situation, without either a this or a that, then there is no need to trouble oneself about birth and death – nor is there any need, after once having gone through that opening which Master Hakuin calls the Great Death. He also tells us that dying it once is essential, but it is still reversible and, therefore, it needs to be died at least four times to really hold.

So in a way, there is no end to training – fortunately. Even the Buddha has something to do: he has to teach us. The Buddha has not gone into Nirvana for good and forever, has not vanished into it – at least, not according to the Zen view. He and Bodhidharma are still here training with us, and thus encourage us by showing that they are continuing too. So just when we feel, 'Oh, it is all too much, I can no longer go on,' if at that moment we become aware of the Buddha on our right and Bodhidharma on our left side, walking or sitting with us, do we then say, 'I can't anymore?' Or are we encouraged – 'Oh, get on with it, it's all right.'

And as to 'birth and death' – well, being used to dying and being reborn umpteen times a day on the Wheel of Change, I need not trouble much about them when the big moment comes. Rather there is a smooth going with it, the more so if we know where we are going. When the wave, having arisen, falls back into the ocean, it has gone 'back home'.

'Walking is Zen, sitting is Zen, / Talking or silent, moving or still, the essence is ever at ease.' As was mentioned earlier, Zen is the Japanese pronunciation of the Chinese chan or chan-na, and of the Indian Dhyana, which mean meditation. So we could imagine that a Zen monk in his monastery does nothing but Zazen. However, although the monks get up early, the day starts with Sutra chanting, and then Zazen only until it gets light. During the day the monks work: 'A day without work is a day without food.' When it gets dark in the evening, Zazen starts, usually until about half past nine or ten o'clock. After that the monks are supposed to do their private night meditation for at least an hour, and by eleven o'clock they may sleep. By three o'clock in the morning in summer, and by four o'clock in the winter, they are up again. They have, therefore, the propensity of instantly falling asleep whenever they are not moving. They do not need sleeping pills, they have few problems, few wishes – and those are mostly connected with sleep and food. It is a very simple life for the first three or four years, and they find out for themselves that 'Walking is Zen, sitting is Zen.'

What is meditation? We naively assume that meditation can only be done on the cushion and that it cannot be taken into ordinary life. But not even monks sit in meditation all the time, and it merely shows that we have never given ourselves into a Daily Life or Sila Practice. Meditation is an inner attitude, first to be practised sitting, but then to be taken into ordinary daily life and lived. Without Sila Practice, attempts at meditation practice will be unsatisfactory because we are not patient enough, not giving enough, not soft enough, nor can we endure long enough to attain that inner calm. So this needs to be cultivated further, from sitting motionless to moving, and to letting it prevail whilst functioning in our ordinary circumstances at work and at home. Once established, it remains the inner attitude, and it is no longer subject to tremors whatever the situation, whether pleasant, unpleasant or neutral. Until then, when circumstances are pleasant, or even neutral, we may keep calm, but can we when circumstances are unpleasant? Basically, meditation is not an activity that 'I do'. It emphatically is not a kind of ecstasy of floating somewhere up there, but simply a state of heart, where there is a 'being at one with' the situation, and a smooth functioning in it.

'Walking is Zen, sitting is Zen.' That is how life is lived, in this new attitude. 'Talking or silent, moving or still, the essence is ever at ease' under all circumstances. Once it has been truly cultivated and is being truly lived, it is not shaken anymore. But we mistake this unshakeable attitude as uniform, displayed by a grim, long-faced expression of, 'I don't mind anything anymore, I am beyond all that.' That is merely callous, and not the Buddha's Way. Where is the energy then, that life energy that is in every living thing?

If you look at the various traditions, they all have teaching stories, and however the particular formulations may differ, they all point at the same verities, at what is universal. Why are such stories universal? Our human nature, our human heart, is the same – there is no ancient or modern, no Eastern or Western, neither Northern nor Southern human nature. On the surface we are all different individuals; further down we are creatures of our culture. Still further down differences begin to cancel each other out because we all share the same human nature, with the same human heart that hopes for something good, wants to be happy, and dislikes pain. Still deeper, and it becomes universal. We share traits with our mammalian brothers and sisters in that we all naturally gravitate to what is pleasant, and naturally shy away from what is unpleasant.

'Walking is Zen, sitting is Zen.' Living out of this attitude is what Zen training helps us to accomplish. 'Talking or silent, moving or still, the essence is ever at ease' does not mean to be free of circumstances, but to be free of my reactions to circumstances; not because I have learned not to care, but because the circumstances are no longer threatening. 'Even on encountering spears and swords it remains whole and perfect, / And poisons too fail to disturb its serenity.' We think again of the Buddha under the Bodhi tree, assailed by Mara's demons poking at him with their spears, lashing out against him with their swords, but they did not jolt him out of his deep calm, his meditation.

A rather awe-inspiring story is told of Master Hakuin's teacher, Shoju Rojin, who had his temple in the Japanese Alps. There in the mountains the winters are very cold and there is much snow. He was considered one of the greatest teachers of his time, yet he had few disciples because of his known severity. Like most masters, this teacher usually did Zazen in his own room and did not sit with his monks, except occasionally over Rohatsu Sesshin. He lived his Zazen, but at the height of winter liked to make sure his calm was unshakeable, that he truly was in the state of 'mushin', empty heart, so once or twice he went into the woods to sit a night there in the snow. Of that full, complete Zazen strength it is said, 'Even on encountering spears and swords it remains whole and perfect, / And poisons, too, fail to disturb its serenity.' He would sit there and wolves would come and sniff at him and jump over him, taking him for a rock.

There are many stories on the same theme: they illustrate what is meant by when I am no longer truly there. I cannot imagine how it is without 'I', only think (or flatter and delude) myself to be without 'I'. Fortunately, usually something happens just then that throws me out of my self-satisfaction, wakes me up again and makes me realize there is much training yet to be done. If I then have the humility to start again, right from scratch, with a beginner's heart, and yet again, then the ripening process occurs of itself if only I persevere without giving up halfway through.

21   *Our teacher trained under Dipankara Buddha,*
     And for many Kalpas patiently underwent austerities
        as a hermit.
     I too went through many births and deaths –
     Births and deaths endlessly without stopping.

22   *On suddenly realizing the non-originated,*
     Neither praise nor blame cause joy or grief.
     I live in a ramshackle hut in remote mountains –
     Wide and steep they range as I sit under the old pine.

Commentary

'Our teacher trained under Dipankara Buddha.' 'Our teacher' is, of course, the Buddha. Mahayana texts talk of many Buddhas; 'our' Buddha, in our world age, is Sakyamuni Buddha. 'Sakya' is the clan to which the family of Prince Gautama belonged, and 'muni' means teacher, so his title is 'Teacher of the Sakya'. Traditionally, before our Buddha there were other Buddhas, and Dipankara Buddha was one of them.

Before becoming Sakyamuni Buddha, he trained 'for many Kalpas' as a Bodhisattva, patiently practising 'austerities as a hermit'. This is told in the Jataka Tales or birth stories. In one such story the Bodhisattva who was the Buddha-to-be, stood on a tall cliff. Looking down he saw a starved tigress with two scrawny, hungry cubs at her heels.

Motivated by his great compassion, the Bodhisattva threw himself over the cliff in order to feed them. To us this seems unreal, a beautiful story extolling compassion, but how can one take it seriously? But what these stories actually point out is something which is deadly serious and awesome, and we had better ponder them most carefully.

All Mahayana schools cultivate the Paramitas. The first six are particularly emphasized, but all go beyond what 'I' can do, even beyond what I can conceive. Because, should I stand on that cliff and see that hungry tigress down there with her howling cubs, I feel, 'Thank goodness I am standing safely up here, she can't get at me here.' Who, frankly speaking, in spite of long training, would even think of throwing themselves down to feed the tigress, let alone do it?

So here we are referring to the first Paramita, Dana or Giving, which goes beyond 'I'. Not only beyond what I can do, but even beyond what I can think. As that, it points to a state of No-I. We are not exhorted or expected to do it: 'I', the self-conscious 'doer', is inevitably wrong. Rather, we are pointed towards a state of selflessness, with the last root of 'I' dropped off. Thus there is just the situation itself – in this case a hungry tigress and two hungry cubs, and a possible meal for them. So you supply, and the situation is fulfilled.

We cling to life, expect to be healthy, and nowadays even feel that we have the right to be so. And if there is something wrong with us, whether it is a toothache, a tummy ache or something more, we feel it shouldn't be, it interferes with our normal healthy state. We no longer realize that it is the nature of things to balance each other. I take it as my right to continue being practically immortal until I am almost at the point where I go, and then the regrets come, and I ask myself whether I have wasted my life? The human state is a very precious one because only from it is deliverance possible. There are various analogies on how difficult it is to be born as a human – even just physically because, although grossly overpopulated, we are by far outnumbered by insects. Although we are not the main populaters on the globe, we certainly are the main ravishers of it, but fondly believe it will go on like this forever. When will we awaken from that dream, attached as we are to our wants? The Buddha points the Way.

So the future Sakyamuni Buddha 'trained under Dipankara Buddha... for many Kalpas [aeons]' and 'patiently underwent austerities as a hermit.' We are also told that during these ages robbers got hold of the Bodhisattva and tortured and killed him. First they cut off his fingers and then his hands, then his toes and then his feet. Then they cut him from the elbows and the knees until, little by little, they had dismembered him. Throughout this whole ordeal he kept up his meditation and wished his torturers well.

Now, we either take in the full impact of that and tremble with awe, or we fend it off – 'Oh well, these eulogies. This is not human, who could actually do it?' But just that is the point; it is not human, it is not meant to be human. It goes beyond 'I', in the fulfilment of the Dana Paramita, going beyond 'I' giving. And perhaps it makes us realize that, if it really comes right down to it, it is more than I can conceive. Perhaps we can also then begin to have an intimation of how much training is necessary to forget 'I' so completely that, even while being dismembered, because he is no longer a human being, the Bodhisattva is truly not shaken by circumstance.

'Our teacher trained under Dipankara Buddha, / And for many Kalpas patiently underwent austerities as a hermit.' What is pointed out by that? The Paramitas run like a theme through our practice, and we will come back to them again and again. Each one carries beyond 'I', but all are needed for a real transformation. I can only give so much, and in full awareness, with all reverence, I am not capable of giving more. I may close my eyes and jump blindly – I often do so anyway, but that is our deluded human state acting impulsively, driven by the Fires. Not just by liking and loathing, but by their corollaries, such as opinions, convictions, etc.

Our modern neglect of inner discipline has made the overlaying surface perilously thin. Scratched only a little, and this force – or the fear of it – soon breaks to the surface, and 'in hot blood' it lets us commit terrible things in good conscience without any real judgement. When these primal Fires flare, reason, and even humanity, are swept away, yet, once cooled down again, if you look at the individual and talk with him or her, they seem to be decent and reasonable. If you talk with a football hooligan or a mugger one-to-one, they may be a bit rough and ready, but most are reasonable people, kind to their friends and family. Only when 'the other', the Fire or the 'bull' roars up, they have nothing to hold on to or to support them. They have no staying power, and so are swept away. The energy erupts, and exceeding the bearing tolerance of the undisciplined person, discharges itself through any crack or weakness because otherwise it would burst the person. Thus, without the discipline of containment, and the inner strength resulting from this discipline, the inner transformation of the elemental power into human values cannot take place. We have every reason to practise this containment, and not only for ourselves, but for the sake of others too, because if such a flare-up comes into contact with somebody who is equally undisciplined, sparks soon fly.

But it would be a grave mistake to judge this elemental force as 'evil' per se. If we must 'picture' it, it is better to think of it as a bull, as in the Zen analogy. It is not inhuman, in spite of all the atrocities that we have managed to produce in our collective history. At bottom, that energy, whether as the passions or as the Buddha-nature, is not human. It is much more than human, and the human is only one of the forms it enlivens. So we human beings had better bestir ourselves to see that it is properly humanized. This is why we first of all need to attain the stature of human beings, because only from that state is deliverance possible.

Only then can we start on the Spiritual Way proper. It is not possible to go this Way for oneself alone, because on it 'I' dwindles, and with it my wants and aversions, and to that extent the un-selfish urge, 'for the sake of all sentient beings', arises. That is why 'our teacher [Sakyamuni Buddha] trained under Dipankara Buddha, / And for many Kalpas patiently underwent austerities as a hermit.' His training was with the Paramitas – Giving, Restraint, Patient Endurance and Energy of Application – so that things can really come together. Through that, the elemental power is itself transformed and humanized, and is now seen as the life-giving and life-forming power informing all sentient beings.

If we really watch our actions and reactions for just one day, with all the afflictions we produce in our delusion, and so put ourselves under restraint, it is a sobering experiment.

We may then think that Paramita training is beyond us, but that is still another deluded judgement. We do not know, but we can make a start and see for ourselves. Many, many Kalpas are necessary, patiently undergoing austerities, to become familiar with that elemental force.

We have all heard that the human state is difficult to attain. And now, having attained this precious human body that for Kalpas we have striven towards and are now living in, what are we going to do in that state? Are we going to fritter it away again? If we spend all our life with nothing but wanting, what will we become next time round? Always wanting shunts us among the hungry ghosts on the Wheel. And if we live judging everything and are constantly irritated, we will end up amongst the fighting demons, and so on. Thus the precious hard-earned human state will slip away, and with it the opportunity of making use of it while it lasts, not only for our own happiness, but also for that of others. The Buddha's Way leads out of suffering, and the opening up can happen in this life; the end of suffering can be achieved, the Great Death can be died in this life. But it is not only just for this now momentary combination called 'I'. If 'I' slips off, something else begins to emerge to fill what has been vacated. Awakening to that, and then living out of it for the benefit of all beings, is the aim of the Buddhist Path.

Yoka Daishi says, 'I too went through many births and deaths – / Births and deaths endlessly without stopping.' Because however much Yoka Daishi, or we, have bestirred ourselves, all those states which we have traversed are still clinging to us like wet eggshells. Now, having at last become human, rather than waste this precious human birth, it would be better to make an extra effort for deliverance. Having come this far, it is possible in this life. With Yoka Daishi it was possible. He says that he too, like the Buddha before him, like all those who walked the Way before, went through many births and deaths, endlessly without stopping. There is no resting place on the Wheel, it churns on and on. And it is the delusion of 'I' with its concomitant desire and aggression of 'I must have' or 'I don't want' that drives it.

So, 'Births and deaths endlessly without stopping' until it opens up with 'On suddenly realizing the non-originated, / Neither praise nor blame cause joy or grief.' Neither elated nor upset – is such a life not bland? That is what 'I' imagine. But we have already heard (see Commentary to Verses 7 & 8) the Bhikku, Nagasena, telling King Milinda that, on the contrary, such a one can savour life to the full, as it is, the good and the bad – and make something out of it, for one's own delectation, as well as 'in joyful service to all beings'. For that nothing special is needed. 'I live in a ramshackle hut in remote mountains – / Wide and steep they range as I sit under an old pine.' That is a favourite analogy; a ramshackle hut in remote mountains. Not much is needed when there is equanimity and real serenity. Nor is it necessary to specially go and find a ramshackle hut in the faraway mountains. When it is possible to live like this, it is also very clear where, this time round in this life and in these circumstances, that place actually is. There is a wonderful saying of Master Rinzai: 'One stands on a mountain peak, solitary and alone. One stands in the dusty marketplace amidst the dirt of carts and horses. Who is front? Who is back?' Some may say, 'Look, he can exist all alone on the mountain peak, how great!' Another will say, 'What is the use of him on the mountain peak, he had better go down to the marketplace.' 'The snowflakes fall, each in their appropriate place.'

It is important that we each find this, our appropriate place, which is not 'mine', as I mistakenly fancy, but a place of harmony, the place karmically fitting this particular, now manifesting, entity. To find that place and that activity is the all-important thing, because there is nothing else that will give us real joy and peace of heart. It may be a mountain peak, it may be in the marketplace, it may be as an artist, it may be as cobbler, or a road sweeper, or Prime Minister. If it is really the appropriate place, and we work towards it, then that is exactly where we belong. Even if it is not fully achieved, as long as it is known and worked towards, that is the important thing. And, quite remarkably, if that movement towards the appropriate place is once instigated and steered, miraculous things begin to open up. The training will very clearly show it. Suddenly things begin to fall into place, as if the whole of nature wanted to move along in that direction, and we only need to go with it.

23 *In the wilderness my hut is perfumed with the calmness*
    of Zazen,
    And it is tranquil and peaceful all round.
    Once awakened, there is nothing further to do,
    But phenomena, ever changing, are not of that nature.

24 *Giving, if practised with attachment, may bring good*
    fortune,
    But even rebirth in the heavenly realm is like shooting
    an arrow into the sky.
    Once its momentum is spent, it plunges down again and,
    Contrary to intention, only invites unfortunate rebirth
    in the next life.

Commentary

'In the wilderness my hut is perfumed with the calmness of Zazen.' In the previous verse Yoka Daishi says, 'I live in a ramshackle hut in the remote mountains – / Wide and steep they range as I sit under the old pine.' The old pine is often a metaphor for 'a long time'. What happens when we try to sit quietly for a couple of hours all by ourselves, with nothing else around, no book, TV or whatever? Are we likely to sit quietly and just look? Sometimes the sun shines and sometimes it rains. And there we sit, two hours, three hours. Do we get fidgety? Do we crave distractions? Do we want to have some entertainment? We come to a beauty spot – 'Oh, how wonderful!' I sit myself down, but all too soon I wish there were not any cars there – 'It is a bit public, isn't it?' 'Is it clouding over?' 'These tiny flowers – I must get some for my rockery.' Or, if at home I think I ought to do this chore, or read that book, or write that letter. We want to be entertained or distracted, want to be with a friend, have somebody to relate to. And why? So that if you are with me and I relate to you, you affirm my being here. And without being constantly affirmed, I begin to feel a bit lonely, perhaps even scared. It all shows that I do not feel very friendly towards myself. Perhaps our first task in this training is to become friends with ourselves. That does not mean to become self-indulgent, but acquainted with ourselves.

But we can find relationship with ourselves by just sitting in the wilderness. Yoka Daishi is sitting like that; he can do so now because he is at peace with himself, at peace with the world – 'my hut is perfumed with the calmness of Zazen.' The calmness of Zazen – of Zen meditation – what does that mean? Meditation is supposed to calm, isn't it? But do we know, even if we have done it for some time, what meditation really means? Does it mean sitting immovable and rigid with eyes fixed and staring? Do we think that is what he is doing all day long?

The calmness of Zazen is something quite different. We learnt it first in the very formal yet supportive position which holds while thoughts wobble about and feelings wash over us, but when that has somewhat settled, and the energy that has been wildly hopping about has calmed down, then it carries like the quiet sea carries a good swimmer.

That calmness permeates, perfumes the hut, it comes from Zazen. Zazen taken only as an activity, as me 'doing it', is not Zazen. At best it is the beginning of calmness meditation, which is nothing but trying to hold together. For that, Sila, or Daily Life Practice, is essential.

Yoka Daishi is now sitting comfortably in the wilderness, at home with himself and his surroundings. His hut is 'perfumed with the calmness of Zazen', and so it is also 'tranquil and peaceful all round.' If the heart is at peace, then peace is everywhere: whether an aeroplane drones in the sky, or people are shouting nearby, it does not matter. And it is also correctly responded to – not getting angry at it, but moving away if possible, or peacefully sitting it out. A Chinese proverb tells us, 'Quietness is not on the mountain peak, nor noise in the marketplace. They both dwell, eternally changing, in the heart of men only.'

Nowadays wildlife films are often shown on television. They are most instructive. We feel that, with the noise at an airport, all the wildlife will be driven away, but, on the contrary, the wildlife comes to the airport. They don't mind the noise, and understand that nobody is going to shoot at them there, they have learned all about planes and what to do. It is only we with our attachments and opinions who judge it intolerable. But if there is tranquillity and peace in the heart, it is not only inside, it is outside, too.

What is it that drives us? Why do we feel coerced by our environment? Why must I do this, that and the other, ever more, quicker, faster? Even if I think I have given my life to something, is it really true? Naturally my livelihood is important, but where is the limit to earning my living? And having got a bit more, striving for still a little more, then it suddenly grips, and I am in the rat race – more, and still more, quicker, better, faster!

Not only money or pleasure, but also reading and understanding – another book and a fourth book, and then a sixth book. The room is overflowing with books and not all of them read. Nowadays we are deeply convinced that the more we read, the more we will understand, but are we quite sure that this is the case? Or is it that the more I read, the more I fill my head with a medley of ideas? And when it then comes down to doing something, we are in a quandary: ideas chasing each other in the head obstruct the response to what is. 'Is this the right way?' Having stood up all my life, I now look for the 'right way' to stand up, or to brush my teeth. It is ludicrous, but we actually do it.

Master Rinzai asks, 'Haven't all of you got a father and mother?' Or also 'What at this moment is lacking?' If we really become aware that actually this moment is the only thing we ever have, then the rest are only the cobwebs we spin, our fantasies whirling around. Five minutes ago is only a memory – we no longer live in what was five minutes ago. And five minutes from now is mere speculation – we do not know what will be in five minutes. A thunderbolt may come down and blow us away. We do not know. The only thing that we actually, truly have and, therefore, know is this moment now. And it is just this moment we fail to live. We disport ourselves in what was five seconds or five minutes ago, in what was yesterday, in a good or spoilt holiday, in what there is going to be for dinner and what to do for Christmas. But now, at this actual moment? This is where our Daily Life Practice points to and is geared to bring us to – this moment. So we try to get used to giving ourselves into this moment, which is where we actually are. And at this moment there is nothing lacking.

'Once awakened, there is nothing further to do' does not mean to just sit around doing nothing. The human body is not geared for that. But there is nothing further to get myself excited about, nothing further to obtain, no need to assert myself or to make myself more. 'But', says Yoka Daishi, 'phenomena, ever changing, are not of that nature.' There is a difference because this is an impermanent body that has a beginning, exists, has a name, and will come to an end. While existing, it needs to breathe, needs nourishment and shelter. But what animates this body and animates all bodies, that is not 'I'. Insight into this basic Buddhist teaching comes only through dedicated training, because we cling to 'I' and are deeply convinced that without 'I' it does not go – that I must do, I must watch, and I cannot do without understanding. It is all not true – this is precisely what our bad dream is about. It is not the calm peace of someone who has nothing further to do.

If we do not have anything further to do we get very restless, and so to keep us occupied right from the beginning we start with what we call the Daily Life Practice. This sounds the simplest thing in the world. We only have this moment here and now – and giving ourselves into it is not difficult. We all do it automatically when we are interested in something, judge something as important or dangerous, but when we judge it as not important, uninteresting or boring, then instead of giving ourselves into it, we wander off, to outer space if necessary, we are not here. Daily Life Practice cultivates this giving ourselves into what is being done at this moment, into the situation here. If we are in it, there is always something being done. We always think of doing as being in the active mode: I walk, I run, I hoe, I weed – this is doing. Sitting here is not doing anything. But sitting here is also doing – we are always doing something. Even if we sit motionless for half an hour, there is still sitting. But most of the time we cannot do it, we soon start getting itchy and fidgety. So we patiently train giving ourselves into this moment just as it is, as wholeheartedly as possible.

'Giving, if practised with attachment, may bring good fortune, / But even rebirth in the heavenly realm is like shooting an arrow into the sky.' 'Giving' is the first of the Paramitas and like all the Paramitas, it goes beyond what I can do, and so needs training. I first start with giving myself as far as possible. If I could give myself completely, there would be no need for further training.

Giving can be done either as a bartering or it can be done as an offering. If it is done in terms of the former, I give this and then I'll get that – I do the Daily Life Practice and contain the anger, and then the anger will go away – that is bartering, and nothing much comes out of it. I will possibly contain myself a bit, for a while at least not flaring up so easily, but a transformation cannot take place just by evasion. What we are after is not a kind of repression. That is not healthy, because then the energy is held down ever more, so that sooner or later, and usually just at the most awkward moment, it erupts again. 'Making a mountain out of a molehill.' 'The straw that broke the camel's back.' Language expresses the wisdom of the ages.

'Giving, if practised with attachment, may bring good fortune, / But even rebirth in the heavenly realm is like shooting an arrow into the sky.' If I am by nature irritable, but hold it down so that it will not flare up, that is better than throwing tempers. It may even lead to rebirth in the heavenly realms, as depicted in the Twelve-linked Chain of Dependent Origination. But although in the realm of the heavenly beings life is long, it is still under the law of change, and does not last forever, it does not deliver from the Wheel. In the course of even just one day we may migrate through all the stages of the Wheel. Waking up on a glorious morning – how wonderful, we are in heaven. Then my tea is cold and the toast is burnt. What happens then? Do I take it philosophically – 'Oh well, that's just how it is' – or do I get annoyed and upset – 'Just when I have such a hard day ahead!'? And now I am amongst the demons or hungry ghosts.

Occasionally I also suffer with the miserable beings, painfully with some illness or hurt, or must endure something unpleasant without redress, like the animals. In Buddhism, the animal state is seen as a miserable one because, whether in captivity or whether in the wild, an animal must take whatever happens to it. It has no redress, it cannot do anything. If a tiger loses a few teeth, he will soon come to a miserable end. Wild animals do not usually live out their full life expectancy, and domesticated ones have to take what is meted out by their owners. We may have a pet cat, but considering how many cats are kept in the world, there are only a few that have a good life, most of them do not. So in Buddhism the animal state is seen as deplorable.

And thus in the daily round, we swirl round through these six states, yet we differ from the residents of all the other states, who spend their allotted life span in one. A wasp, for instance, will reliably behave exactly as a wasp always does. It will fly about; it will hunt for food. And an ant will always behave as an ant, under all circumstances, whether good, bad or indifferent. A lion will reliably behave as a lion behaves – if it is hungry it will hunt, otherwise it will loll around with nothing to do. And we so-called human beings, do we always under all circumstances, good, bad or indifferent, reliably behave in truly human fashion? We all know what 'truly human' is. In Buddhism this means not only in deed, but also in word and in thought. Is there anybody who can say, that in the last six days they have behaved thus, 'truly human' without one 'Oh blast', or 'That fool!'? And yet we want to be good and understanding. However, we do not have to learn anything new for that purpose. What we need is the strength and the patience to be able to do what in our hearts all of us truly want to do but often, regretfully, fail to bring off. Hence the need for practice. 'Giving, if practised with attachment', as a barter for something I want, although it may bring good fortune, does not effect the transformation into a true human being. 'But even rebirth in the heavenly realm is like shooting an arrow into the sky.' However high you shoot it, 'once its momentum is spent, it plunges back down again.' No transformation has taken place; and the good Karma, now spent and exhausted, will instead only invite 'unfortunate rebirth in the next life.'

'Contrary to intention' is another version of the old Zen saying that 'all intention misses the target.' How come? If we have no intention to practise, we would not do it, would we? So we believe intention to be necessary. But we all know that if we do something self-consciously, intentionally, it is likely to miscarry. So again we come back to the Daily Life Practice of 'just giving myself'.

With that, a transformation begins to set in. Experiment – when wanting something desperately, take a deep breath and, not thinking of the object that you want, stay with the energy that drives the want. Hatch it out. Stick it out, and sooner or later it will change. The raw energy that is in the want, in the 'must have', undergoes a transformation if truly hatched out. If repressed, it will only go underground. But there is no other way that can effect this transformation than giving ourselves into and patiently enduring the rampant energy, unpleasant, as it is while it lasts. But once the energy is truly transformed, the True Nature or True Face becomes naturally apparent.

Try putting this giving into every living moment, just as it is. We are a great many people on this small globe, and it is inevitable that sooner or later something happens that annoys. Give that energy houseroom, live it and do not let it escape; rather, make good use of it. There is a gauge for whether this is done correctly or not: if something quite trivial goes contrary to one's expectation, how much does one work oneself up about such nothings? So the moment that energy rears up and goes into the well-worn track, stop and take a deep breath in. Hold it for a moment. Now the body is as big as can be, and the rising energy has room and fills it. Then hold the breath for a moment and reverently address the energy: 'Please burn me away.' Endure its singe, but be careful now with your physical responses because you are highly charged. Be ultra-polite in your speech, so that the energy does not discharge itself by way of mouth.

Move slowly and keep good form. Sooner or later the energy, being dynamic, will burn down like a fire going out. Now it is over, and you feel physically lighter as well as relieved. This physically lighter is the gauge of energy transformed rather than wasted.

Anger is energy; so is wanting. The 'object' of either is unimportant; it is only the lightning conductor. Without that conductor, there is only 'I' and the rising energy. If the latter is contained, then the energy, being by nature dynamic, acts in lieu of a suitable conductor. It must now go for what is still there: that is 'I'. This is why I find it unbearable. But if endured, then the raw energy and 'I' will, little by little, both be transformed and begin to resemble each other, so that finally a merging can take place.

To sum up: energy thus transformed, when it has neither been discharged nor been pushed underground, has not lost any of its power, but is now a little more human. It is not that the body has become lighter, but the actual sensation of it is lighter, because all the energy is still there. This is why working with the emotional energy is so important. By its transformation insight arises into the enigmatic saying that, 'The passions are the Buddha-nature and the Buddha-nature is the passions.'

25   *Far better, then, is to ascend to Absolute Truth,*
And with one step to enter the realm of the Tathagata.
Just stick to the root and do not trouble about the branches;
It is like the moon reflected in a lapis lazuli bowl.

26   *Now I know that this wondrous Mani Jewel*
Inexhaustibly benefits self and others.
The moon is reflected in the stream, a gentle breeze
   in the old pine tree;
Deep and quiet night – what is it for?

Commentary

In Verse 24 doing good is compared with shooting an arrow into the sky: when its momentum is spent, it falls back down to earth again, no real change has taken place. Doing good is certainly fundamental, and thus the basis of religious practice, but if it is done with self-interest or with intentional will, then it will not go very far. Whatever is done with premeditation is still within the realm of Samsara – bound on the turning Wheel of Change. Calculated action, if good, will result in good Karma, but when the accumulated merit has been exhausted, it goes back to what was before, or worse.

So Yoka Daishi continues, 'Far better then is to ascend to Absolute Truth / And with one step to enter the realm of the Tathagata.' Wouldn't that be wonderful? I am quite certain that we are all raring to take that one step, but the question is how to do it? The Buddha himself assured us that it is possible to enter the realm of the Tathagata with one step – it is only a question of waking up. Awakening from what? From what in Buddhism is called 'delusion' – and not only general delusion, but from what could be called the nightmare of feeling myself to be a separate, completely different entity, totally 'other' than everything else. Underneath this state of alienation there is naturally always fear, because I feel exposed, all alone. The Buddha found the way out from this delusion, awakening to what we truly are. The Buddhist Teachings, collected together, fill libraries, but the Buddha summed them up in one short sentence: 'Suffering I teach and the Way out of suffering.' That suffering is the delusion of 'I-alone'.

Let us come back to the Buddha's proclamation of, 'All beings are fully endowed with the Tathagata's wisdom and power, but sadly, because of their attachments, human beings are not aware of it.' Now, if I hear this I might say, 'Fine. If this is the one step that is necessary, I'll just drop all my attachments.' But I can only drop what I actually have, and I naively believe that I have attachments – the Buddha says so. Yet I find that I cannot drop them, so there must be another nexus somewhere connected with it. Let us carefully begin to look into attachments. I prefer coffee to tea – that is an attachment, isn't it? Will that make a difference, do you think? Or would it, perhaps be attachments to my ideas and my convictions – to what I am convinced is this, that or the other? And then I begin to look further. What could I not do without? Or, what would I not like to do without? Thus I begin to see what I am actually leaning on, what props me up. There I will find a whole host of ideas, opinions, convictions – all mine, if I am honest, but factually there is no 'I' that owns them. What I naively think of as 'I', because it seems continuous, is an ever-changing bundle of attachments. Nor is it I who have them – I am them. The question is, how to stop them? I cannot drop them. That is why we need a practice to, little by little, wean us from 'our' attachments, as we first think of them. It is rather frightening to accept that, without attachments, there is no 'I'.

The most basic and important Buddhist Teaching is that of the Three Signs (or Marks) of Being. The first, Anicca, is that everything is subject to change, nothing is permanent. This body has a beginning, whilst it exists it is given a name, and then it ceases to be again.

The second mark is Dukkha – dissatisfaction, unease and suffering because I cannot really accept change. I can say, 'Oh yes, summer is over, autumn is coming', but even that already has a melancholic tinge. The more distant or abstract the change, the easier it is to accept it. The huge cycles of change like the Ice Ages, etc., are not a problem, but when change comes very close to me personally, do I accept it so philosophically? When something that I am fond of recedes from me, can I then just say, 'Oh yes, change is quite natural.' If I am desperately waiting for something and want it, and it is not forthcoming, do I then say, 'Oh well, things will change, sooner or later.' Or do I react against it, am sad, impatient, or angry? Change when it comes very close, is not very congenial to me, and yet it is inevitable.

This is where the delusion of 'I' comes in, and so we have No-I, Anatta, as the third mark. No-I cannot be understood because how can I understand a teaching of No-I? It just is not on, but there is a possibility, and that is to go on with a conducive, traditional training that has a couple of thousand years of experience behind it. Following the Buddha's teaching, we can, with practice, slowly wean ourselves from that deeply ingrained conviction of being a separate 'I', different from everything else. Such training has to be gradual, step by step, otherwise it is too frightening.

In a good solid training, the feeling of a separate 'I' is slowly ground away. To the extent that I am ground away, my delusions, notions, etc., become less, and instead what really is, the inherent wisdom and power of the Tathagata, or the Buddha-nature, appears. With 'I' shrinking, the Buddha-nature can unfold and be trusted. Thus a merging can take place, and that is the purpose of the exercise. That such a practice is not always enjoyable is obvious. Let's be honest, I usually undertake a practice in order to get something out of it. This practice makes me lose all the way.

I want to understand. But there are many things (and we will learn that too in the course of the practice) that the head cannot understand, that are either irrational or inconceivable. As mentioned above, no 'I' can understand a state of 'I'-lessness. But there is another part of ourselves, just as real, which in Buddhist text translations is often wrongly called 'mind', but which connotes heart, spirit, sentience, life and mind, and for which we have no equivalent expression in Western languages. Here we always translate the crucial term (in Sanskrit, citta) as 'heart'. It is not the exact equivalent, but rather better than 'mind'.

The heart has very little to do with my heady assumptions, and often enough goes contrary to them. We are deeply convinced, are we not, that if only we understand, if only something is clearly and carefully explained to us step by step, that we can then also do it? But there are many things which, even if they can be explained to a certain extent, cannot be explained completely. In particular, this refers to everything to do with experience: familiarity and skills learned with the body rather than mere understanding in the head.

Why are we so much more keen on asking 'how', than on actually trying it? Perhaps because I do not want to fail, but we learn much from our failures. If I am frightened of failing, I become ever more rigid. In horsemanship, a proverb says, 'He is no good rider who never kissed the sand.' In training too we think we need to be able to do it correctly from the start, and get discouraged when we find we can't. But we just need to try again and again, and to fail again and again until it has become physically familiar, not just in the head, and that takes some time.

So the head wants to understand, and is deeply convinced it can understand. I believe that if I am clearly told, then I can do it. Also, I want to understand and to know, and when I know everything, then there will be peace, yet underneath there is an urge which says, 'That is not all.' This is why in our daily life, as it is nowadays, there is an ever-increasing emphasis on speed, on more, better, a compelling demand to get some lasting fulfilment and satisfaction. Our mistake is to seek it 'out there', and thus the needs of the heart have been neglected. The heart is not interested in knowing, its needs are quite different. When we do something that we really enjoy – watch a play, read a book that is fascinating or play music – are we then aware of 'I'? Or does, at some stage or another, a kind of merging occur, and we are suddenly at one with the music, or with the hero or the heroine, or are involved in the story, or whatever, and are not there anymore?

Where am I then when that has happened? Gone! And then the curtain falls, the book comes to an end or my attention span drops, and suddenly, there I am again. Where was I? Swallowed! Vanished! Peacefully forgotten. Where and in what do we nowadays seek this forgetfulness of the heavy burden of ourselves? Newspapers, television, horror films, alien abductions, etc., all reveal that we need pretty strong stuff nowadays, in order to get hoicked out of ourselves. We are pretty far gone, and the ordinary will no longer do.

But basically the need to be distracted from ourselves, from 'I', shows that what the heart really wants is to be part of something, and to act or play its part in that context; not just to be an onlooker, but to be once more re-united with and part of what is. Forgetting oneself in some activity – selflessly helping others – it comes together, if we can forget ourselves in it, be at one with it. Then the heart can partake in something that is more than 'I', not intentionally 'I', but as a response in which it fulfils itself. This is the field of religion – 're-ligio', being 're-united'. But in our spiritual ice age, as it is now, all religious qualities are missing. We no longer have any sense of any power that is greater than 'I', and consider ourselves centrestage. Troubles are inevitable. Fundamentalism and the like also miss the point because they are based on my/our opinions, convictions and interpretations, and not on a true spiritual value.

Not long ago a proviso of 'God willing', or something like it, would give us pause. Now it no longer does. Spiritually impoverished, we do not understand anymore what it means, and how it helps to fold the hands and bow. We do not know the warmth of the heart, nor its depths. We no longer know real gratitude or true selflessness. So we are cut off, with a heart that starves and aches to partake. A traditional training will help us to get the heart flowing and partaking once more, and shows us values that are above and more than 'I', because only in that can the heart find its own fulfilment.

'Just stick to the root and do not trouble about the branches' we are advised. The 'root' is the basic teaching of the Buddha; these have been commented on, elaborated on and further explained, so that today there are many variations. We need to be acquainted with them, but not to forget that they are but facets of the basics. I may feel, 'Oh my goodness, all that has to be learnt in Buddhism, it is just too much. How can I ever remember all that?' But that would be chasing the branches, hopping from branch to branch – nothing much will come out of that. Stick to the root: once the root is clearly seen, the branches also fit together in a natural, organic way. It only looks inexplicable if I do not see the common root. Yoka Daishi tells us to stick to the root, to come back to the One Root and to the One Essence out of which everything develops.

'Like the moon reflected in a lapis lazuli bowl.' Lapis lazuli is a blue stone. If a bowl made of such a stone is filled with water, and on a moonlit night the moon is reflected in it, it is hard to tell the difference. The one is like the other in the same light, they shine and reflect each other. Knowing/ not knowing – in a way knowing, in a way not knowing. It cannot be expressed but it can be lived. We can talk about life, but can you show me life? Where is it? It is not a 'thing' but yet we all live it. How can one show it? You cannot take it up like a glass of water and, 'Ah, now I know what life is.'

But as long as we are alive, we live it. When we have woken up from the dream of an isolated 'I', we will live out of the wisdom and power of the Tathagata, reflect it, manifest it, but cannot put it into words. Master Obaku calls this 'a tacit understanding'. Just this is what 'the moon reflected in a lapis lazuli bowl' means.

Yoka Daishi then continues, 'Now I know that this wondrous Mani Jewel / Inexhaustibly benefits self and others.' In the Tibetan tradition we encounter the Mani Jewel, the wish-fulfilling gem, with Om Mani Padme Hum – 'Hail to the Jewel in the Lotus.' The Mani Jewel, as the lotus, is the flower or throne on which the Buddha sits. It refers to that wondrous jewel which the Buddha left for us – the three great teachings of Impermanence, Suffering and No-I, which we are to remain aware of as guides on the way of training. We are all endowed with his jewel, are born with it, always have been with it, and never will be without it, whether extant or non-extant. It is inexhaustible, and Yoka Daishi fully realized it. It is inexhaustible in that it benefits self and others, because 'self' and 'others' here are no longer separate.

'The moon is reflected in the stream, a gentle breeze in the old pine tree; / Deep and quiet night – what is it for?' The picture that is painted here is rather beautiful. That is true awakening – not just an insight in the head only, but actually physically in the body. Then there is real peace too. 'The moon is reflected in the stream' corresponds to 'the moon reflected in the lapis lazuli bowl.' Both evoke night because the moon does not shine by day. And 'a gentle breeze in the old pine tree', hardly perceptible – the night is 'deep and quiet', but alive, it breathes. Into that natural rhythm, I intrude and clamour, 'Nothing ever happens!' 'I want to know.' 'I want to have.' I want, want, want. Thus I break the rhythm, the peace, the harmony. We mistakenly think that a state of such harmony is inactivity, but by no means. The night will fade, the stream will run dry or into spate, the moon will wane, and so it will go on. What is shown here is how to go or flow or turn with it just as it moves, but with the same serenity, unperturbed, as the moon reflected in the stream, as the gentle breeze in the old pine tree, as quiet and deep as the night.

Awake and listen to that long, soft groundswell in the midst of the hurly-burly of our daily life, even in the midst of the more unpleasant things that we human beings do to each other. Keep to that quiet state – not being carried away oneself, and thus showing others that it is possible, and helping each other. That is important, and is the greatness of the truly human state with its compassionate understanding, which is true wisdom, and evokes gratitude for so much that we all share, for life is not only suffering but joy too. And there is so much we have to be grateful for: grateful for our parents, however much we may gripe about them, to the sunshine, or to the rain when the earth is thirsty, to those who have looked after us, and in particular to our teachers, without whom we might not have come into contact with Buddhism. And we should be most grateful that we have the incredible good fortune of sitting here as human beings and reading the Buddha-dharma.

We are told that four conditions are needed to be able to realize the Buddha-dharma. The first is to be born into the human state – this is already one of the great blessings. The second is to be born at a time when the Buddha-dharma exists, because there are also long aeons when there are no Dharma teachings. The third is to be born in a place where the Buddha-dharma is known. If we had been born 200 years ago in this country or in Europe, we would never have heard of the Buddha's teachings, would we? And finally, that we come to hear about it, and being so interested or touched by it, we want to follow it – that is the greatest blessing. Thus these 'four necessities' inspire us to enter the Path and follow the Buddha's footsteps to the same insight that he had. As we are all sitting here reading about them, these 'four necessities' have all come together in us. Is that not something to be profoundly grateful for? And perhaps that gratitude is equally important in itself as well as being a great source of strength and energy. With that we are able to resolutely and humbly walk the Buddha's Path without stopping, until it comes to that same insight, where the state of 'the moon reflected in the stream, a gentle breeze in the old pine tree; / Deep and quiet night' has really come about and is bearing much fruit – as the Mani Jewel inexhaustibly benefits self and others. Not inexhaustibly in the sense that it can be used for more and more and bigger and better things, but that it will continue to nourish and succour inexhaustibly.

Yoka Daishi movingly describes the inner landscape he has entered. A clear night with the moon reflected in the stream and the gentle breeze in the old pine, all is quiet. It is achingly beautiful, and then comes his little barb – 'what is it for?' We always want to have a purpose, and we cannot let things be. There Yoka Daishi sits, with the moon reflected in the stream, a gentle breeze in that old pine, deep and quiet night, and he points, 'what is it for?' We cannot settle into a situation when it has become quiet. We think we want the quiet – but when we have it, we cannot take it. That night we know it will not remain dark and quiet. The night will go, the day will come, the ordinary daily activities will be engaged in again. A good many of them we do not like either, but neither can we give the whole of ourselves and blend into that quietness of the night – the moon, the stream, the pine, the wind – losing ourselves and becoming what is, instead of wondering what we are going to do tomorrow, or whatever other thoughts come up at night. We cannot let be – I must assert myself to assure myself that I am still there. But when we come to that state of Yoka Daishi's, we need not ask 'what is it for?' After a day's work when there is nothing to do we fully relax into rest and, when there is something to be done, fully give ourselves into the doing. Then, working or resting, ever at peace – and that peace is infectious in that it affects and benefits all alike.

27   *The jewel of the Buddha-nature is inalienably imprinted*
      on the heart ground.
   Mist, dew and clouds make the enlightened one's robe.
   His bowl gentles dragons, and on his staff that subdues tigers
   The golden rings chime, oh, so clear!

28   *These are not just figments of my empty imaginings,*
   For the traces of the Tathagata's precious staff are
      intimately familiar.
   I neither seek for truth nor shun errors,
   And have come to know that the Two Truths are empty,
   without shape or form.

Commentary

'The jewel of the Buddha-nature is inalienably imprinted on the heart ground.' Although not much emphasized in Indian Buddhism, the teaching of the inborn Buddha-nature took on a new meaning in China. Self-sufficient, growing out of itself, it lacks nothing, and is what we really are. An awakening to that inborn Buddha-nature is possible, not by long and thorough training over millions of years, but can be realized in this very life. This teaching helped the Chinese to accept Buddhism, and it also helps us here in the West. It propounds that if we wholeheartedly put ourselves into the training and really live it, then an awakening is possible in this very life.

Our first need is insight into ourselves. Underneath all our convictions and basic assumptions, which we take as absolutely given and have never even queried, underneath all the phantasmagoria of ideas, volition, fantasies, what is actually truly there? To find out we need both the map and the scriptures, and actual training under a teacher who keeps us on track. Such training needs to be traditional, that means one with long experience in how to point the Way, without being carried away by sentimentality or by fashionable trends, but dealing with what is grave and constant in human experience.

'The jewel of the Buddha-nature is inalienably imprinted on the heart ground' – on everybody's heart ground, because it is that human heart that we all share. The newborn baby does not need to be taught how to suckle, it can do it by itself. How does it know? Nobody has ever yet tried to explain to a newborn antelope how to get on its legs and find its mother's udder, it just does it. How? This inborn information is specific to our different forms; for an antelope, for a newly-hatched turtle, for all forms, including ours. In moments of shock or danger something else takes over – that is the inborn Buddha-nature, the power and wisdom of the Tathagata, which then can and does emerge directly. We can all recall such instances.

In my later years in Japan, I used to spend a few days in April and August on a tiny island in the Inland Sea. The south side of the island was very steep; there were three coves with deserted fishing villages, so that one was quite alone there. I stayed in a guest house on a crag, and went swimming and walking. In half a day one could walk the length of the island.

The road hugged the cliff and was very winding. On the sharp bends there was always a statue of Jizo, the Bodhisattva who looks after children and travellers. Often it is just a stone with a rag tied around it, but always a simple offering is placed in front of it, perhaps just a green branch in a jam jar. I had become used to bowing whenever I passed such effigies. Rather tired at the end of one long day of walking, trudging along and only half with it, I went around a very sharp bend and bowed before the Jizo standing there. As I came up from the bow I saw that right in front of me was a sheer drop down a steep cliff. If I had not stopped to bow, I could have walked straight over it. Well, yes, perhaps they put that statue there in order to prevent people going over. But, on the other hand, you could also say it was the Bodhisattva himself who prevented me going over – and gave me my first real feeling of the importance of bowing. It stops us in our tracks when we are running headlong after something. In the very act of bowing, the heart bows too, and opens towards the Buddha-nature. The body knows that to bow is to lay oneself down. With the bow I hand myself over, and at that the Buddha-nature emerges naturally. 'The jewel of the Buddha-nature, inalienably printed on the heart ground' has always been there and always will be there. It is where we come from, and where we go back to at death.

'Mist, dew and clouds make up the enlightened one's robe.' We have to look carefully at such sentences. If we take that materially, does that mean he goes naked? Or does it rather indicate that this jewel of the Buddha-nature has no form, and that it is not possible to say 'I have got it' or that 'it is mine.' As long as 'I' am there, there is also attachment.

When that is gone and only the Buddha-nature is there, it includes everything; nature as it is – 'mist, dew and clouds make up the enlightened one's robe.' Nobody can say, 'I have got it.' If anybody does, they do not know what they are talking about.

The next two lines are rather beautiful. 'His [begging] bowl gentles dragons and on his staff that subdues tigers / The golden rings chime, oh, so clear!' 'His bowl gentles dragons.' Although it is an ordinary begging bowl, he can catch dragons in it; and the dragons in the bowl become quite gentle. We have already mentioned the difference between the Western dragon and the dragon in Far Eastern mythology (see Commentary to Verses 17 & 18). The latter, though fierce and strong, is gentle enough for children to play with. This is the quality that is referred to in 'his staff that subdues tigers'. In olden times when a monk went on pilgrimage or was sent as a messenger to a far-off place, he took a long walking staff with five rings on top. As he went along, the staff hit the ground and the rings chimed. This was partly in order to make a noise so that wild animals would get out of his way. When snakes are about in the jungle or wherever, they go away of their own accord as soon as they hear a noise and loud footsteps, but there is another side to it. When you hear the jingle of the rings, the message is: 'Here comes somebody who has no animosity. He has no fear and so is not full of aggression.' And there we are again with that great teaching of, 'no fear'. No fear for himself. No fear, therefore, of others or anything, and no fear when the spiritual power suddenly rises up. In our spiritual ice age we have forgotten about it. But if you look in the Bible you find that not only the Almighty, but all heavenly messengers on approaching a 'mortal', invariably begin with, 'Fear not!' Otherwise, in that overwhelming presence it is not possible to hear, or to hear correctly.

So the staff is just this 'Fear not!' Without that, the inborn wisdom of the Tathagata cannot really arise. And, therefore, the staff subdues tigers with the rings that chime so beautifully, telling the surroundings, 'Fear not! I come in peace.' Just that is the tremendous message of 'Fear not' which is the beginning of the Bodhisattva Way.

Yoka Daishi then continues, 'These are not just figments of my empty imaginings', assuring us that he is not saying it for the beauty of it or because he feels uplifted, but because, 'the traces of the Tathagata's precious staff are intimately familiar.' Something that is infinitely familiar we do not just know in the head, rather it has become a natural quality and propensity of ourselves, always at hand.

But to become intimately familiar, training has to be careful and patient. If not, you may bring it off once or twice for show, but at the moment when it really counts, it deserts you. What, however, has become intimately familiar arises of itself when needed, and works and responds. 'The traces of the Tathagata's precious staff' have then become 'intimately familiar.'

We are always inclined to ask, and I have heard it asked often, 'What does Buddhism teach about this?' or 'What should I do about that?' But Buddhism only teaches us to become aware of the inborn Buddha-nature, its wisdom and power. Its basic Precepts stipulate just ordinary decent behaviour. It does not teach what I should do under such and such circumstances. It leaves it to the individual and the situation in which he finds himself.

Next, Yoka Daishi tells us, 'I neither seek for truth nor shun errors, / And have come to know that the Two Truths are empty, without shape or form.' Now, we must not misunderstand this and take it for cool callousness. In most religions we find analogies about fire. Somebody has to find it, even at the price of stealing it, but, stealing not being on, there is usually a penalty attached. First of all, however, it is a question of finding it and then of guarding it. We are familiar with the Buddhist teachings of the Three Fires – Desire, Aversion and Delusion. We are also familiar with the flare-ups of these Fires, the 'afflicting passions'. Fire, if not guarded, goes into a conflagration and does much damage, but if it goes out, there is no warmth, no life. In Northern Buddhism, 'The passions are the Buddha-nature and the Buddha-nature is the passions.' It must be emphasized, however, that the one is not the other, but both are of the same energy or essence. This, 'heated up' by 'my' likings and loathings, flares as the passions, but if allowed to go out completely, then all is dead and rigid. So this Fire has to be carefully guarded lest it spills over as the 'passions' and goes into unlimited aggression/infatuation. But when carefully guarded, kept alive, it lights the way and warms the heart – a symbol for life itself, everlasting.

Perhaps a good analogy for the guarding and transformation of the power of the passions is a mountain brook or river in spate. The sheer power is tremendous, and so is the damage that it can do. But if that same brook is carefully channelled, its power can be made to produce electricity, a power that gives light to see by and heat to warm us and to cook with. To see clearly is wisdom, and warmth of heart – to feel for and with each other – is compassion. Yet even if we have both wisdom and compassion, they are of no use unless there is the power, the strength, to put these two aspects into action, to make them function and work, just as electricity also is the power that drives machines. Thus action, seen as right action, is possible. But unless wisdom is there to 'light the Way', that same power goes haywire, like when a high-voltage cable breaks or lightning strikes.

And so, 'I neither seek for truth nor shun errors.' That sounds pretty stiff, doesn't it, but is it really? The inborn wisdom and power of the Tathagata, the Buddha-seeing, is seeing all things the way they really are. Once awoken to that, there is no need anymore to seek for this or to shun that. This and that no longer exist, and the 'seeker' is gone, too – that was all in the delusion of 'I'.

Yoka Daishi continues, 'And [I] have come to know that the Two Truths are empty, without shape or form.' The first of the Two Truths, as given in the doctrinal formulation, is the seeming or relative truth, which is very clearly here. If I stub my toe on the door it will hurt. And the door? Well, in one way one cannot say that it is not there, but in another way it has no real lasting quality. Sooner or later it will wear out, and is then no longer there. That is one aspect of the Two Truths. The other is the Buddha-nature, which is but a name, and of itself has no shape, no form, no material or any other existence. But it works in all of us, as with the baby that knows how to suckle from the moment it is born. Does the baby know about the Two Truths? Does the baby know about the One Truth? Or does it just obey its own inner nature which, as yet, is still harmoniously together, at one with all that is? And this obedience to our own inner nature, to that inborn wisdom and power of the Tathagata is the at-oneness which is called enlightenment.

Finally, the Two Truths are only concepts in the head. We ourselves have created them, and they are quite useful for an approximate intellectual construct, but in themselves they do not exist. In the same way we like to think in terms of body/matter and mind/spirit. But where is the boundary between body and mind? You cannot take them apart, they are one. We are only conceptualizing, and then we mistakenly take these abstract concepts as concrete entities. It is the same with the Two Truths. They are concepts in the head; in themselves they do not exist. We can use them intellectually to help us approximate a certain understanding, according to which we can then work, but we must not take them for actual reality.

In his great *Song on Meditation*, Master Hakuin says, 'To take the form of no-form for form. To take the thought of no-thought for thought.' It may sound a little odd, but if we look at it, not with two eyes and double vision but with the Single Eye, then we will see how right that is. 'And [I] have come to know that the Two Truths are empty, without shape or form.' And it is out of this emptiness, out of this spacious roominess which is also inside and not only outside, that it is then possible to adapt to the situation as it is, seeing clearly.

That is important, and we need to do so in our ordinary daily life – not to impose our will on the situation, because that is certainly not going to blend in, but to look and see what the situation itself demands. To cultivate that sensitivity is part of our training. We remember Yoka Daishi saying earlier, 'In joyful service to all beings according to their needs' – to take in the situation as it is, and to respond to the situation within the needs of the situation. It seems a tall order, but it is not really so. It is something which comes quite naturally once we have lost most of our attachments and can open up. The wider we can open up, the wider the angle is to see and to point, and the more natural it is to take in what is there. We are seldom aware of how much we project our own ideas onto our surroundings, although a proverb tells us that, 'There are none so blind as those who do not wish to see.'

29 *Without form is beyond both, empty and not empty,*
    And just this is the true form of the Tathagata.
    There are no obstructions on the heart mirror;
    Brilliantly clear it illuminates as many worlds as
        the sands of the Ganges.

30 *All ten thousand things are contained in one shining jewel*
    That has neither inside nor outside.
    Mere empty emptiness denies the law of cause and effect,
    And creates muddles which invite calamity and misfortune.

Commentary

'Without form is beyond both empty and not empty, / And just this is the true form of the Tathagata.' One of the great arguments at the time of the Buddha, and for a good many centuries after, was the nature of reality – whether something is or is not. Accordingly, adherents were called 'Eternalists' or 'Nihilists,' and the issue was debated energetically. From his own experience, the Buddha and those great ones who came after him found that, actually, you could not really say that something is, for although it is true that something 'is', it does not last, and so at the same time it also 'is not'.

Nowadays in science we have an approximate analogy, in that light sometimes behaves as if it were particles and sometimes as if it were waves – you cannot pin it down, it just sometimes is 'this' and sometimes 'that'. And in the same way 'without form' is beyond form, and thus 'empty and not empty'. Forms exist but they do not last, they are not eternal. Moreover, 'eternal' is not everlasting in continuity – that would be an unchanging entity. The existence of such is denied in Buddhism – change and, therefore, no self-nature. Eternity is not connected with time at all, it has nothing to do with time. The opposite of impermanent (not lasting) is everlasting, but is that eternal? We have all had experiences of eternity, but never for more than a moment. Sometimes when looking at a sunset, or a beautiful view, or listening to some music that really moves, or perhaps a poem, suddenly things and the heart 'stand still' for a moment, and then they shift back again. But for that moment we were not – that is the timeless moment. You can neither say it is, nor that it is not: it cannot be tied down. Simple cultures, which we tend to call 'primitive', talk of 'the time before the beginning.' That also refers to that timeless moment.

Our teaching and training point us towards this moment. We are told again and again 'Give yourself into what at this moment is being done.' If wholly given into, then the time-lessness of the moment comes up, of each moment, because, if clearly perceived, all we have, can have and live in is this moment just now. What was five seconds ago is gone, it is only a memory now, in the past. Nor can we know what will be in five minutes because it is not yet here. We expect things – and ourselves – to go on according to our assumptions, but they often do not; we have no guarantee. So it is just this moment, now, always only now, yet we fail to live it. We would rather disport ourselves in memories of the past, which is gone, and in planning for a future which is not yet here, and so we live only in our thoughts and emotions, and do not really savour life. One reason why we feel that life is not fulfilling is because we do not give ourselves into this moment, just as it is, and fully live it. This moment need not always be joyous, but it is all we have. If we refuse to live it, as is our wont, all that unlived life begins to pile up against us, and we become ever more rigid, troubled and worried, chasing after fanciful notions instead of realizing that all we want is a full and complete moment. A full and complete moment is all we have, and in it we have all – eternally, every moment. Paradoxically, this gives full and lasting satisfaction, and only needs that we give ourselves into each moment, and do not conjure up pictures of the bygone past and phantoms, or of what we would like or dread in the future.

The great Zen Master Hakuin said, 'How sad. How sad. In the midst of water, pitifully crying from thirst.' That is really what we are doing, not willing to see that 'without form is beyond both, empty and not empty.' And, as already quoted in the same *Song on Meditation*, he suggests, 'Taking the form of no-form as form. Taking the thought of no-thought as thought.' It is worth pondering, not by logic, but in the heart.

'Without form' is not the opposite of form. We have to be careful because Zen language, although direct, expresses Mahayana understanding. And so, 'Without form is beyond both, empty and not empty'. And just this', says Yoka Daishi, 'is the true form of the Tathagata.' Translated, 'Tathagata' means 'the one thus come and thus gone', and is an appellation of the Buddha. Is that not rather like the 'eternal moment' mentioned above? 'Thus come and thus gone' cannot be got hold of, but it can be lived, and that is what counts. 'And just this is the true form of the Tathagata.'

Yoka Daishi continues, 'There are no obstructions on the heart mirror, / Brilliantly clear it illuminates worlds as many as the sands of the Ganges.' The heart mirror is a favourite Buddhist analogy, and is particularly stressed in our Zen School. We have already mentioned it in connection with the two poems written to establish the successor to the Fifth Patriarch (see Commentary to Verses 19 & 20). 'And just this is the true form of the Tathagata. / There are no obstructions on the heart mirror.' There never have been any. It is only the delusion of 'I', of my ideas and notions that overlay its shining surface. My pictures obscure it, and I must clear them away. 'There are no obstructions on the heart mirror': I myself am the obstruction. Once the mirror is really polished and clear, and is perceived as that, then 'I', my intentions, convictions, notions, ideas and ideals are no longer projected onto it, and so it is 'Brilliantly clear [and] illuminates as many worlds as the sands of the Ganges.' The Ganges is a long and mighty river, and the number of grains of sand in it is incalculable – it is a favourite Buddhist analogy for inconceivable multitudes. Buddhist cosmology, which is also the old Indian cosmology, conceives of multiples of worlds in order to convey a sense of the vastness of the cosmos which is in the human heart.

If for a moment we refrain from the arrogant Western judgement of, 'Old stuff, now we know better', and just reflect in the Buddhist mode, then there are any number of worlds, each one with its own Buddha, with its own central mountain, its own sun and moon, endlessly. We can get quite dizzy picturing them, but we refuse, saying 'Oh well, that's just old Indian cosmology. They just did not know any better.' Yet we religiously believe in our own universe in which we live, furnished with all our projections, all our science and all our ideas and notions. Of these we have as many as grains of sand in the Ganges – just look at every fact and fancy we create in our minds and in which we adamantly believe.

Since we believe in the universe of our own creation, we should not think, 'Ah, these are old stories, nowadays we know better', because, however much better we think we know, as our dreams show us at night and during the day, we inhabit universes beyond count. If we compare them, we would see that each of us has such universes, and although they are seemingly different in form, all have a Mount Sumeru, a sun and a moon and so on. This consideration might turn us from our 'I'-notions to what is being pointed at in these cosmologies. They are interior maps rather than outdated descriptions of the world outside, pointing at the heart mirror inherent in each human being, whether ancient or modern, East or West, or whatever. The reflections come and go, the pictures differ. Two or three thousand years ago thunder was a bolt or hammer thrown by a deity. Nowadays, since the so-called Age of Enlightenment, we no longer believe in a thundergod, we believe it is electricity, a natural force, which we no longer hold to be divine, and perhaps in another thousand years we will call it still something else. Our collective pictures change, but thunder was, is and will be just thunder, whatever we call it, and if we realize that a great amount of unnecessary controversy dies. Even the arrogance of knowing better, from which we all suffer, might come to an end, and that would further mutual understanding and tolerance. Although I may project something different from what you do, and your projections may be different from mine or from someone else's, all our projections, however manifold, coarse or fine, are in themselves empty. If we can realize that, then there is peace. 'There are no obstructions on the heart mirror'; it just reflects the forms as they come and go.

Yoka Daishi continues, 'All the ten thousand things are contained in one shining jewel / That has neither inside nor outside.' 'The ten thousand things' is a term the Chinese used to indicate 'everything'. This includes all the possible pairs of opposites, which comprise all that is physical and mental, but which being opposites, also cancel each other out. Picture a circle. On the rim there are all the ten thousand things, each one connected to its opposite by a radius through the centre. Light and dark, white and black, you and I, this and that, all make up the rim, but going away from the circumference towards the hub, the opposites merge together in one still point. They do not interfere with each other at that point, they fall together in oneness. But is that really a point? There we go again: it is a point, and at the same time it is not a point. We can each have our opinion about it as long as we realize that it is our individual way of seeing it. And from whatever angle I see it, there is also an opposite. Only in the middle do the opposites cancel out.

So the ten thousand things are, and are not, and are all contained in one shining jewel. Since this shining jewel is both centre and circumference, it has neither inside nor outside. Just to make quite sure that we are not mistaking this jewel for something physical, something that has form, it is explicitly stated that it has neither inside nor outside. What kind of jewel could that be? Without either inside or outside, surely such a 'thing' cannot be? So this shining jewel, in which all ten thousand things are contained, actually is not. It is merely a concept in the mind, a phantom, yet it is not quite so outlandish as we may think. What we call the 'laws of nature' operate in this way, devastatingly so if we do not obey them; but they are our concepts, and as such, as entities, they do not exist. We arrogant fools think we can discover and conquer nature. Remember Icarus!

Snowdrops grow, whether we know or do not know how they grow. The snowdrop does not care what we think, it just grows in obedience to its own nature and laws, and it is by obedience to these laws that it can unfold and grow. However large an oak tree may be and however many leaves it may have, its leaves will all unmistakably be oak leaves – each one individual and unique, which makes for diversity, yet they are all oak leaves. This we can usefully bear in mind: as unique individuals we should not forget our common humanity, and should conform to it rather than clinging to our individual opinions. And when you next pass a tree, bow to it and say, 'Thank you for a great lesson.'

At that the heart opens up, and with gratitude we realize that we are continuously surrounded by teachers who show us the Way by what they are, by how they grow and unfold in obedience to their own laws. Although the same laws are inherent in us too, we are ever prompted to disobey them by our appetites and notions. This disobedience, this clinging to 'I', is the source of our troubles, problems and sufferings. The Buddha saw clearly that, because of our attachments, we human beings are not aware of the inborn wisdom and power of the Tathagata. This wisdom and power is to grow, develop and unfold according to those inherent laws.

So, 'All ten thousand things are contained in one shining jewel / That has neither inside nor outside' – that both is and is not. 'Mere empty emptiness denies the law of cause and effect, / And creates muddles which invite calamity and misfortune.' '"Mere empty emptiness" ... if everything is empty, nothing is worth striving for; it's all for nothing!' So I won't live it, I refuse it. However much we would often like to, we cannot quite refuse living life as it is, even its darker sides. 'Mere empty emptiness denies the laws of cause and effect', and we are governed by these laws, whether we like it or not. In Buddhism the laws of cause and effect are seen as Karma. Again, it does not matter how we define them, but disregarding them only invites further confusion and calamity, and we all have ample experience of this if we care to remember. So denying the laws of cause and effect, by whatever name we call them, only 'creates muddles which invite calamity and misfortune'. A verse from the oldest Buddhist scripture, the *Dhammapada*, puts it starkly and simply: 'To avoid doing harm as much as possible; to do good as much as possible; to purify the heart; that is the teaching of all the Buddhas.' In a way we all know that, but fail to live it.

So we are told 'to purify the heart.' But actually, once we restrain ourselves to do as little harm as possible and to do as much good as possible, the purification of the heart is well under way. We must be careful not to split 'good and bad' into opposites, and heed the 'as little' and 'as much as possible'. It does not mean good, better, holy – that is only one opposite.

When we read Buddhist texts about purification, purifying or pure, it can practically always be translated as 'empty' and 'emptying' – pure and empty are interchangeable terms. And so we are encouraged to 'empty the heart,' and with that we come again to that emptiness of which the penultimate line speaks. Aware of our propensity to be one-sided, Yoka Daishi warns, 'Mere empty emptiness denies the law of cause and effect.' What we conceive of as 'empty', as opposed to 'full', is dead emptiness. This 'nothing' is not pure but just callously forgetful. In purifying the heart, it is emptied, little by little, of all the myriad forms, configurations and appetites that cause our errors, attachments, and so on. If the heart is empty, such an empty heart will naturally not only realize the wisdom of the Tathagata, but will just as naturally also act in accordance with it; not having to think about it, not wanting to do good, not wanting to avoid bad, just naturally responding, as all other living beings respond, to the situation according to their nature. Aware then, that ours is a human nature, and with the Buddha as the shining example, we will hopefully respond to the passing situations in a truly human way under all circumstances, good, bad or indifferent. 'Only from the human state is deliverance possible', we are told in the scriptures, but we have to forge ourselves into such true human beings. No scripture, however true, can do that. And that is Bodhidharma's injunction: not to rely on scriptures only, but to 'make them one's very own' by means of diligent practice.

31   *Equally ill-conceived is to deny being and instead
        cling to emptiness
     Like jumping into fire to save oneself from drowning.
     Let go of delusions and take hold of the truth.
     However, both letting go and taking hold are still sham
        and deception.*

32   *If a trainee mistakes discipline as his aim rather than
        a means,
     He in fact takes in the robber mistaking him for his
        own son.
     At that, the good fortune of the Dharma is lost,
        accumulated merit wasted,
     And all that because of the picking and choosing
        of the heart.*

Commentary

At the end of the previous verse we heard, 'Mere empty emptiness denies the law of cause and effect, / And creates muddles
which invite calamity and misfortune', but now Yoka Daishi
adds 'Equally ill-conceived is to deny being and instead cling
to emptiness.' Seeing everything as empty is easily mistaken
for seeing everything as 'equal'. There is then neither good
nor bad, all is the same – and so I can go out mugging! In
this world in which we live there certainly is both good and

bad, but to see no difference between them is equally ill-conceived. Keeping the Precepts prevents us from going into such fanciful notions, which are merely excuses to do anything and everything we like.

Therefore, Yoka Daishi says, 'Equally ill-conceived is to deny being [to deny this relative world of ours] and instead cling to emptiness.' After all, this our world, Samsara, is not always pleasant, and so one seeks to escape. This is why we have taken up the Buddha's Path that leads out of suffering. But to deny Samsara, and to try and evade it by clinging to emptiness, is 'Like jumping into fire to save oneself from drowning.' Although I have never drowned, nor have I been burnt to cinders, I would suspect there is not much difference – either way I perish. You might say, 'But that is marvellous! After all, in Buddhism it is said that "I" is a false conception.' But whether I burn or whether I drown, it is not liberation from the ever-revolving Wheel, it does not constitute the transformation of the energy that has become wild because of 'I' picking and choosing. The delusion of 'I' goes on, and I am by no means off the Wheel.

Here we meet another basic Buddhist concept which we tend to have trouble assimilating. Not only are there the karmic accumulations, but there is the awkward question of what is 'reborn', 'reincarnated', or whatever. The difficulty for us is the Buddha saying there is no 'I', and that the notion of such an entity is merely a delusion. But if that is so, how can a mere delusion be reincarnated or come back? So we have to look deeper into it.

We either welcome the idea of coming back again because we want to continue and are frightened of death, or we vehemently deny such a notion. The Buddhist, on the other hand, does not want to go on. Rather, he wants to get off that continuously grinding Wheel of Rebirth with its Six States or Realms. To a Westerner, it might seem consoling – 'Oh well, I'll have another chance next time' – but are we going to have another chance next time? We might not be born into the human state.

Even if we are born amongst the heavenly beings, release from the Wheel is not possible from their state, and in all the other states there is not much chance of accumulating sufficient merit to get off the Wheel, nor to realize who we really are, so the human state is very precious. The Buddhist realizes this, and even if he cannot get off the Wheel this time, he strives to accumulate enough merit to at least be reborn as a human next time so that he can continue his efforts. Hence the demand for good behaviour to ensure rebirth in that realm next time.

So, whether jumping into the fire or drowning, it only means returning again, and next time it might not be a return in a human form, and so a great opportunity is missed. Liberation or deliverance or awakening means to be no longer tied to that Wheel. For that the deep root of 'I' needs to fall off. With 'I' and fear gone, there is nothing more to hold on to, nothing to lose. That opens into Life itself, and now there is a flowing with it. As the Zen saying expresses it, 'The heart flows with the ten thousand things, this flowing is truly mysterious.'

It is no use at all to try and grasp what is meant by 'mysterious'. It means a real letting go. When there is nothing left, the door is found. When we hear about a mystery, we want to understand it, don't we? But what we can understand with our reasoning is always 'something', and that is not what a mystery is. A mystery cannot be understood, and in front of a mystery the only gesture possible is to fold the hands and bow. That is what the true mystery is about. Then, miraculously and mysteriously, in the act of bowing in front of a mystery, which is not understood but clearly perceived as a mystery, the heart can open, and suddenly a oneness comes over.

There is a long poem in the Islamic tradition, *The Conference of the Birds*, which is another version of this theme. It tells of a flock of birds who set out to find Allah, who is mystery. In their quest they meet many dangers and obstacles. One by one they fall by the wayside as the search becomes ever more difficult. In the end only a few, tattered and straggly, make it to Allah's throne, but what they see is a roaring flame that sucks them in and consumes them. At that very moment all who had set out together sit happily chirping, in their original state, in the heart of Allah. The pointer in this story is that a mystery is not something to be understood, but that in the reverent bowing the heart opens and there is a merging, a 're-union'.

'Equally ill-conceived is to deny being and instead cling to emptiness.' Whether something is 'this' or 'that', they are just opposites in the head, still all in this relative world. It is only trying to avoid the one by running away to the other, 'Like jumping into fire to save oneself from drowning.' And so Yoka Daishi says again, 'Let go of delusions and take hold of the truth.' Let go of the delusion of 'I', but he immediately explains, 'both letting go and taking hold are still sham and deception.'

When both – letting go of the delusion and holding on to the truth – are sham and deception, what then can we do? 'I' letting go and 'I' taking hold are both intentional, are volitional and, as such, karma-producing, and so they bind us to the Wheel. Even the best intention is still karma-producing, and so not without result. Hence 'letting go and taking hold are still sham and deception.' And what happens if neither is done anymore? This is the state the Buddha, the Great Being, found himself in when he had nothing left and sat himself down under the Bo-tree.

'Let go of delusion and take hold of the truth.' The truth, that is where we always have been. 'However, both letting go and taking hold are still sham and deception.' It needs a complete letting go – this is what we train for. An old Zen master compared it to hanging on a cliff, one arm holding a stout root, the other arm and the legs dangling over the abyss. And he asks, is it possible to let go and plunge down? As a question, this is dealt with in the interview room, but we can look at it as a pointer.

What is that stout root on which we hang? In our ordinary life we carry a variety of wishes and wants around in us, some smaller, some larger. They all fan out and beget further ones, like water from an upturned glass will spill all over the table. But when seriously ill, there is just one wish – to get well again. 'The very sick man has only one wish.'

Most probably we can all remember an occasion when all our widespread, messy wishes and wants have concentrated into one only, and nothing else mattered. If only I could have this, or if only I could get rid of that, then there would be peace and happiness forever. This is the one root on which we then hang. Is it possible, with my whole life at stake, to open the hand, to let go? The Buddha admonishes us to be heedful, not blindly impulsive. We must first fashion the root to hang on before we let go. And after that, Master Torei says, 'begins another Life', which is no longer 'my' life.

'If a trainee mistakes discipline as his aim rather than a means, / He in fact takes in the robber mistaking him for his own son.' Discipline is essential to bring one up to the point of letting go, but often when something is done over a long period of time or rather forcefully one can get rather stuck to it, and then the discipline becomes the ruler and master. Everything is then seen in terms of discipline. It is no longer a question of getting off the Wheel, or of warm-hearted understanding and compassion. Sticking religiously to the rules has become the end, and then it does not work. It is a great temptation, and not for nothing does Master Yoka Daishi mention it.

So, 'If a trainee mistakes discipline as his aim rather than a means, / He in fact takes in the robber, mistaking him for his own son.' That is a well-known Chinese proverb – to take in the robber, thinking he is your own son, and then at night the robber walks out with whatever he can get hold of. For, 'At that, the good fortune of the Dharma is lost, accumulated merit wasted, / And all that because of the picking and choosing of the heart.' That is mistaking the discipline for the end, and it becomes rigid and arid. 'At that the good fortune of the Dharma is lost.' This is rather disturbing, is it not? He has fastidiously observed the discipline, and yet he loses the good fortune of the Dharma. Again, we must never mistake the discipline as the end because that results in a rigidity which misses the most important point of the Buddha's teaching – it lacks compassion. What is only rigid turns back to 'I', cannot also be warm, and so cannot have true understanding and compassion.

'At that, the good fortune of the Dharma is lost, accumulated merit wasted, / And all that because of the picking and choosing of the heart.' We have already mentioned the significance of the term 'heart' in Buddhist texts. Its connotation includes heart, soul, spirit, mind, all compounded. As long as there is the delusion of 'I', 'my' picking and choosing, the basic energy inherent in all of us is roused into passionate 'I must have' or 'I must get rid of'. This energy is in all of us, but gets diverted by 'my' picking and choosing. Hence it is not the situation, is not the object, it is 'my' response to it that matters. In the Confucian view, events by themselves are neutral, they are just as they are, but how we perceive a specific event depends on us – we react depending on our own likes and dislikes. Although we are very rarely aware of it, this picking and choosing affects our language and our thinking. The ten thousand things are made up of opposites. We can only think in opposites: we can think of good only in contrast to bad, etc. In the selection that we continuously make, picking and choosing is continuous, and because it is continuous, we, in our culture, interpolate a 'doer', 'I'. Nothing can be done without a doer, but in the Eastern way of thinking there is no necessity for such a doer, because it is an open, neutral system. The selecting and discarding goes on naturally, and there is no need for an active doer.

In our picking and choosing we act from a natural affinity, which has nothing personal in it. We deceive ourselves if we make it personal, and thereby our problems arise and multiply. I call it sympathy and antipathy, but, it must be repeated, it is not personal and has nothing to do with the object. It is merely my reaction to it, my seeing it, and my judging it.

So there are three great hindrances in the training: to mistake discipline for the end rather than the means, wasting accumulated merit, and, while continuing in the cycle of picking and choosing, to believe it is 'I' who makes these choices. These hindrances bring up aggression, disagreement, disappointment, suffering, and the general unsatisfactoriness of life which the Buddha called Dukkha, and out of which he pointed the Way. 'Suffering I teach and the Way out of suffering'. And he clearly defined the Way out of it: 'Impermanent are all compounded things, strive on heedfully.'

33   *This is why the Zen school insists on thorough insight*
      into the heart.
   By the power of this wisdom the deathless is suddenly
      entered.
   The enlightened one takes up the wisdom-sword,
   The banner of Prajna, the flaming Vajra-diamond.

34   *He not only crushes the clever capers of those of Other Ways,*
   But vanquishes even the greatest demons.
   He lets the Dharma-thunder roll and sounds the
      Dharma-drum.
   Clouds of compassion rise and rain down sweet dew.

Commentary

The last lines of Verse 32 were that, if not thoroughly trained, 'the good fortune of the Dharma is lost, accumulated merit wasted, / And all that because of the picking and choosing of the heart'. The training tries to prevent such calamity and, therefore, Yoka Daishi continues, 'This is why the Zen school insists on the thorough insight into the heart.' For that, the training must be heedful, careful and meticulous.

The Zen school is often thought to be severe and strict. Not so: it is only very thorough in order to make quite sure that none of 'my' self-centred predilections remain, 'the picking and choosing of the heart'. Whenever we 'rear up', fired by 'my' notions and by wanting things 'my way', we inevitably incur some kind of misfortune. If we really take this to heart, we become more careful and attentive, and with this new attitude the rough stone that I am is polished until it becomes smooth.

Yes, 'The Zen school insists on thorough insight into the heart'. This is why we carefully line up our cushions, why we are careful entering the Zendo (the meditation hall), are careful in our daily life with what we handle, what we do, with all we touch and how we touch it, and how we function. It is very strange at first but becomes increasingly rewarding, so that, by means of this training, we begin to feel a real relationship and a real satisfaction with all our doings and a fulfilment in doing them, even with the smallest thing. Things seem to be alive, and we are connected with them. As the corollary of thorough insight into the heart, we become 'fully alive', which also means without fear. 'By the power of this wisdom the deathless is suddenly entered.' The power of this wisdom is at the same time 'deathless' because, with that entered, our last fear, the death of 'I', has come to an end.

'The enlightened one takes up the wisdom-sword, / The banner of Prajna, the flaming Vajra-diamond.' What does it mean? The sword of wisdom is wielded by the great Bodhisattva Manjusri, and it is Manjusri who is enshrined in most Zendos. His flaming sword of wisdom cuts through the bonds of ignorance and delusion. In the Zendo his sword is symbolized by the Keisaku, a flat wooden stick. The Jikijitsu, the head monk, goes around carrying this sword, which cuts the bonds of ignorance. To somebody experienced, it is quite visible if somebody is snoozing comfortably or daydreaming, though he may be sitting motionlessly. Then the sword which cuts the bonds of ignorance falls down and wakes him up. While he walks around the Zendo, the head monk carries the Keisaku over the shoulder ready to be used as a sword, but when he stands still he holds it upright before him as 'the banner of Prajna'. Prajna is the 'Wisdom Gone Beyond', the wisdom of Buddha-seeing, seeing all things the way they really are. As that, the sword is also the flaming Vajra-diamond. A diamond can cut everything, and it flames with the light of clear seeing.

What is a diamond actually? In composition it is simply coal dust, carbon. And if we remember that 'the passions are the Buddha-nature and the Buddha-nature is the passions', it is the same energy. Either it wildly flares up as the passion of 'I must have' or 'I must get rid of', which is the source of our quarrels, our wars and all the horrors that we perpetrate or, if really and truly gentled, the same energy manifests as the Buddha-nature that informs all forms and to which now all action conforms. The diamond is the hardest of all minerals and, therefore, the most valuable jewel, yet it consists of nothing but coal dust: that, too, is a useful consideration. Industrial diamonds – for drilling, cutting and grinding, etc. – can now be made artificially. If you take a piece of hose, fill it with coal dust and blow into it, a black dust cloud will come out of the other end and drape itself over everything – a perfect picture of what happens when the 'passions' explode! But if you take a pipe made of something so strong that it cannot burst even under tremendous strain, load the same coal dust into it and blow through it with real pressure, then at the other end out comes a diamond.

How very interesting. Do we remember the need for form? Form is important, and so, 'the Zen school insists on thorough insight into the heart.' Training makes the body straight and the heart strong like that pipe, so that 'my' gripes, 'my' wants and 'my' lusts do not continuously blow me about. Even though the whole energy may erupt, if contained, and the form holds, then the transformation into the 'diamond' takes place.

So we take up a special position when we sit Zazen which is conducive to holding together when we don't want to anymore, when we are bored, when our legs hurt, when thoughts invade. But the form holds, and thus the 'diamond' is fashioned, however slowly, rather than trying to get away from what I do not want.

In the same way, when the 'passions' arise, instead of trying to shove them back or trying to explain them away or letting them discharge into the situation, we fold the hands and say, 'Precious energy, I am still there. Please burn me away', and allow it to burn and grind 'me'. This energy is precious, is the only force (this is where the diamond comes in again) that is stronger than 'I', and so is capable of transforming the very root of 'I'. In the presence of a picking and choosing 'I', it is the elementary energy of the passions. With 'I' burnt away, it is again what it always was, the Buddha-nature.

As to the Vajra-diamond, with it 'He not only crushes the clever capers of those of Other Ways, / But vanquishes even the greatest demons.' That sounds rather warlike, but if we look carefully we might discover another aspect. How does he crush the 'clever capers' of 'Other Ways'? Surely fighting will only increase the discord? Instead he recognizes them for what they are. Thus he is not carried away by them, sees the beginning and where it points to, and by just being what he is and standing clear and firm, he may possibly deflect them.

So what are these 'clever capers' of 'Other Ways'? Some may be nothing but clever capers, but they can distract people very much. Others are not so funny. Some of the present cults with their suicidal tendencies and manipulating, not to say brainwashing, are not so funny, and can be downright dangerous. We live in a spiritual ice age, but our heart needs warmth and longs for some value that is more than 'I'. To fill this emptiness within has always been the sphere of religion, for if the heart has only 'I' to like and to value, it is not enough. Then the longing can get into strange byways from which it is hard to find a way out. These days New Age ideas sprout like mushrooms after rain, and vanish almost as quickly. Some of them are downright silly, others quite sinister. To see them clearly will prevent us being caught up in and carried away by them.

'The greatest demons' – what are they? Do they come from outside, or are they inside ourselves? There is the demon of selfishness, the demon of anger, the demon of greed, the demon of fear – those are the real demons. Once they have got us, they hold us and are very difficult to vanquish. They all have to do with 'self', and this is why it is said that to fight oneself is the hardest fight, to conquer oneself is the greatest victory.

But thorough training can vanquish even the demon that sits inside us. And how is the greatest demon vanquished? By means of the Daily Life Practice, of always staying 'at home'. What does that entail? If we really give ourselves to what at this moment, now, is being done, and come back to it again and again, then we are in the moment, here. Then we do not need to look out for or observe because it becomes perceptible quite naturally. Thus even the slightest manifestation of the demon surging up becomes instantly conscious. I may sit here quite comfortably, but seeing you doing what I dislike will annoy me and, before I have even become conscious of annoyance, my hands have already tensed and stiffened up. If I am 'at home', that is, in the here and now, that bodily sensation registers, and I recognize it – 'Aha, here she blows!' All I need to do at that moment is to unclench my hands, take a deep breath, and look again. The heat has gone out, and I can speak and act dispassionately. With nothing further than remaining 'at home', the greatest demon is vanquished. But if I am not 'at home' and, therefore, do not notice this clenching, the annoyance/demon comes up to the level of the heart, and I suddenly fume – and a moment later when I shout at you, the demon has escaped. If I am 'at home', he cannot escape and gets vanquished before he has arisen. But we do not notice these little physical gestures which yet give all the information we need. This is partly because we deem it beneath our notice, and in any case feel that it is all in the mind, and that the body is not nearly so important. 'The spirit is willing but the flesh is weak.' Forget that weak flesh – it is not so. The body is very willing, it gives us all the information, if only we pay heed to it.

Vanquishing even the greatest demon does not mean going out and cutting off his head. We cannot vanquish the demon by brute force, but only by being there and recognizing him. To do so, we need the experience which comes from the training, with which also comes the clear seeing, the Buddha-seeing – seeing all things the way they really are, 'coming to be and ceasing to be'. Such looking then gives insight into what is. Yet all attempts at explanation and description are only pointers – we can talk about it, but cannot really convey the essence. Only if you drink the water will you yourself know how cold it is.

When even the greatest demons, including death, are vanquished, then 'He lets the Dharma-thunder roll and sounds the Dharma-drum.' That also sounds warlike, but the Dharma-thunder can be a very gentle voice, although sometimes it needs to be a real thunder to overcome the growling of the demon. If we take this to heart and are no longer afraid of the universe, we have also found the inmost part of our own heart. And we have found the one that dwells in the own heart, have discovered him as the Buddha rediscovered that ancient road that leads to an ancient city. At the moment the voice is heard, perhaps in the rolling of the Dharma-thunder or the sound of the Dharma-drum, the heart opens. That 'drum' need not be a war drum; it can equally be the sound of sunshine. We only need to open the heart and let it in.

Then 'Clouds of compassion rise and rain down sweet dew.' We usually hear only about the harshness of our training, how demanding it is to effect real changes, and it all sounds rather austere, but if that were all it would be rather like bread that has not risen and is soggy and bottom-heavy. Obviously that is not the purpose of the training, and so there is another side too, and that is where the Dharma-drum comes in. It is not only the rousing war drum; it joyously beats to the dance of life.

In a Zen monastery both are beaten, one to 'endure what is hard to endure', but also one inviting joyous laughter. There is room and opportunity for both, and it is useful to remember that in this training there is nothing to be wasted. When something good comes along we fold the hands and gratefully and thoroughly enjoy it, knowing it will not last, and so do not hang on to it or want it to continue forever. And the strength that accrues from that joy is then helpful at the next stretch, which may perhaps be difficult. That too we can then accept gratefully as good practice, and it will not last either – 'coming to be and ceasing to be'. To refuse the joyful side, the time when things are easy, and not live them gratefully is perhaps the greatest misunderstanding. The two sides need to balance each other, and just this is what the Buddha meant when he advocated the Middle Way, which is neither too ascetic nor too indulgent. Between those two extremes, rather than erring too much to this or the other side and getting further carried away into shallowness, the practice keeps us to the Middle Way, and leads ever deeper down until what has always been there is seen clearly for the first time. It cannot be shown as a picture, it cannot be expressed in words, but it can certainly be lived.

Again we are reminded of the Buddha. Although on his Awakening he clearly 'saw', he also realized that what he had thus 'seen' was not expressible in words, and wondered how to communicate it. There are various versions in the Scriptures, but generally it is said that it needed the great Brahma himself to come and plead with him to somehow make his insight available. Although the Buddha described the stages of the Way that he himself had found, nowhere in the Buddhist scriptures will we find an account of what he actually 'saw'. What is described in a multitude of different formulations is the Way.

As we become familiar with these stages, we will see that the various formulae lead to the same basic teachings. People are different, and incline more to this, that, or still another. Out of compassion, the Buddha taught various formulae to enable us to find one that our heart inclines to. All of them lead out of 'I' to the Buddha-nature but, unless our heart specifically inclines to one, whenever I begin to weaken I will be tempted to stop. If it really is the way of my own heart, then the heart wins out, and it is possible to continue even when I no longer want to. This is the all-important point, and the reason why there are so many Buddhist ways.

So, 'He lets the Dharma-thunder roll and sounds the Dharma-drum. / Clouds of compassion rise and rain down sweet dew.' The Buddha is called the All-wise and the All-compassionate One. Those two appellations belong together: the clear seeing of the Buddha inevitably evokes the warmth of the heart, which is compassion. Compassion is different from our usual feeling of pity. The latter is natural, but real compassion is actually more than just feeling pity for something. Real compassion is not affected by anything, and is thus able to promptly do something about it.

A Bodhisattva is one who, doctrinally, has lost his 'I' and is now nothing but compassion. The first iconographic gesture of such a being is not that of compassion but of fearlessness that has tremendous power to fully function even under the worst or impossible circumstances. That is what real compassion is about, and the great Bodhisattvas show this in their behaviour. And they are there to help us in our practice, too: we can remember them, feel their strength and hold on to it when things get really tight.

The Buddha, then, is found in one's own heart and so the outside Buddha is not something to hold on to any longer. Rather, when the Buddha in the own heart is really and truly realized, then his compassion holds us together when we are in trouble, and this is why the 'clouds of compassion rise'. Not that the clouds will do anything, but from them rains down the sweet dew of compassion which touches us all. And not only just when we are in trouble, for actually we are in a constant state of trouble, the state of our delusion of 'I'. So these clouds rain compassion, a sweet rain that touches our hearts. They not only help us in an intrinsic and important way, but they make us aware of our delusion, incite us to aspire to something more. And with that we come to the great Buddhist teaching of bodhicitta, 'the aspiration towards enlightenment'. Once that has awoken in the heart and is cultivated and nurtured, for which we need the continuous compassion of Buddha and Bodhisattvas, then we can really follow the Path. And then we will also, by our own practice, become meticulous, diligent and grateful. Thus, all the qualities of the heart begin to engage and help us follow in the footsteps of the Buddha.

35 *Majestic like an elephant or dragon, of boundless*
      benefit to all,
    Those of the Three Vehicles and Five Natures are made
      to awake.
    Hini, the luscious grass is found only on the highest
      Himalayan slopes;
    From these pastures comes the rich milk that is my delight.

36 *One Nature pervades all natures.*
    The One Dharma contains all dharmas;
    Just as the one moon is fully reflected in all the waters,
    And all the moons of all the waters are of the one moon.

Commentary

'Majestic like an elephant or dragon.' These are huge animals that cannot fling themselves about carelessly, so they are always considered as paragons, indicative of the whole stature of a Great Being. In one of his stories, Zhuangzi says that 'a fish the size of a house does not fit into a valley brook.' And so, 'Majestic like an elephant or dragon' points us towards something which we think we have no need of nowadays: form. And this is not the form of an elephant, not the form of a dragon, but the form of a human being, the real human being, liberated from the tyranny of 'I' with my judgements, fancies and opinions.

We all know what good form is, and we usually rebel against it, at least when young, because we think it is something like a straitjacket that hems in all individuality. But good form becomes 'fitting' to the human being, like a well-worn jacket, and it also proves to be a real support. Good form in our case is 'human', and to become so, training for it slowly, works off all kinds of excrescences that I have: the self-will of 'I want it my way', which is the source of our problems.

There is another term for the true human form, which is particularly disliked nowadays and that is of the 'gentleman' or 'gentlewoman'. A gentleman is not born, has nothing to do with aristocracy. A gentleman is made, is educated, is brought up. This means somebody who is no longer the complete shuttlecock of his emotions and opinions as they arise and overpower him, shunting him through all the Six Realms of the Wheel. A gentleman has sufficiently gentled this tremendous emotional energy so that he can be absolutely relied upon to be able to function even in the middle of an uproar of the passions, so that he is also capable of realizing that there are others about and be considerate of them. All that makes him a trustworthy and responsible human being. And if you look at the Southern Buddhist texts, the term 'ariya' means 'noble' as, for example, 'the son of a noble family who is leaving home'. Is that the son of an aristocratic family? By no means, but he is the son of a family who have brought him up to the stature of a human being, and who now can truly enter the religious life.

The nobility comes from the full state of a human being. It does not come from birth or from anything else – it needs to be cultivated. We all have the chance of cultivating it, even if our culture neglects it. We can look at the Buddha's teachings: they give us exact information on how to behave and what to do. His teaching of the inborn wisdom and strength of the Tathagata already guarantees that it is possible to come to that human state if only we apply ourselves. We are meant to attain it karmically because we are born into it. And the very fact that we are shows that it is possible, and is in itself the guarantee that we can do it – rather like a little child is guaranteed to grow up to the full stature, at least physically, of the human form.

So, when 'Majestic like an elephant or dragon' is truly manifested and has become irreversible, there is someone who really knows the Way and has really walked it, who has become truly gentled in nature, and so is 'of boundless benefit to all.' Such a person, although perfectly natural, is impressive because his heart is free of any kind of egoism, so its warmth cannot help but flow over. And since we all have that same kind of heart, touched by such flowing warmth, there is no need for great words. When you come into the ambience of such a flowing heart, you suddenly feel, though you don't quite know why, that there is something there, and you want to go after it. That is when the bodhicitta, the 'aspiration towards enlightenment' really arises. If we only hear about it, it may be intoxicating – it touches, and then it is gone again. But when we actually come into contact with such a person the experience is lasting, and so, 'Majestic like an elephant or dragon [and] of boundless benefit to all'.

'Those of the Three Vehicles and Five Natures are made to awake.' The Three Vehicles are made up of the Sravakas, Pratyekas and Bodhisattvas, who represent the three main types of religious aspirant. There are different classifications of the Five Natures, but we take it as meaning all beings. So the Three Vehicles and Five Natures are doctrinal versions of 'every thing and every being'; and all, without exception, are 'made to awake', for, touched by such a Great One, they themselves set out on the Way.

When the sun shines it does not just shine on one particular shrub or one particular tree or flower. If it shines, it shines because shining is its nature and everything that grows somehow orientates itself toward the sun. You can easily see it with pot plants – wherever you place them in the room, before long they will turn their leaves towards the source of sunlight.

'Hini, the luscious grass, is found only on the highest Himalayan slopes; / From these pastures comes the rich milk that is my delight.' High up on the Himalayan slopes a bluish kind of grass is supposed to grow that is particularly rich and stands quite tall – people who have travelled there specifically mention it. Every summer, with great difficulty, the herdsmen bring their flocks up to these highest slopes so that their animals can feed on the luscious pastures and will give particularly good milk. Here 'the highest Himalayan slopes' means 'as high as possible'. That, strangely enough, is where the richest food is.

We think, 'I need this for my life', or 'I must have this in order to be happy.' We are, in fact, fairly insatiable. Nobody wants what they have – the grass is always greener on the other side. My problem is my hunger or desire, and I want it stilled! But it cannot be stilled by getting things from the outside, because the problem that I have is actually myself.

What I really want is not the momentary 'picture' that I have mistakenly projected. What I really want, underneath the surface of desires, is the fulfilment of the heart. These projections are my problem, but I do not realize it.

So, in order to get that luscious grass that really gives me delight, that stills my wanting this, that and the other, I have to go 'up'. I cannot solve my problem at its own level, which is usually my real difficulty, yet I still want to solve my problem here, on the same level. I have had a serious disappointment; I have had a great wish thwarted; I have been slighted in love; I have got a problem with my boss; I have got trouble in the office; my next-door neighbour is someone who for some reason I cannot bear anymore. I want to get rid of 'my' problems whatever they are, including difficult relations with my children or my parents. The problems are innumerable, but they cannot be changed here where things are as they are. They cannot be changed if I myself am unwilling to change – and I am usually unwilling to change. And even if I am willing, I think I cannot do so until my problem is solved. This is the dilemma in which we usually find ourselves.

Here it is very clearly said that this luscious grass, the solution for all my problems, is found only on the highest Himalayan slopes. So somehow I have to get up there to get my fill, and on those pastures to find the milk that really is my delight – not the ephemeral pictures that I chase, but the rich milk that is only to be found up there, and that stills all my hunger.

'One Nature pervades all natures. / The One Dharma contains all dharmas.' One Life, we could say as an analogy. This One Life, which is life, you cannot show it – there is no such 'thing' as life. But we are all alive, and life pervades all of us as long as we are alive. 'One Dharma contains all dharmas'. If Dharma is translated as 'law', one law contains all laws.

Hopefully, more often than not, we live according to the law of a human being, though not necessarily perfectly. An elephant lives according to the law of an elephant. Short of human beings, because of our attachments, all our other sentient brothers and sisters truly live by their respective laws, but that One Law underlies and pervades all laws. A tiger will always be a tiger under all circumstances – good, bad or indifferent; it will never behave like a mouse. And a mouse will always be a mouse under all circumstances, and reliably behave like a mouse.

Sometimes we read stories where animals suddenly begin to behave in a different way. They talk to somebody who is open and receptive; and plants do likewise. That is an intimation that, if there is that One Dharma, that One Law, and if the inherent Law of the state in which we are – in our case that of a human being – is realized, then there is harmony with that One Law, and in that One Law we can all communicate with each other.

'One Nature pervades all natures. / The One Dharma contains all dharmas; / Just as the one moon is fully reflected in all the waters / And all the moons of all the waters are of the one moon.' This realization re-unites and merges us again with all that is – with the miracle of Life and Nature, in which we clearly see all things as they really are, 'coming to be and ceasing to be', and willingly go with it. Sometimes it hurts, and sometimes it is joyful, but there is no need to make unnecessary artificial difficulties and whirlpools.

If we can realize and really live – or at least remind ourselves again and again that all things are Buddha-things – then we lay down the Buddha-spoon without too much clatter because we will be reverent. And we will take up the Buddha-glass reverently. And we will reverently converse with each other in a proper human fashion, and will live life in that manner, to our benefit as well as to that of others. And do so joyfully too, because the burden of 'I' has been laid down.

37   *The Dharma-body of all the Buddhas pervades my own
nature,
And my own nature is also the same as that of all the
Buddhas.
One realm fully encompasses all realms,
Neither shape nor heart nor Karma are there.*

38   *At the snap of a finger, the eighty thousand teachings
are perfected
And all the bad Karma of three Asamkya-kalpas is
instantly extinguished.
Words and phrases from outside are but shadows
That cannot reflect the light of my deepest insight.*

Commentary

'The Dharma-body of all the Buddhas pervades my own
nature, / And my own nature is also the same as that of all
the Buddhas.' The Dharma-body (Dharmakaya) or Law Body
can be understood as the laws inherent in this universe and,
therefore, also in us. In this sense 'body' is not something
material, but rather like an essence which, although imma-
terial, is unmistakable. So the Dharma-body is the essence
or principle of the Law. This Law was not laid down by the
Buddha, who did not set up any law, nor was it created by
some deity. It is the natural law, the way all things really are

and, as that, it just is. It is, and functions, in forms. Out of it all forms come and into it all forms return, yet it is not different from form and it informs all forms. To be in harmony with that Law, having realized it and acting in accordance with it, is exactly what makes our joy, releases us from all stress and makes it possible, in all situations, to act according to the demands of the situation.

So 'The Dharma-body of all the Buddhas pervades my own nature', but we are not aware of it. Awareness can only arise when what conceals it, the thought coverings – and I am the main thought progenitor – are removed. We remember the question of the Sixth Patriarch: 'Before thinking of good or bad, what is the True Face?' The True Face, or own nature, or Buddha-nature – there are many names for it. And so 'The Dharma-body of all the Buddhas pervades my own nature.' It is inborn. Having awakened, Yoka Daishi is naturally aware that the same principle is working in him too because, as a natural law, it pervades the whole earth.

Remember the last lines of Verse 25 of the *Daodejing*: 'Man obeys the laws of Earth, Earth obeys the laws of Heaven, Heaven obeys the laws of Dao, and Dao obeys its own inherent nature.' All of them exist harmoniously together, and this is the source of right action. If man recognizes and obeys the laws of the Earth, he is naturally in complete harmony with everything, with heaven, the Dao or Dharma, the essence of the Dharma. But we have always had great difficulty with obeying, especially nowadays, and we do not like to do so.

Being in harmony is itself our joy in life, makes for a full life. If we are out of harmony we cause eddies or disturbances which fret us. And so, 'the Dharma-body of all the Buddhas pervades my own nature' and 'my own nature is also the same as that of all the Buddhas.' It is the same Dharma-body, the same Dharma-essence, but it would be utterly mistaken to take this literally, in the sense of 'I' or 'my own', as something personal to be grasped or gained. To be one with it is the important thing.

Yoka Daishi continues, 'One realm fully encompasses all realms, / Neither shape, nor heart, nor Karma are there.' This one realm, this one Dharma-essence, is the basis and informing principle of everything that exists, and it encompasses all realms. It is and always has been, but, as the texts carefully say, it has no location, is not a 'thing'. It is not something, somewhere, a place or a realm to be found. It acts everywhere and informs everything, but in it – being no-thing – neither shape nor heart nor Karma are to be found. They could not be there: a principle has no form. Heart or Karma are thought-forms, conditioned phenomena, and so cannot be part of an essence or principle.

Analogies should not be stretched too far, but this might be indicative. Crystals are classified according to an interpolated three-dimensional axial system which is inherent. Crystals grow or form exactly according to a particular axial system, and the angles of the axes can be measured precisely. But even when cutting a crystal and looking for those axes, of course they are not there, and in fact do not exist. Nevertheless each crystal, regardless of outward form, in its structure grows in harmony with and in obedience to that inherent non-existent axial system.

'And my own nature is also the same as that of all the Buddhas.' It is clearly realized as the same. This nature, as the principle, functions in and informs specific forms and bodies, but itself has no form, and in it are no forms. There is no heart in it and no thoughts. Not even Karma can function because, if there is nothing, what can Karma work on? This is beautifully expressed by the Sixth Patriarch as 'When all is empty, where should dust settle?', When all is empty, how can Karma operate?

'At the snap of a finger, the eighty thousand teachings are perfected.' In the 1950s finger-snapping was the vogue with all the 'Zennists'. Everybody was good at it, trying to express understanding because the books said, 'This is it!', and nothing more to it. Try that in a formal interview and you will see what happens! At that time it was the vogue, and everybody thought they knew what it meant, but there is a difference between Yoka Daishi snapping his finger and someone full of ideas snapping their fingers.

So, 'At the snap of a finger, the eighty thousand teachings are perfected.' The so-called Twelve Divisions of the Teachings fill two huge library rooms, but the Buddha summed up his teaching simply as, 'Suffering I teach and the Way out of suffering.' The eighty thousand teachings are really only elaborations. It is useful to see the Buddhist teachings as one organic tree: one does not need to go into the finest little branches to see what it is all about. The Three Signs of Being and the Three Fires are the foundations that carry all the Buddhist teachings. Everything else consists only of further refinements and descriptions and of suggestions for ways of training. This is why we can safely say, 'At the snap of a finger, the eighty thousand teachings are perfected.'

At the same time, with the delusion of 'I' gone, 'All the bad Karma of three Asamkya-kalpas is instantly extinguished.' A Kalpa is a very long span of time. An Asamkya-kalpa is a period that is limitless, that seemingly has no end, but three such periods are mentioned and, according to Buddhist teaching, the universe lasts for four of them. In other words, all the bad Karma 'that from beginningless time has been accumulated', as we chant in the *Repentance Sutra*, is instantly extinguished. We read in the Sutras that, sooner or later, whatever karmic deeds have been produced will come to a ripening and will start to act on us. There is a subtle aspect to these karmic actions, for they relate forwards as well as backwards in time, and we find that difficult to grasp. Karma, in the Buddhist sense – rather than the New Age one – is very deep and profound. If we look at a rug, for example, there is a specific pattern that stipples itself in the fabric. The threads go through, sometimes they come up, and then they go underneath again and are no longer seen. In the same way the Dharma or Law weaves a pattern – not intentional, but as the consequence of its function. And for that carpet pattern to come about, there is not only the retribution for what was, the fruition, but also a connecting trend forward to what is to be. We never know with our short-sighted thinking what it may be, and this is why it is so important to be willing to go with it. Therefore, it is silly to hold the teaching of Karma responsible for the fact that, if I have a lung disease like pneumonia or tuberculosis, it means that in a previous life I was shot in the chest.

'All the bad Karma of three Asamkya-kalpas is instantly extinguished' if the whole insight is clear. At the instant of

'I' really falling off there is the awareness of what the own nature really is, and that moment is not more than the snap of a finger. All the teachings are perfected. The Japanese Master Hakuin talked about the Great Death died in life. He said it has to be died at least once, but to hold and last, it needs to be died four times. 'I' is very deep-seated and, unless died four times, it resurrects itself again with a vengeance.

In the Buddhist teachings it is said that it is very difficult to be born as a human being. There is a traditional analogy that describes how rare such a chance is. In the vastness of the world ocean floats a board with a hole in the middle. Also in that ocean lives a blind turtle who, once every hundred years, needs to come to the surface for a breath of air. What is the probability of that blind turtle putting its head right through the hole in that board as it surfaces? That is how rare it is to be born as a human being. Are we going to make good use of our human birth or not?

Yoka Daishi continues 'Words and phrases from outside are but shadows / That cannot reflect the light of my deepest insight.' However it is expressed in words, the essence of it cannot really be conveyed. It can only be pointed to and, therefore, Yoka Daishi says that words are but shadows. Sesso Roshi once used the analogy of a worshipper in a Shinto shrine. He said that what happens in the heart of a sincere believer as he bows in the Presence of the deity cannot be put into words.

'Words and phrases from outside are but shadows.' They can lift us out of ourselves, but they cannot give us insight. They are stepping stones, and we should make good use of them, but never forget that the essential is something else.

To live out of what happens in the heart of the believer as he bows, not only at that moment, but to continue to live out of that, and to let it carry one in all one's doings, that is important. That is what Yoka Daishi means when he says, 'The Dharma-body of all the Buddhas pervades my own nature, / And my own nature is that of all the Buddhas', and at that all 'the eighty thousand teachings are perfected.' If that is truly lived, it is, to put it in almost Christian terms, as if walking under a cloud of grace.

'Words and phrases from the outside are but shadows / That cannot reflect the light of my deepest insight.' We need to be careful about that deepest insight – it has to do with bowing, with reverently bowing in that Presence. Therefore, the heart is always in it, and it is not just an intellectual understanding, for which we can easily mistake insight. In the human form there is the warmth of the human heart which, with insight, opens up our narrow self-centredness, and it is out of this that the whole further story of the Bodhisattva develops. Yoka Daishi lived out of this deepest insight, and from it comes his *Song of Realization*.

39 *Beyond blame or praise,*
    And limitless like space,
    It is right here, always calm and serene –
    But when you look for it, it cannot be found.

40 *It cannot be grasped nor thrown off*
    And, while you can do neither, it is as it is.
    When (you are) silent it speaks and when (you are)
        speaking it remains silent.
    This bliss-bestowing gate stands wide open without
        bar or bolt.

Commentary

Verse 38 ended with, 'Words and phrases from outside are but shadows / That cannot reflect the light of my deepest insight.' This deepest insight is 'Beyond blame or praise.' Nothing can be added to it, nothing can be taken away from it, it is 'limitless like space'. Space does not mind stars, meteors, even man-made machines moving about in it, and is not even aware of them. 'Limitless like space' – all the little human fancies which plague us are quite irrelevant in that context.

That is precisely what makes it so difficult to accept, particularly for us Westerners, who have, for two thousand years, been brought up in a culture with the idea that there is something that looks after us and that cares about us. This Eastern teaching is quite different. There is nothing that cares, but only a very accurate register of what happens and is done. This is where the concept of Karma comes in: whatever is done for a purpose or is done with intention is karma-productive. Nothing cares. If I put my finger into water it will inevitably get wet, and if I put it on a red-hot stove it will inevitably get burnt. We have always wanted to outgrow those natural consequences of our deeds, to put ourselves in control – not to be wetted by water, not to be burnt by fire.

'Beyond blame or praise, / And limitless like space.' If something happens to me which is unpleasant, am I prepared to admit that it is because of my own foolishness, my own silliness, my own carelessness? Do we not try, if at all possible, to blame it on something or somebody else? If we cannot find anyone to blame it on, then we can at least say that it is my bad luck, but that it is my own fault is something that I very rarely, and only after a good bit of training, am capable of admitting.

We think we know it all, but if it is 'limitless like space', can we possibly have a concrete notion or realization of 'limitless' or 'space', as opposed to some kind of abstraction? Although we talk glibly about it, in spite of all our scientific knowledge nowadays (which is quite fantastic and magnificent), we do not and cannot concretely 'know'. If we are in a place that seems limitless, we even get frightened. People easily get seasick, partly because of the waves, and partly because there is a limitless horizon far away, and in big empty spaces like the plains in Africa or Russia, particularly if alone, panic grips us. 'Limitless like space': it dwarfs us, and that is really why it is frightening, but that is the world we find ourselves in.

Though 'limitless like space' and 'Beyond blame and praise', it is also 'right here', and it is 'always calm and serene'. Limitless and right here! Master Rinzai used to say to his disciples, whether monk or lay people, 'Listen – who is it who is here listening to the Dharma and understanding what is said, right now?' Or 'He is standing right in front of you. Open your eyes!' You either become aware, or you will have to wait a long, long time. Of course 'It is right here, always calm and serene.' If it pervades the universe it must be right here too, not just in some bygone age or in the outer reaches of space. It is just a question of becoming aware of it.

We are not aware of what is 'right here, always calm and serene' – and it is not only around us, for we are part of it, and it is in us. In the midst of the greatest turbulence there is that quiet space out of which appropriate actions come. Such actions will always be in response to the situation, not partial or biased as my actions are. Therefore, it is also said that all intention misses the target. What is asked is action in response to the situation, a listening to what is right here in the situation, and also in us. Limitless, it pervades and permeates what we are, whether we are aware of it or not and, therefore, 'when you look for it, it cannot be found.'

Yoka Daishi goes on, 'It cannot be grasped nor thrown off.' We cannot get hold of it. We are all alive, but can you look for life, can you find life outside a living body? 'Life' itself – we have made these abstractions in our heads with our thoughts. Not realizing it, we now believe that they are actual entities, but they are not. 'It cannot be grasped' – can you grasp life? Can you actually take it in your hands? Can we grasp even our own life? Yet we live it. A Zen master would say, 'Show me life!' How are you going to show it? By having a long discussion about what it is, and how it ends when clinical death takes place? How else are we going to show it? We may think we can throw off life because we could commit suicide, but if one particular body dies, is Life, which is in everything, extinguished? So Yoka Daishi says, while you can neither grasp it nor throw it off, 'it is as it is.'

The important thing is whether it is realized, listened to, adapted to and lived in obedience to and in harmony with, or are we going to do our own thing? If we do our own thing, as we usually do, then we are going to have trouble: we create eddies and crosscurrents, put ourselves under stress. The fact that we seem to be under more and more stress, and that there is more and more talk about stress, should actually show us that we are running ever more according to our own will. We have to run faster and faster because it is uncomfortable, and we want to get away. 'It cannot be grasped nor thrown off, / And while you can do neither, it is as it is.' This willing adaptation and going with it is exactly what we learn in our training. Willing adaptation, and to a certain extent even limiting, is what we learn and need for our life in harmony with what is.

Regarding this limiting and going with things as they are, there is a story about two monks. They met in a little temple where they had stayed for the night, and found a lot in common. The next day they left together. They came to a river, and the ferry had just gone. One calmly walked across the water. The other one sat down and waited for the ferry to return. The first one beckoned to him, 'Come along!' The other refused. 'Come along, you know you can do it.' Again,

'No'. The ferry returned, and the monk was ferried across. The first one was waiting for him on the other side, and scolded, 'Why didn't you come across? You know you could have done it, and I could have helped you.' The other replied, 'It hasn't been of use to you, because you are waiting for me. What's more, if I had known you were such a one, I would not have taken up company with you.' And that is the important point: 'If I had known you were such a one ...'

This leaving it as it is, rather than trying to impose oneself onto it, that is what we have to learn. This limiting oneself to staying within what is has a remarkable effect, and in a human being it also releases the warmth of heart. All Mahayana texts assert that insight/wisdom and compassion belong together; one cannot exist without the other. Actually they are the same; they are the two sides of the same thing. The one who wants to get above, the so-called magician, has not got any warmth of heart and does not care about any human feelings. Since we are in the human realm in both Buddhist and human terms, it behoves us to realize our commonality and how we are connected, and thus to cultivate goodwill and compassion for each other. And so, while 'it is as it is', there is something for us to do in our sphere because we are what we are, and in that there is a proper part for us to play.

'When (you are) silent it speaks and when (you are) speaking it remains silent.' What could that mean? If during a Sesshin, sitting and not speaking, we are quiet inside, and if we are not hounded by continuous thought-streams, then occasionally a real calm can arise. There is an intimation in that quietness; a listening which is not listening to something, but a listening inside, listening with the heart. What is then in the heart – the wisdom and power of the Tathagata – can make itself heard. That is why we do things like having Sesshins. While we are in the middle of all kinds of outside activities, yapping with each other, mostly about things which are quite unimportant, gossiping away in order to drown out what we are frightened of, we cannot hear. 'Speaking, it remains silent.'

'The bliss-bestowing gate stands wide open without bar or bolt.' Whether we want to go in or not depends on our practice that renders us willing enough to stoop and go through. From the Hassidic Jewish spiritual tradition comes this beautiful short story. A famous rabbi was asked by his most brilliant student, 'How is it that in the old days many saw the face of God, but nowadays nobody can see that Countenance?' The old rabbi smiled and said, 'Well, my son, nowadays nobody can stoop so low.' When 'I', as such, am no longer there then that gate opens fully and completely. When the attachments are gone, along with 'I', the wisdom and the power of the Tathagata can function freely in the given form, whatever it may be.

41 *If asked what teaching I adhere to,*
    I reply that it is the power of the Mahaprajnaparamita
    Which surpasses ordinary human understanding,
    And not even the vault of heaven can encompass it.

42 *For many Kalpas have I persevered in training,*
    And do not want to beguile you with idle words.
    I hoist the Dharma-banner of Sakyamuni's teaching
    To which I too have become heir.

Commentary

'If asked what teaching I adhere to, / I reply that it is to the power of the Mahaprajnaparamita.' Wherever we go we are asked what we are, where we belong – not only in Buddhism, but everywhere. In the Zen school it is often asked 'What song do you sing?', which comes down to the same thing. We have to declare where we have got it from because we are not self-realized, and could not possibly be. So, the first thing is 'Where do you come from? Who is your teacher and what is your line?' Yoka Daishi says, 'If asked what teaching I adhere to, / I reply that it is the power of the Mahaprajnaparamita.'

We in the West may be interested in the Buddhist teachings and practice, but rarely in the religious aspect, and so we miss the other half of the message. We are attracted to what suits us, how it helps us, and soon start tinkering about with it so that it turns into how we like it. We ignore the religious side, the folding of the hands, the bowing of the head, we forget the Buddha and the Dharma. It very soon becomes something like psycho-babble, and then we are surprised that nothing comes out of it.

What goes with the religious attitude? The most important is the opening of the heart, saying yes and willingly undertaking the practice. It is not only the doing, however faultless, but how it is done – whether the heart is engaged or not. If music is played faultlessly, accurately to the last note, but the heart is not in it, then it does not move, and is as dead as a dodo. So it goes with our practice, too: if we want to give it life, we must not forget the Buddha and the Dharma. That is where we get our understanding from, and it is also the framework it flows back to, which supports us in adversity and in ordinary daily life so that we can smoothly go with it. So, Yoka Daishi, fully enlightened, states, 'If asked what teaching I adhere to, / I reply that it is the power of the Mahaprajnaparamita.' 'Mahaprajnaparamita' can be translated as 'The Great Wisdom Gone Beyond'. The Sutras and Commentaries belonging to this cycle are fundamental to all Mahayana schools. Every morning and evening we chant the Heart Sutra, which is its heart, the gist of this whole teaching.

'The Great Wisdom Gone Beyond' – what does that actually mean? Gone beyond what? Into the supernatural or something like that? Do we recall Master Rinzai's list of the Buddha's supernormal powers (see Commentary to Verses 13 & 14)? 'In the eye not to be deceived by form, in the ear not to be deceived by sound, in the nose not to be deceived by smell, in the tongue not to be deceived by taste, in the body not to be deceived by touch, and in the mind not to be deceived by notions and thoughts.' These are the real powers of the 'Wisdom Gone Beyond', and they only function if the delusion of 'I' is really seen into.

Together with the delusion of 'I', the endless desire, fear and aversion have fallen off. That delusion gone, the whole phantasmagoria is gone too, and the sight is truly cleared. This clear seeing is the Buddha-seeing. All things are seen the way they really are, and that is precisely how the 'Wisdom Gone Beyond' perceives. Not gone beyond the ordinary, but gone beyond 'I'. Looking at all the Paramitas, they start with Giving and end with Wisdom. With Giving, we start with a little, perhaps a flower for the Buddha-altar. Then in Daily Life Practice we give ourselves ever more and ever deeper into what is being done. Then sooner or later, helped and strengthened by the exercise in all the Paramitas, we can give ourselves fully into and away. That then is Giving 'gone beyond'.

The Paramitas are often translated as Perfections, which is a very bad translation for us because we love perfection, and would like to be perfect or something like that. But how can a delusion become perfect? What a silly idea! It is the going beyond 'I', the forgetting of 'I' which opens up the whole power of what is. That is precisely what the Great Wisdom is all about, the Wisdom Gone Beyond. Therefore, Yoka Daishi explains what this entails: 'the power of the Mahaprajnaparamita ... surpasses ordinary human understanding' because without an 'I' there is no longer that ordinary understanding that swerves from yes to no, from right to wrong, always caught by and between opposites. We

Westerners are particularly prone to that, and so are especially aggressive. For us, our world is separated into good and bad, or right and wrong, into prime opposites that are at war with each other. So we take sides and fight the 'other', hoping that in the end the good will win. But are they all so irreconcilable and totally separate? With us, yes, and we make our choice and there we stand.

In the East, fortunately, this is not the case. There the opposites are related and have not been cut apart by notions, as symbolized by the concept 'yin yang'. On the contrary, each goes about the other's business: if one gets top-heavy, the other one begins to assert itself and makes it come down again, and if that then gets top-heavy, like a seesaw, the other comes up again. They go about each other's business, and so to want to get rid of one, to do away with it for good and forever, is simply not possible, and inconceivable to an Easterner. So, unless infected by our Western way of seeing, they are, by and large, more tolerant, especially in the field of religion. They find it easier to accept the ordinary difficulties that are part and parcel of the dark, sorrowful and painful side of life. That is something we have yet to learn.

Truly it is the Mahaprajnaparamita, the 'Great Wisdom Gone Beyond', that surpasses all our ordinary understanding. Even if we can intellectually follow what it means, that the 'ten thousand things' are not separate, we cannot live according to it without the relevant training. For, says Yoka Daishi, not only does it surpass 'ordinary human understanding', but, 'not even the vault of heaven can encompass it.' It is always there, and pervades everything. It has many names: you can call it the Dharma or the Buddha-nature or the True Face. It is whatever it is and, since it connects everything, it also means that every form is informed by it, and every form is part of it. If only this could be grasped then, instead of feeling like a separate 'I', such insight could open the power of the Paramita, the power and wisdom of the Buddha. This Wisdom/Power metaphorically stands on its own feet, not in a defensive/aggressive belligerent way, but just peacefully is. And it cannot be bowled over by anything – not because it stems itself against anything, but because it just is, and acts out of its own gravity. It is unmistakable when that informs a human being.

Yoka Daishi goes on, 'For many Kalpas have I persevered in training / And do not want to beguile you with idle words.' He knows that, in order to come to real insight and be able to live out of it, there are two stages. In Zen training it is said that to come to the first insight is relatively easy, but to then really live according to it takes long and bitter training. To have really 'digested' the first insight so that it pervades the whole body and being is called to have become at one with it. There is no need to try and act according to it, rather it is impossible not to be in accord with it. This irreversible state is hard to attain. For that reason Yoka Daishi describes it as 'for many Kalpas have I persevered in training' and so 'do not want to beguile you with idle words.' He knows what he is saying.

What does it mean, 'to beguile with idle words'? It means talking about something from hearsay, or from my notions and from the standpoint of what I think, how I interpret it and how I see it, but without having the whole of the Buddha-knowledge carrying it. So our training continuously needs to be tested: every insight, every action, every word and every thought needs to be tested. Does it conform to the Buddha-dharma or not? If it does, fine. If it does not, then once more it has gone off the rails, as it very often does. For this reason, real acquaintance with the Buddha-dharma is necessary because, being what we are, we are prone to stray. If we do not have the framework of the teachings, and continuously test ourselves against it, we will very soon be off and away down a blind alley or worse. Again, training and the teachings need to match, need to go hand in hand.

In the fifties a lot of interest arose in Zen, particularly in the States, but the iconoclastic side of Zen was misunderstood. It was propagated with the snapping of the fingers as, 'This is it!' or 'If you meet the Buddha, kill the Buddha!' and all such fads. It was quite a shock to see Zen as practised in Japan. Two Americans visited a monastery where the master spoke very little English. He showed them around and, passing the various Buddha statues, he naturally always bowed. By the sixth bow, one of them could bear it no longer. After all, he had been nourished on, 'If you meet the Buddha, kill the Buddha', and now he saw this master bowing to all those Rupas! He blurted out, 'All your bowing and scraping, that's not Zen! Why, I could spit at it!' Do we know how we would react if somebody said that they could spit at something that we hold very dear, which means at least as much, if not more, than our own life? Even if somebody would just spit at one of our pet ideas, how would we react? What did the Zen master say? Quite unperturbed, in his funny English, he said, 'Okay, okay, you spits, I bows.' Perhaps we can take that to heart.

This story clearly shows the long and thorough training needed to be able to react like that, for when something happens that I don't like, that I do not fancy, that hurts something inside me. I am a touchy, insecure creature – something rises in me and strikes swift like a snake. There is nothing wrong with it; it is a natural survival response which is still in us from when we climbed down from the trees and ran about in the jungle. It has never been humanized and urgently needs to be, for under the veneer of urbanity much has been left underneath, and this is precisely where our troubles come from. And that needs to be gentled, humanized.

Yoka Daishi says, 'I do not want to beguile you with idle words', idle notions. And to make sure this is understood, that idle words have nothing to do with what he says, he declares who he is: 'I hoist the Dharma-banner of Sakyamuni's teaching / To which I too have become heir.' We need to remind ourselves again and again what the Dharma-banner of Sakyamuni's teachings is, and adhere to it so that it leads us to the living spirit. The living spirit underlies everything else, but if we chop and change about we will not reach its fullness, will not be quickened by it, and thus deluded, turn down one of the many blind alleys.

So Yoka Daishi declares where he comes from, and that it is not his but the Buddha's teaching, with all that this entails. He, therefore, sees no reason to use idle words: 'I hoist the Dharma-banner of Sakyamuni's teaching / To which I too have become heir.' Having become one with it, he can speak in the same way. In my own experience, I had the good fortune to be allowed to work under two masters, Master Sesso and Master Sojun. They came from different teaching lines, but what they taught was exactly the same because they both were heirs to Sakyamuni, and their teaching and training methods, therefore, were those of Sakyamuni. That does not mean that there is not an individual flavour to it because, as individuals, people differ on the surface but not in the essentials. As Master Hakuin says, 'In the end, the nose is still vertical and the mouth is horizontal.' The teaching is the same and the training is the same.

If we are really serious about the training, then going 'my way' is certain to lead us astray. What is asked is the gentleness of handing ourselves over. That is foreign to us Westerners, this gently saying yes and carefully following the footsteps of the teaching. If I think 'I must do it', and believe 'I must do it right because I must not get anything wrong', then I get as stiff as a ramrod, and either become more insecure or more swollen with 'I'. But that is not following the Buddha's Way, is not his teaching. We are reminded of the Austrian horse-riding proverb: 'He is no good rider who has never kissed the sand.' If we are frightened of making mistakes then we might just as well not even start. We are goal-orientated, and intend to get away from where or what we do not like, determined to get what we want; so we heedlessly shoot off, driving ourselves more and more. But, as some of us older ones have realized, there is no such thing as a goal.

When the heart opens it takes in what the situation itself says. In the situation itself we can hear the voice of the Dharma, into which the Buddha had insight, and we can be re-linked into the Dharma, into what really is. What the human heart really wants is to be re-linked with the harmony which pervades everything and where it has its being.

The Dharma, or Law or principle, informs all forms. To have insight into that, to be one with it and, therefore, to act out of it, is what the heart is longing for. With that, its longing is fulfilled and, being fulfilled, there is now an active and joyous participation in and with all that is.

43   *Kasyapa was the first to whom the Lamp was transmitted,*
     And for twenty-eight generations it was handed on in India.
     Then Bodhidharma himself brought it across the sea
     To our own country, and is its first patriarch here.

44   *As is well known, his robe was transmitted for six generations*
     And many came to listen and entered the Way.
     Truth has no need to be established, and as for the false,
       it is originally empty.
     If both, being and non-being, are put aside, the not-empty
       is voided.

Commentary

In Verse 42, Yoka Daishi said that he 'hoist[ed] the Dharma-banner of Sakyamuni's teachings', to which he had become heir. Now he reminds us again of how this banner of Sakyamuni was handed down through the generations. We feel deep gratitude to all those who, after the Buddha, have followed in his footsteps and have kept his teachings and his insight alive by walking the same Way. At five-day Sesshins, with people taking shortcuts across the lawn, the first traces of a path appear within a couple of days: just so with our own practice. We are deeply grateful to those who kept the Way open for us to tread it, and are aware that our own walking it will keep it open for those who come after. This is what Yoka Daishi reminds us of.

'Kasyapa was the first to whom the Lamp was transmitted.' It is said that once when the Budhha was expected to give a talk, he silently held up a flower instead. All waited for him to speak, but he just sat there and held up the flower. Among the multitude, Kasyapa suddenly smiled. At this, the Buddha acknowledged Kasyapa – 'the transmission from heart to heart'. We need to acquaint ourselves with the patriarchs and with the stories of their lives because they show what is necessary for following the Buddha's Path. Kasyapa was the first to whom the Lamp, the teaching, was transmitted. The teaching is often compared to a lamp or a light, like a candle lit by another candle, and so on. The candles differ, but the light is always the same.

'And for twenty-eight generations it was handed on in India.' The twenty-eighth Indian patriarch, Bodhidharma, then brought it across the sea to China and became the first patriarch there. We have another lesson to learn from this because we know only too well that, historically, this is not true. Nobody knows who those first twenty-eight patriarchs were. Bodhidharma's existence is itself somewhat questionable, but traditionally he is revered as the first patriarch of the Zen School. Its actual history can be studied, but only the tradition gives hints of how to practise.

The transmission from India to China, from one culture to another, is of interest for us here. It took some time before the Buddha-dharma took root in China but, being a well-travelled religion, it has been shown that its roots can grow in any soil as long as its spirit is transmitted. If the spirit is tinkered with because 'it does not suit us', then it goes wrong. So Yoka Daishi says, 'Then Bodhidharma himself brought it across the sea / To our own country, and is its first patriarch here.' There are pictures of him in all Zen temples.

So from Bodhidharma to Eka, and from there, 'As is well known, his robe was transmitted for six generations / And many came to listen and entered the Way.' The robe is symbolic for the genuine Dharma that is handed down. The sixth generation after Bodhidharma is, of course, the Sixth Patriarch. After that the robe of transmission is no longer referred to. We have already related the story of the Huineng's arrival at the monastery of the Fifth Patriarch and of the poetry competition to decide the succession (see Commentary to Verses 19 & 20). On the strength of his poem, the Fifth Patriarch summoned the young man to him and, being satisfied with the genuineness and completeness of his insight, handed him the robe and bowl of Bodhidharma, but told him to leave. This was done not only to settle the insight so that it really became irreversible, but also because in his monastery there were monks of twenty and thirty years standing who naturally would be upset and wonder whether the young man, who was not even a monk, could be given the robe of succession, so it was suggested that he go away to mature and only come back again later.

When it was noticed that the young man had disappeared, and also that the robe and bowl were gone, a few of the monks were so upset that they ran after him. There was envy, but also a genuine suspicion that he might have stolen them, that he was not the proper successor. Nobody could imagine that they truly might have been given to him. A burly old monk eventually managed to overtake him. But on being overtaken – and this is the important point – the young one just laid down robe and bowl. The elder monk made a grab for them, but found he could not lift them. Begging bowls, although big, are not heavy, and neither is a monk's robe. Why could he not lift them? The traditional stories just tell us he could not, so we need to look at what this points to. He laid down what was rightfully his. Would we do that willingly if someone tried to take away something of which we were the rightful owner, particularly if it is something of greatest import like the robe and bowl of succession? It must have mattered enormously to him, must have been dearer than his own life or he would not have got them in the first place. Those who have laid down their lives for what they considered more have always been considered heroes, but that young man also laid down what meant considerably more than his own life. Moreover, something that was not only proof of transmission, but carried with it the responsibility that he would hand it on undiluted to future generations. All this he laid down. With nothing left, the last root of 'I' is really and truly laid down. The heart empties. If all is laid down, no person can pick all that up. This is why Myo, the pursuer, could not lift them.

But he too was a well-attained monk, and at that moment he realized that he stood in the presence of the genuine Sixth Patriarch. If we read the Sutra, we see the immediate change, which seems ludicrous if we read it without understanding. First he runs after him for days and finally overtakes him, but now respectfully addresses that youngster: 'Elder brother, I have not come for robe and bowl, I have come for the Dharma.' What happened to him at that instant was a total change of heart. At that the Sixth Patriarch asked,

'Before thinking of good and bad, what is the true face of the elder Myo before father and mother were born?' Thus, twice startled and shocked 'out of himself', the elder Myo 'saw', had insight.

That is how the Zen Way goes. Please ponder that carefully, and do not go into the many byways that are, of course, always open – 'I' only too easily engages in them. Stick to the Way, and cultivate not yourself or anything, but just that giving, and again giving. Not giving yourself over, but wholeheartedly giving yourself into what at this moment is being done, with the Precepts as guidelines.

Yoka Daishi continues, 'Truth has no need to be established and, as for the false, it is originally empty.' Why does truth not need to be established? Because it simply is. Whether I admit it or deny it, it has nothing to do with true or false, only with the way things really are, which is the Buddha-seeing. We talk and argue about it, because we have our own notions about it. We may even be quite sincere but, because we have seen just one tiny aspect of it, now, fools that we are, we believe that we really know it. But we do not: truth just is as it is and does not need to be established, does not need to be affirmed or discussed. It is as it is, needs not to be listened to or to be obeyed.

It is a strange thing that we always have trouble with that listening and even more with obeying. But unless we really listen, we cannot hear. Even in conversation, we usually only listen to the first few words and then quickly form our own ideas about what we are going to say, formulate our answers, and do not listen any more. Or we might listen on a surface level only, and miss the real message. What we listen to with the ear is only the sound. When we listen with the intellect, we can hear the words but they do not really convey what has been said. If we really want to listen wholeheartedly, the whole body goes forward to truly take it in. That is listening with the heart, and then the meaning behind the words is also perceived. So the real listening is listening with the whole body, as often expressed in Zen texts: 'To see with the ear and to listen with the eye.' To really take it in, the whole body, 'body and heart', need to open up; only then can a truly satisfying response ensue. Thus, an answer need not necessarily be intellectual, but arises, flashes forth from that open attentiveness. Just this is what we need to learn for dealing with each other, for our relationships, and for our general understanding, so we start practising this listening, listening with the whole body, with the opening of the heart. This opening of the heart is already the first beginning of the insight into the way things really are.

'Truth has no need to be established and, as for the false, it is originally empty. / If both being and non-being are put aside, the not-empty is voided.' This 'originally empty' is what we seek. It is our own ground of being, and the heart clamours to be re-united with it. What is false, what is unnatural as we often term it, cannot itself exist, only our view of it. Truth is as it is, but Truth is not just beautiful, as we would like to have it: it is awesome, not to say horrific. The false and unnatural cannot exist – only what is in the laws of nature, of the Dharma, exists, and that is empty. What temporarily exists is a flood of ever-changing forms 'coming to be and ceasing to be'. It is useful to ponder that from time to time.

'True' and 'false' are just another pair of opposites, as are 'being' and 'non-being'. In the phenomenal world they exist phantom-like, ever changing, so can be put aside; 'coming to be and ceasing to be', as the Buddha said. Other such pairs of opposites are creation and destruction, birth and death. In the analogy of the wave and the ocean, the individual waves go up and down, form and dissolve, but inherently are nothing but ocean.

45 *The twenty teachings on emptiness are not revealed*
       to begin with;
    The (True) Nature is the same as Tathagatahood.
    If the heart is swayed by the dust of the sense objects,
    Then heart and things are like traces dulling the surface
       of a mirror.

46 *If the traces are wiped off, the brilliance emerges;*
    Heart and things forgotten, the True Nature shines forth.
    Oh this sorry world of the Decline of the Dharma,
    When sentient beings are poorly endowed and find
       control difficult!

Commentary

'The twenty teachings on emptiness are not revealed to begin with.' Why not? I am interested, and would like to know about them. There is a saying, 'Do not tell the frog in the well about the vastness of the wide ocean.' Why should I not be told of the vast ocean? We do not even suspect that the vastness of the wide ocean might terrify us.

Just ponder, why are we so afraid of losing control? This basic fear is the other side of 'I', like the palm and the back of the hand. Where there is 'I', there is fear. Where there is fear, there is 'I' and, as expressed in the *Heart Sutra*, when the heart is free of hindrances 'there is no fear.' The twenty teachings on emptiness do not have any 'I' in them. They are awesome to even a medium-sized 'I', and to our big-sized 'I' they are shattering, so they are not revealed to begin with. They have to be approached slowly, by diligent training that whittles away 'I', so that they can be entered without shattering results. It is of the nature of 'I' that, wherever something is hidden or not disclosed, that is what I fervently want to discover.

'The twenty teachings on emptiness are not revealed to begin with.' Not only would they be too frightening, but they would also prevent us from even beginning. To dwindle away is the last thing we want, and so to begin with there are all kinds of encouragements to enter the Path. Slowly then, by our own experience as we undergo the training, the grip begins to loosen, and as 'I' recedes, the True Nature begins to emerge. This '(True) Nature is the same as Tathagatahood.'

Although the Buddha pointed out that human beings are fully endowed with the Tathagata's wisdom and power, they are not aware of it. In a way, other beings are not aware of it either, because what makes us human beings is our conscious awareness. But since that has mostly become self-conscious, we are deluded: Avidya, or not seeing clearly, has existed from the beginning. Or, in Christian terms, since we have eaten the apple of good and bad, we have fallen into the world of opposites, which distorts seeing. But the True Nature sees clearly, which is the insight of the Tathagata, and that is also the wisdom and power of Tathagatahood, and so is the same as the Tathagata, the Buddha, the True Nature. This insight is what the Buddhist strives towards, and what the Buddhist teachings point out.

To approach it directly is very difficult. Yoka Daishi says, 'If the heart is swayed by the dust of the sense objects, / Then heart and things are like traces dulling the surface of a mirror.' 'If the heart is swayed' – in other words, indulges in preferences, such as I and you, this and that – then the whole is split into opposites, giving rise to what the Chinese call the 'ten thousand things'. Then the heart is swayed by preferences, and what falls into the senses, the sense objects, pull us because of our picking and choosing. 'I like this, but not that.' 'This is beautiful, that is ugly.' The Third Patriarch carefully admonishes us that, 'The great Way is not difficult, it only avoids picking and choosing', which he later calls the dis-ease of the heart, as well as being the cause of the dis-ease. And so, if 'swayed by the dust of the sense objects', 'heart and things' or 'I' and things are 'like traces dulling the surface of a mirror.'

'If the traces are wiped off, the brilliance emerges.' However scratched the metal surface may be, if you go on polishing, the scratches are polished away sooner or later, and the brilliance inherent in the metal emerges of itself. Thus, says Yoka Daishi, 'Heart and things forgotten, the True Nature shines forth.' 'Heart and things', or myself and objects, are both forgotten. Can I do that? Naturally not, but it does happen. As a matter of fact, it happens every day, only we are not aware of it. If I try to forget them, I cannot do it. If it happens of itself, there is no problem. But although it happens of itself, it is only sporadic, and suddenly I am back again, and the world is as it was. To make it continuous needs a training that gently but inexorably undermines this split into 'I' and 'objects', so that both heart and things can be forgotten. At that moment, 'the True Nature shines forth.'

What does 'wholehearted' mean? That we give our whole heart into the moment, or into what is being done at that moment, and so for that moment lose the sense of 'I'. Then this becomes more and more of a habit, of just pure doing, responding to the moment, to the demands of the moment, rather than 'I' doing it my way, rightly, wrongly, liking it, not liking it. All this falls off of itself, is simply no longer there. 'I' and objects forgotten, there is just doing.

In this functioning 'the True Nature shines forth.' This True Nature itself cannot be said to be, but it pervades, informs and functions in everything. Take electricity – is it, or is it not? Can you see it as such? Can you touch electricity? You can get an electric shock, but that is not touching electricity, that is touching a wire that conducts it. Electricity may be thought of as a force but, by itself, as such, it is 'nothing', cannot be seen or touched, yet in its functioning it can be made use of, or can harm us. We can die from an electric shock, but we can also use electricity to iron, cook with and keep warm by, we can get light from it, and its power can drive machines. Its function is perceptible, electricity itself is not. And so when 'Heart and things [are] forgotten, the True Nature shines forth.' To try and grasp True Nature is merely foolish. This is one of our difficulties, as the Sixth Patriarch points out. It is only perceptible in its functioning.

With real sadness Master Yoka Daishi says, 'Oh this sorry world of the Decline of the Dharma, / When sentient beings are poorly endowed and find control difficult!' There are said to be three periods after the life and ministry of the Buddha. For some time there is the clear and simple Dharma of the Buddha when ease of understanding prevails.

As we read in the scriptures, many of his direct disciples seem to have had little difficulty – the Buddha explained carefully, and suddenly they saw. Why does that not happen any more? That is a very real question, and the answer is that we are too engrossed in our delusion, divided in ourselves, split. So we are told that after the first period when deliverance was easy, with less 'I' and less fear, there comes a middle period, when it is no longer so easy to awaken. Finally, during the last period of the 'Decline of the Dharma', it is next to impossible. This is the period we are supposed to be in now. Even Yoka Daishi a long time ago said, 'Oh this sorry world of the Decline of the Dharma', so this world of the Decline of the Dharma dawned on us a long time ago and is still continuing.

'When sentient beings are poorly endowed and find control difficult.' There is a twist here. We find control difficult because we are poorly endowed, and we are poorly endowed when we find control difficult. We can all decide to do something from now on, but it is unlikely that we will really bring it off smoothly. We cannot control ourselves. It has been said from of old that to overcome oneself, to be able to control oneself, is the greatest of victories. It is so difficult because the root of 'I' is so deep, seems to be the very life-spring of our being. There is also the split between head/'I' and heart/emotions. To have all that truly dissolved needs hard and devoted labour. It cannot be said often enough that it is not possible for 'I' to do it. This is why it is necessary to undergo a training that, little by little, restrains my usual predilections. Consequently, I feel hemmed in and want out, but instead of getting out, it gets still tighter. Then just at the moment when I think I'll die, something changes.

We see this progression in all religious traditions, but it is made especially clear in the story of the Buddha's life. We cannot do better than continuously mull it over, because the stages are analogous to our own walking the Way. No historic record exists of the Buddha's life, but that is not important. The stages inform us of what we will encounter on that Way, and how little by little things begin to fall off: when he is no longer a prince, nor a famous disciple and heir of great teachers, when finally even his last five disciples leave him, there is nothing left. This is the road that we too need to go – until nothing is left.

We need to look into this 'nothing left'. It may also be read as 'no attachments'. If I am a multi-millionaire and my millions mean nothing to me, that is fine – they have no power over me, may be used to good purpose. If I give them away, become a beggar, and moan that I am cold and hungry, then that is of no use at all. 'Nothing left' means 'nothing to lose', to have no attachments left. The final attachment is 'I', but the root of 'I' is deep. As already mentioned, in Buddhist tradition, what needs to fall off are four things, in sequence: first 'I', then the sense of a human being, then of a sentient being, and finally a life. If life also falls off, then really deep down the Great Death is died – just as for the Buddha when he sat under the Bo-tree and Mara tempted him, or as in Christianity when Jesus was on the cross. When the very life also falls off, everything is gone. One thing that we do know is that this is an insight each one of us inevitably will have at the moment of death, but of what use is that insight to anybody else? Master Hakuin calls it the Great Death, dying to the whole 'I'-complex while still alive. His great disciple, Torei, said, 'Then begins another life.' Again, the Buddha's life – after his enlightenment begins his ministry for the benefit of all beings.

So in spite of, or perhaps because of, the Decline of the Dharma, when looking around at the increasing difficulties that we have, it might be helpful to keep the legend of the Buddha's life in mind and, with that as an example, 'strive on heedfully'. In spite of being poorly endowed, to submit to the teaching, to keep control, and to give ourselves into the practice. Such restraint and holding ourselves in control will gradually dry out and starve off the hindrances. That then clears the sight, and the True Nature, the Tathagatahood, which is inborn in each one of us, can shine through. This is the great message that Yoka Daishi passes on to us. We need only to be willing to follow it. This might be useful to ponder carefully, and little by little, to put it into action. Do not be afraid of losing 'I', a bit of 'I' – it rather eases the burden. I am my own obstacle. It might also help to think in terms of offering it up.

Perhaps we could begin to train ourselves whenever we have any difficulty, whenever any annoyance or sorrow arises in the heart, or any this or any that, we might then possibly kneel down in front of the Buddha and lay that burden down at his feet. As we are less and less weighed down by whatever it may be, we might feel lighter, released from our burden, until finally we can, with reverence, lay ourselves, that final burden, at the feet of the Buddha. At that moment we will know who we really are.

VERSES 47 AND 48

47   *Erroneous views increase as the distance from the*
       Buddha increases.
     As the Dharma declines, Mara's strength grows,
       and with it hatred.
     Even though they hear the Tathagata's sudden
       teachings expounded,
     It would not shake them out of decline, as a brick
       is smashed at one stroke.

48   *The heart instigates all actions and the body suffers*
       all the consequent misfortunes.
     So do not complain about or blame others.
     If you do not wish to incur unlimited bad Karma
     Do not slander the Tathagata's Wheel of the
       True Dharma.

Commentary

'Erroneous views increase as the distance from the Buddha increases.' That seems to be fairly obvious. It's rather like 'Chinese whispers' – even a short sentence is ludicrously changed when being passed on from one to another. That illustrates our normal way of half listening and not retaining properly, embroidering what we have heard with our own ideas. Go to see a film with a few friends and afterwards get each person to write down the story. You will have as many different versions, and they will often not just be variations of the same story, but inherently different.

'Erroneous views increase as the distance from the Buddha increases.' It does not say that the Dharma changes, only that views about it become ever more erroneous. Although very sad, what declines is our understanding, not the Buddha-dharma, which is the way all things really are. Presumably if twenty Buddhas sat down to a game of Chinese whispers the sentence would remain unchanged because each would have listened and then handed on without any additions or subtractions. We cannot do that, but we can learn to listen attentively rather than hearing something and, believing we have understood it, pass on our short-sighted erroneous views to others.

Yoka Daishi says, 'As the Dharma declines, Mara's strength grows, and with it hatred.' Mara is the deceiver, but who is the real deceiver? Who is Mara really? Mara is one of the gods in the pantheon of the thirty-three, and certainly the god and master of this world of desire in which we live. But if we look a little closer, is Mara outside or is he inside? We do not believe in an outside god, but 'I' is a god inside me, isn't it? Holding sway absolutely, everything centres around it: even the most pious believer could not be as concerned about his deity as 'I' am about 'myself'. My least little whim and wish is almost a command to be obeyed. We are totally under the sway of it. Have we ever thought that we all have our own Mara sitting in our heart? The less we listen to the Dharma the more his strength grows, and with it hatred and aggression, which is very clearly coming up more and more in our times.

The belief in an order, whether religious or social, declines as the Dharma declines, and so the Mara inside grows and freely disports himself. I rise up against everything that does not please me: thus, 'Mara's strength grows and with it hatred.' If we carefully look at this, we will find it tremendously helpful. The Dharma and Precepts are our support. Not only do they help us to behave in a normal human way, but also, by means of that restraint, the inner strength grows. As the inner strength grows, the wisdom and power of the Tathagata can slowly come through, and hence Mara's strength weakens. But hatred, anger, fanaticism and intolerance are widespread in our world, which has no valid religious or cultural supports. With more and more hatred in the world, more and more factions that fight, more and more wars, we naturally become more and more afraid, and have less and less peace outside and in our hearts.

'As the Dharma declines, Mara's strength grows and with it hatred. / Even though they hear the Tathagata's sudden teachings expounded, / It would not shake them out of decline, as a brick is smashed at one stroke.' This fits us in our days of decline. Even though we hear the Tathagata's sudden teachings expounded, does it actually make any difference?

There is a Japanese story of a great general, who was an ardent follower of Zen, and who used to take his Zen master with him on his campaigns. One day a magician visited the camp and asked, 'What is the use of all this Zen business? It's nothing special. I can work real miracles, have got powers that could be useful to you. Look at that waterfall. I can go right through and not a drop of water will touch me!' And he did go through it, and came out bone dry. The general was impressed, and asked the Zen master to do this. The Zen master went through, and came out drenched. Accused of being a deceiver and of having no powers, the Zen master laughed and said, 'So, he came out dry, but what is the use of that? You get wet from water and burnt by fire, and that is just how it is!' We may ask, 'So why should I do a training like this? After all, I already know that I get wet from water and burnt by fire.' But the general was already well trained in Zen and took the lesson.

It is a question of clearly seeing what is, saying yes to it, and then either accepting it or finding a way around it that accords with the situation as far as possible. If a man comes rushing at you with a cudgel you try to duck out of the way, and do not stand still so that he can hit you over the head. This clear seeing and responding to the situation is what is at stake. That is what the real training is about, not fancy fireworks. So 'Even though they hear the Tathagata's sudden teachings expounded, / It would not shake them out of decline', would not stop them wanting to have their fancies, would not enable them to drop them suddenly 'as a brick is smashed at one stroke.'

'The heart instigates all actions and the body suffers all the subsequent misfortunes.' The heart is roused by my picking and choosing. I am the picker and chooser – 'I must have... I won't have...' That makes it hot. When hot, it is blind. The actions that come from such blindness are karma-productive. 'The heart instigates all actions and the body suffers the consequent misfortunes.' The thought is the father of the deed, and consequently the body suffers. How so? In a fired-up state, I think that I can do things I am not really capable of, or I overdo things and suffer unfortunate consequences. If I am a glutton, I gorge myself at a banquet, generally only think in terms of food, and the body suffers. Or I starve myself for an idea, and the body suffers. Or I get carried away by ambition, and work and work in order to get to the top or to get more money, and then I have a nervous breakdown and the body suffers. If you look around nowadays, every other article in the newspaper is about stress. We moan about how stressful our life is, that we have no time at all, which in a way is true. But why do we have no time anymore? Because should we find ourselves with a bit of spare time, it frightens us. Then we have to go and 'kill time' – such idioms are very helpful. What is stressful to me, is not necessarily having to work so much. It is equally stressful if I do not have to work and just sit and rest, perhaps even more stressful. So 'the body suffers all the consequent misfortunes.'

Master Yoka Daishi says, 'So do not complain about or blame others.' We bring it upon ourselves, by not looking at things clearly and by being carried away by what we know as the Fires. We complain that we have not got what we want, or that we always have bad luck. That is one possibility. The other is to blame somebody or something else – I easily find a scapegoat. But difficulties have always been part and parcel of our lot because human life is part of life on this globe, as are light and dark, joy and suffering. The Decline of the Dharma also manifests in my expectation that I can completely avoid any of the dark side and have only light.

'If you do not wish to incur unlimited bad Karma / Do not slander the Tathagata's Wheel of the True Dharma.' If you do not wish to incur bad Karma, then do not spurn the supports of the Dharma, the teaching and the practice. If we do not kick against these, then no Karma is produced. 'All intention misses the target', because it is productive of Karma. This is another reason why obedience to the teachings is so important. Obedience can be translated as 'listening' – not mere lip service to the teachings, but heeding them and what they stand for, what they point to. If we do so, then it is not difficult to hold on to the supports, even if there is a roaring inside of 'I want', 'I must' or whatever.

In former times, all Buddhist temples used to have a picture of the Wheel of Life at the entrance, and an elderly monk there to explain it all to visitors: the Six States, the Twelve Links which hold it together, Mara the demon who grips it, and in the middle, the Three Fires of Desire, Aggression and Delusion which keep it in motion. That Wheel has many connotations, and the understanding of it has many layers, although on the surface it looks deceptively simple. The Buddha cautioned Ananda not to take the teaching of the Chain of Dependent Arising lightly, that it was 'deep and profound'. That depth and profundity becomes clear when 'I' is truly out of the way. So when we are once more in the process of setting ourselves up, proclaiming our notions of this or that, we can be quite sure that at that moment we are ignoring, or even slandering, 'the Tathagata's Wheel of the True Dharma.' Whenever we are blinded and gagged by our notions or convictions or are defending ourselves, then we are certainly far away from it.

If, on the other hand, the Tathagata's True Dharma really means something, we can peacefully say yes to whatever it is. We can use it as support and go with it willingly, holding on to it even when temptations seem overwhelming. If only we hold on to it, it will hold and we can endure. In each such bottleneck a little more of 'I' is ground away until there is so little left that what has always been there not only shines through but comes through, and now it, instead of the misleading notion of 'I', informs all our actions, all our talk and all our thinking. That is where the Buddha's Way leads us, not only to our own satisfaction, but so that we are harmlessly in harmony and friends with everything that is, able to hold out a helping hand to whoever just at this moment could do with one. That is where compassion proves to be the other side of wisdom.

49   *Only sandalwood trees grow in a sandalwood grove.*
     Only lions inhabit the primeval jungle,
     And they alone play about in that vast wilderness.
     No other animals live there and no birds fly.

50   *Only the lion cubs follow at the foot of their parents;*
     When three years old, they roar full-throated.
     How could jackals pursue the Lord of the Dharma?
     Thousands of shape-shifting imps gape open-
         mouthed.

51   *The complete and sudden teachings have nothing to do*
         with human sentiments;
     If there is doubt, nothing is settled and quarrels are sure
         to arise.
     This is not just the babbling of an old mountain monk,
     My fear is that your learning might land you in the cave
         of either eternalism or nihilism.

Commentary

'Only sandalwood trees grow in a sandalwood grove. / Only lions inhabit the primeval jungle.' When we first read this, both of these lines seem strange, and we have to look more closely to see what we actually really have here. 'Only sandalwood trees grow in a sandalwood grove.' 'Well, naturally', we might say, 'that is why it is called a sandalwood grove.' But perhaps there is more to it than that.

We human beings are strange creatures, hanging on to one extreme or the other. We feel ourselves to be special, and nowadays any imposed conformity, together with discipline and obedience, are much resisted. Instead we easily fall for any trends and fashions – from clothing to thinking and doing. When these grip us we want everybody to be like us, all the same. Nature, however, is structured. There is nothing unstructured in this universe, and certainly not in our world. If it were unstructured it could not be. So, instead of quarrelling about whether the sandalwood trees in the sandalwood grove are all the same, we just see that they are not all the same: some are bigger, some smaller, it just depends.

There is still another point. We can find conformity quite difficult: 'Only sandalwood trees? But I don't want to be an ordinary sandalwood tree! Why can't I be a pine tree with spiky needles?' 'Only sandalwood trees grow in a sandalwood grove' – in conformity with each other. We human beings have so much trouble realizing that we are all human. We make many artificial distinctions, and then believe in them rather than in our common humanity. One person might be young and tall and thin, while another is old and small and fat. They differ in appearance, but does that cancel out their commonality? If we look at it like this we see what we have in common and what the individual differences are, which are there, but which do not really count very much. We go on, 'He is rich, and he is poor' or 'He is high up and a president while I am only a coal miner.' But what do these individual differences have to do with the actual fact that we are all human beings? Wanting to be unique is something that is very much cultivated in our time and makes it very difficult for us to conform.

'Only sandalwood trees grow in a sandalwood grove. / Only lions inhabit the primeval jungle.' Of course we know nowadays that in the primeval jungle, or at least in what is left of it, there also are lots of other creatures. Yoka Daishi must have known it too, so why does he say here that only lions inhabit the primeval jungle? The primeval jungle is dangerous; only a lion can live in such a dangerous place.

In *The Zen Teachings of Rinzai* there is a passage which describes what a liberated man can do. He can walk about in the wilderness, in these primeval forests, without being attacked by wild beasts, and he can go into the three deepest hells and play about there as if it were a fairground. When I first read that passage I was very upset about the lack of compassion. I was preparing myself to hear Master Sesso Roshi's teisho (presentation on the text) the following day, and was curious how he would comment on it. The next day Sesso Roshi took it up and said, 'We must look at such passages with the "single eye" of Zen. A "liberated man" must remain free, because if he goes into places of such suffering and is not completely free, he will himself become entangled and become merely another inmate. Of what use is he then? He must remain free, for only then can he hold out a helping hand.' Suddenly we look at those lines in a different way.

'And they alone play about in that vast wilderness. / No other animals live there and no birds fly.' When the lion enters the primeval jungle, all fancy ideas, the bogeys, the longings, the speculations, the fears – and we are stuffed full of them – have all gone away, and so, 'Only the lion cubs follow at the foot of their parents.' In those dangerous primeval places where 'no other animals live... and no birds fly,' it is easy to get lost and come to grief, so only the lion cubs can safely follow the steps of their parents into those trackless places. There, helped by their parents, they can grow up into lions. We can take it that this also applies to our training. If done properly, my strong sense of 'I' begins to weaken, and with it my notions, my wants and dislikes. At the same time fear also lessens. It is only possible to grow up when fear, and thus wanting more and more, begin to fade.

So, only the lion cubs follow their parents, learning by following them. If, as the texts say, we are all Buddha-children, do we follow in his footsteps, or do we find it too arduous? The lion cubs, following their parents, thus learn the way of lions. Do we follow the Buddha's footsteps long enough to grow up? Yoka Daishi says of the lion cubs at three years old, they can 'roar full-throated'. The Buddha's teaching is likened to such a full-throated lion's roar – the good news of the end of suffering.

'How could jackals pursue the Lord of the Dharma?' They can only yelp at his heels. 'Thousands of shape-shifting imps gape open-mouthed.' Who are those shape-shifting imps? They are what I believe, what I am convinced of, the ideas I have, what I have coaxed myself into believing is so – all these millions of sprites in our mind, our fancies, which are made up of whatever we have read, incline towards or have mistaken things for. These are the 'thousands of shape-shifting imps' which 'gape open-mouthed' when the lion roars.

We think that our imagination and fantasy run freely, and are also convinced that we can imagine the unimaginable. What we do not realize is that, even in our keenest imaginings, we can never for a moment leave the realm of our actual concrete experience. It is only the shape-shifting imps. If you look at the early Far Eastern portrayals of elephants, which the painters had read about in the scriptures but had never actually seen, they depict elephants with curly trunks like the tail of a pig. We can also have a particular idea about and portray the body of a lion with the head of a woman; or we can picture the body of a man with the head of an elephant (that of Ganesh). This is putting two well-known things together in a way in which they do not normally combine, thus trying to convey something other-worldly. But it is still not other-worldly, it is just different bits jumbled together in a way that do not naturally occur. This is also the difficulty in writing science fiction, or portraying it in films – we cannot go outside our concrete physical experience. This experience may be very wide now because we have seen pictures of so many things, but bound by it we are. We cannot know what is not physically experienced, and so would naturally deny it. It is very important to realize this for two reasons. First, so that we do not let our ideas run away with us too much, and rather view them with healthy scepticism, and secondly, so that we do not, by sheer intensity of belief, give credence to imagined attributes. For instance in the fifties, when I was first introduced to Buddhism, there was great expectation about the 'Wisdom of the East'. Every Eastern monk was thought to be already enlightened and there was much imagination about it.

What we often imagine to be reading in the Zen texts are actually our own ideas, and we believe them because of the intensity of our imagination. It is exactly this which is a screen right in front of our eyes, through which we cannot see. Be very careful. The first thing on the Path of the Buddha's own 're-discovery' and, therefore, on the Path to our own heart, is to find those screens which we have built up with our convictions and towards which we think we have to strive. These are exactly the 'thousands of shape-shifting imps' that 'gape open-mouthed' when they suddenly hear the full-throated roar of the lion.

'The complete and sudden teachings' are, in the Mahayana classification, the final and distilled teachings of the Buddha. Here the different branches of the Southern and Northern traditions and the various branches within the northern one – the Tibetan and the Chinese – all cancel out. It comes to what in Sanskrit is called the Ekayana, the One Vehicle only. This is what the complete and sudden teachings proclaim – not this, not that, not historical developments. Actually all of them proclaim always the same. This is what we need to learn and realize.

'The complete and sudden teachings have nothing to do with human sentiments.' The teachings are as they are, the principle is as it is. Life is as it is. Life on Earth is as it is. Now it is winter here in the northern hemisphere, whether we like it or not, and in the southern one it is summer. Now it is getting dark, and this morning the sun was shining. That is just how it is. It has absolutely nothing to do with us human beings or with our human sentiments. We are here not because we have a right to be here, we are here on sufferance, and we either comply with it, at least to a certain extent, or we have a lot of trouble. And so 'the complete and sudden teachings have nothing to do with human sentiments', but it is very important that we realize them as a framework, according to which we can align and adjust ourselves.

Master Yoka Daishi continues, 'If there is doubt, nothing is settled and quarrels are sure to arise.' If we are not aware of the inborn wisdom, doubt arises. What these teachings proclaim is just this principle. We are endowed with the wisdom and power of the Tathagata, it is in us, but 'I', deluded by my convictions and sentiments, feelings, appetites and fears, naturally doubt, and 'I', being insecure, am myself the delusion. So there is an uneasy awareness that something is missing. The illusory 'I' wants to shore myself up, one way or another. But I can never be entirely secure because life is not secure, nothing in this world is lasting. This is the Buddha's teaching of change, suffering and No-I. In my delusion I do not see this, and believe that security can be achieved for myself and for our world. So there is an inward doubt and an outward striving for security. What does secure in this sense mean? Doesn't it mean to have it as I want it, and that it lasts? It is as simple as that. We know that this is naturally not possible, that nothing can remain settled forever, so insecurity not only continues but, since I do not look and do not take it in, it increases.

Hence, as Yoka Daishi cautions, 'quarrels are sure to arise.' Naturally, because if I try to shore up my patch and someone else tries to shore up his, we will soon come to a border where we infringe upon each other. Have we become more quarrelsome these days? We certainly have become more and more unrestrained in our wants, and we no longer have any feeling for there being limits. If you look round or read the newspapers you see 'road rage', 'trolley rage', even 'golf rage' nowadays, and it is no longer safe on aeroplanes because people start fighting. We cannot contain ourselves anymore, yet we say that what Yoka Daishi said a thousand years ago does not apply to us! It does, only much more so, because there is much more doubt and much more fear in us, so 'nothing is settled and quarrels are sure to arise.'

Yoka Daishi continues, 'This is not just the babbling of an old mountain monk', because that is the first label that is used against someone who talks like that. An old mountain monk, how can he know anything about the world? Yet during his long time on the mountain he has come to know himself, with all the ups and downs that a human being can have and feel. He has come to see things as they really are, the complete and sudden teachings are clear. So he expresses his worry: 'My fear is that your learning might land you in the cave of either eternalism or nihilism.' He talks of 'my fear' out of compassion, as the Buddha did when he saw into the nexus of our human sentiments that cannot and will not take facts as they are, cannot and will not see that we are living in a world that is just as it is. We have always tried to change the world according to how we wish it to be, but have not succeeded. Rather, we are getting further away from it. The more we tinker, the more messes we produce. The more messes we produce, the more doubt there is. The more doubt there is, the more quarrels arise. And so the Buddha saw the pity of us deluded human beings struggling and trying hard to change something which, in itself, cannot be changed, trying to make something safe and secure which can never be safe and secure. Out of pity and out of compassion, he spent the rest of his life showing the Way out, talking about the principle and teaching it to all those who came to him. Many took it to heart, had their doubts settled and, therefore, had no more quarrels.

'This is not just the babbling of an old mountain monk.' Even so, when we take the teachings to heart, is it not so that we first get interested in them, and then want to find out more about them? But learning without practice, without making it part of daily life, has no effect. Nowadays we are far too clever. If we think about the teachings, there are, of course, the Three Signs of Being, the Three Fires, the Wheel of Life, the Four Noble Truths and the Twelve Linked Chain of Causation. I have heard them, read them, know them, but what do they mean to me? Instead of once more being uplifted by them, we greedily rush after more and more. Such pursuit, however, does not encourage us to walk any further, does not change our attitude to life. But when things get difficult it is the simple teachings that support and carry us. The Twelve Divisions of the Teachings, as they are technically called, fill libraries and, even if it were possible for one human being to imbibe them all, what use would it be? Do they benefit me or rather give me a swollen head? When on my death-bed, what use would they all be?

'My fear is that your learning will land you in the cave of either eternalism or nihilism.' We think that eternity lasts forever, but when we really contemplate it, it is inconceivable and so, to us, it is nothing. Nothing, to us, is simply the absence of something. What in the Buddhist teaching is meant by Sunyata is the voidness of all things mental and physical – what is, just is. Hence, eternal is not what lasts, but what always is – which is this moment, now. Then it is gone, and there is another moment, now. The moment before now is only a memory. The moment to come is not yet here, and at most is only an anticipation, it is unreal. What actually is and always is, is now, here and now. Do we live that here and now?

So we begin to understand what is meant by the term 'eternal' – this moment here and now – and also by the term Sunyata, which even when translated as 'void', we misunderstand as merely 'nothing'. What does Sunyata really mean? Here we again need the 'complete and sudden teachings'. It is a voidness which has nothing to do with me, where none of my ideas, fancies or sentiments have any place, they just do not exist there. Then things can open: when 'no-thing', no trace of 'I'-delusion is there anymore, then what actually is can be perceived and can also be partaken in. And the fullness and completeness of the principle unfolds itself and continues to unfold itself and, in its unfolding, continuously changes. This partaking in it is what the heart truly strives for. That has nothing to do with me, nothing to do with human sentiments, it is just the whole situation, and partaking in it in accord with its spirit. From the point of view of 'I', this is sometimes easy and sometimes hard, but since 'I' am not there, there is nothing easy and nothing hard. I tend to mistakenly regard this as completely lifeless, neither up nor down, all boringly the same, all the more so when I read that there is neither any joy nor sorrow. I begin to feel that it is all nihilistic, all dead, and mistake this as the Buddha's teaching. I cannot approach what actually is unless I have done sufficient training, so I get stuck in the view of nihilism, that nothing is. That game has been played umpteen times, and not only by Buddhists. As human beings, dangling between yes and no or this and that, knowing the opposites, we are always suspended between them. The Buddha's message is, that they can be surmounted in a completeness that is inconceivable from either of the opposites. This he taught not only intellectually as an exercise, but as a Way that can be concretely walked all the way. And he also said that, as a Way, it was not something new that he had invented, but rather that it was an old, ancient road to an ancient city that he had re-discovered. This city is the human heart which, whether ancient or modern, whether East or West, is very much the same. On the surface we individually differ, but that human heart is common to us all.

52 *No is not No, nor is yes Yes;*
Even a hair's breadth difference and it goes a thousand
miles apart.
When 'Yes', a Naga girl suddenly becomes a Buddha,
When 'No', Zensho Bhikku falls living into hell.

53 *From when I was young I have enjoyed scholarly pursuits.*
I studied the Sutras, Sastras and Commentaries,
Quibbling about names and form and forgetting the body.
All is like diving into the ocean to count the grains of
sand there!

54 *The Tathagata strongly condemned such pursuits,*
For what is the use of counting up the treasures of others?
My former achievements and efforts now seem useless,
But for years I was blown about like dust in the wind.

55 *If the seed-nature (where we come from) is not properly*
understood,
The Tathagata's complete and sudden teachings cannot
be reached.
Although the Two Vehicles are devout, they lack the Way
of the Heart,
And as for those of Other Ways, they are intelligent
but lack genuine Wisdom.

Commentary

'No is not No, nor is yes Yes.' What a strange thing! Surely no is no and yes is yes? But in this world of change in which we live there is no such thing as an absolute no or an absolute yes – 'Even a hair's breadth difference and it goes a thousand miles apart.' If there is just a hair's breadth difference from giving in and being in harmony with the situation, at that moment it flies a thousand miles apart. Who is the one who is apart? Isn't it 'I'? If I have not given in, I somehow feel continuously exposed, and this is what makes me so self-conscious. The moment that I am exposed, I become self-conscious. If I am really at one with a situation, then there is no feeling of separation, of either this or that, there is just a smooth flowing with it. Can we remember situations where we acted quite naturally, and others where we were self-conscious and acted artificially? In the latter we feel under pressure to do what we are not used to, but what is so difficult about going into that too, and giving ourselves into it smoothly?

In a monastery a new monk is judged by the way in which he adapts himself to the conditions there. The smoother and quicker he does, the more he is considered a good vessel. The obstacle is the wanting to stick to my way. We all know that my way does not lead to happiness or peace of mind or we would not be interested in Zen training, so we learn to give in. In that giving in, strangely enough, our real individuality develops. Before that there is only a bundle of ideas and wants.

'When "Yes", a Naga girl suddenly becomes a Buddha.' 'Naga' is not a cobra, but the spirit or divinity that is in the cobra, which is revered in India, so Nagas are spiritual beings. A Naga girl is not necessarily very high in the Buddhist hierarchy, but Nagas are connected with the Buddha because when he sat deep in meditation the Naga king reared up behind him and spread his hood so as to shield him from the sun. So 'When "Yes", a Naga girl suddenly becomes a Buddha.' Bear in mind that Yoka Daishi wrote a long time ago, about 600 CE, when the doctrine prevailed that a woman could not become a Buddha, which continues to this day, so when a Naga girl becomes a Buddha, we suddenly break free from notions and opinions.

'When "No", Zensho Bhikku falls living into hell.' Zensho Bhikku was an Arhat, one who has attained enlightenment, and he was convinced he knew. Then something happened, and he had a violent outburst of rage. He was infuriated, not only because he had such an outburst, but even more that he could have it at all, for someone with the status of an Arhat cannot feel rage anymore. So he started to slander the Buddha-dharma, saying that it is not worthwhile, that there is something wrong with it because an Arhat can no longer have anger, and here he was, an Arhat, and perhaps even more than just an Arhat. At that moment the Earth could not carry him anymore. The story goes that it opened up and swallowed him, and he fell living into hell.

Here we have a double: 'When "Yes", a Naga girl suddenly becomes a Buddha.' Saying yes, and with that yes giving into the situation, there is nothing that can stand in the way. It is a yes to and in the situation, not a rigid yes. And when no, a rigid unconditional no, not wanting to take what is, then even an advanced Bhikku falls living into hell.

'From when I was young I have enjoyed scholarly pursuits.' Some of us do. When we get interested in Buddhism, we are likely to start reading and reading. The more we read, the more ideas we get. If we are not in training, we continue with it. 'I studied the Sutras, Sastras and Commentaries, / Quibbling about names and forms and forgetting the body.' It fills the head with more and more ideas, with more and more of my interpretations, just as it suits my notions, 'quibbling about names'. When we just stick to more and more reading, what can come out of it except wildly opinionated views of this or that? We do not realize that we read selectively, that in fact it is just my picking and choosing. And to someone else the same may seem to be quite different, but that is also his picking and choosing. We construct our own views for ourselves and think that this is the Buddhadharma. The more we pursue this the more real it seems, and it becomes the darling of our heart which we hold on to and defend. This does not only happen with the Buddhadharma, but is universal. We Westerners are particularly prone to it, and so have firm divisions – 'I am Theravada', 'I am Vajrayana', 'I am Mahayana', and 'I am Zen'. We can go on splitting, further and further: 'I am Chinese Zen' and 'No, that is all long ago in the past, I am Japanese Zen.' All Oriental art can come into it as well, all the beautiful pictures, then the Samurai stories get added to it and that becomes my idea of Zen. It has gone off into the blue with not even the big toe on the ground anymore. With that barrage going on in me, I cannot see or hear what actually is there.

Such ideas get in the way and act as screens that obscure what is actually there. It is most important to pierce through this rather than letting it build up ever more. So in Buddhism, particularly in Zen training, there are said to be three stages. First, 'hearing with the ear', which in our case is more likely to be reading with the eye. 'From when I was young I enjoyed scholarly pursuits. / I studied the Sutras, Sastras and Commentaries', but that alone is not enough. If the hearing or reading is interesting, if it warms and touches me, then naturally I want to find out more. But instead of reading more about it, the second stage, 'pondering with the heart', suggests to really contemplate and to truly mull over the fundamentals, rather than selectively building up a picture from what I like. But even that is not helpful unless it is very soon followed by 'practice with the body', the third stage. Master Yoka Daishi says, 'Quibbling about names and form and forgetting the body.'

'All is like diving into the ocean to count the grains of sand there!' Even if they could be counted, does it help us if we know how many grains of sand there are in the depths? Does it make us happier, does it make us more friendly towards ourselves and others? Do those intellectual pursuits building up in the head have anything to do with the way things actually are? As a matter of fact they take us even further away, they separate us. They are mere intellectual gymnastics which make us feel more isolated and self-conscious, and more at war with what is, ourselves included.

So we take the body into our training. Besides 'keeping the form', one of the most helpful ways of training with the body is the bowing. We do a lot of bowing because, although the head may not understand, the body and the rest of us understands that this is the age-old gesture of giving ourselves away and of laying ourselves down. If we do the Daily Life Practice with a continuous inner bow, then we cannot go wrong. Then we will also find that our convictions, opinions, stubbornness, self-will and isolation slowly begin to soften. Instead, a feeling of relationship and connectedness arises which lights up our life, and that has an effect on others too. So, although the training helps us out of our isolation, it is also of use to others, and necessarily so. We are not alone. This being of use to others is the heart of the Northern or Mahayana teaching. As concrete insight, it is emphasized again and again in the Zen School.

Yoka Daishi tells us that, 'The Tathagata strongly condemned such pursuits', that is, collecting more and more ideas, busily accumulating concepts. And he asks, 'For what is the use of counting up the treasures of others?' Yes, we need a framework, but then to search for more and more details, how this person saw it and that person realized it; such pursuits will not bring us much nearer. Hence the proverb not to mistake the pointing finger for the moon.

So Yoka Daishi tells us, 'My former achievements and efforts now seem useless' – whatever he had done, all his scholarly pursuits after this and that. From this we might easily get the mistaken idea that there is no need for any learning. Merely clinging to the teaching at word level is what Yoka Daishi means when he says, 'But for years I was blown about like dust in the wind.' We had such a period in the sixties and seventies – either expecting that it would come of itself, which is one of the fancy ideas, or waiting and thinking that it will come by just doing practice, and making the practice the end rather than the means. Both are extremes, and neither will help. There is a Dutch proverb that says, 'God helps the sailor, but steer he must himself.' There we have the two sides together. We need both the framework of the teachings and the practice; it does not go without practice, and practice without the framework very soon turns back again to 'I'. This is what we need to keep in mind, for inevitably when practice without the framework of the teachings turns back to 'I', the pictures and the inner film begin to swallow us up. That is where convictions and notions come from; they are fired by that inner film. They have nothing to do with insight into the Buddha-dharma.

We have to work very hard to get the framework of the teaching into our system, we have to be diligent in our practice, and use the framework to measure and check it against. Do our little insights as they come up match the framework or not? If it is only the insight of others, and we think that we know and understand, then we are already deceiving ourselves. Having done all the necessary studies, Yoka Daishi said that, once he had had the real insight, his former learned achievements and efforts seemed useless. That does not mean that they were altogether useless, because he would not have come to this insight if he had not done those studies before. But once that insight has lit up, then the studies seem useless. In a way, useless because the wisdom and power of the Tathagata are inborn, but cannot be uncovered without knowing the teachings and following the Way. Once uncovered, studies are useless, yet without them it is not possible to come to that insight.

'If the seed-nature (where we come from) is not properly understood, / The Tathagata's complete and sudden teachings cannot be reached.' The seed-nature is the inherent nature or Buddha-nature or the True Face or the True Nature – it is irrelevant what names we give it. It is where we come from, go back to, and live out of. We remember the Sixth Patriarch: 'Before father and mother were born, what is the True Face?' Of this seed-nature, the Buddha said that all beings are endowed with it but, because of our attachments, we are unaware of it. We have often spoken of these attachments and how, when it comes right down to it, 'I' am the attachment. It is very important for us to realize that this 'I' has very long and deep roots, and in Buddhism, four ever deeper layers of this root of 'I' need to be penetrated, loosened and uprooted – the layer of an 'I', a 'human being', a 'sentient being', and 'a life.' That is scary and awesome. It cannot be learned by reading books or by listening to talks or whatever, nor by listening to any kind of ideas that come up in our deluded heads. There is something quite decisive and no-nonsense about it. We come face-to-face with the seed-nature and merge, for good.

All traditions warn not to take this uprooting lightly or to search for it out of mere curiosity. A strong 'I' cannot take the impact, it gets either shattered or killed. Only when 'I' has been so weakened that it has faded away, and when all the four layers of 'I' have melted down, then the awesome mystery can be seen and opened up to. We practise towards this meltdown. Skin after skin of the touchy, opinionated, wanting, deluded 'I' is peeled off, and so the whole bundle which I think of as 'I' is worn away. I need to have patience and be willing to endure such stripping, and allow it, even though each one feels like a little death. If I am not willing to die all these little deaths, then the Great Death of which Master Hakuin talks cannot be died.

'If the seed-nature (where we come from) is not properly understood, / The Tathagata's complete and sudden teachings cannot be reached.' They can be expounded, talked about eloquently, read and studied, but without practice it does not reach the heart. That is why, 'Although the Two Vehicles are devout, they lack the Way of the Heart.' So, we may be devout, we may be learned, but the really important things cannot be learned, cannot be found by those who 'lack the Way of the Heart.' The Two Vehicles are the vehicle of the hearers, the Sravakas, and of the Pratyekabuddhas, as they are technically called. In the Northern Buddhist teachings, the hearers are those who, although they hear the teachings, cannot really make use of them. They cling to the teachings and that is all. The Pratyekabuddhas have seen into the consequences of cause and effect, but they also lack the 'heart'.

'And as for those of Other Ways, they are intelligent but lack genuine Wisdom.' The Other Ways are the philosophies and the convictions of various schools. Philosophy is the love of wisdom and, from of old, was one of the great disciplines of learning, but it did not necessarily have a spiritual dimension. Nowadays it is nothing but intellectual gymnastics, rootless fancy ideas, clever rather than intelligent, mostly sophistry. That is what we engage in nowadays, and meanwhile the heart becomes more and more hungry. And because it receives no adequate nourishment, it gets caught up in all the changing fancies that are floating about and even creates new ones.

Not without reason does the Zen School rightly call itself the Buddha-heart School – the heart of the Buddha, and the Way of the Heart. That is where the insight is contained and from there it has to come out. When it is no longer encrusted by all the views and presumptions that make up the hard and brittle shell of 'I', which is other than everything else, and when all that has melted away, then the wisdom of the heart is truly released. For good measure, Yoka Daishi says, 'Although the Two Vehicles are devout, they lack the Way of the Heart.'

56   *There are those who, foolish and childish,*
     Mistake the empty fist or pointing finger for Truth.
     But mistaking the pointing finger for the moon
         dissolves all their merit
     And, like phantoms they bob about in the sense fields
         of objectivity.

57   *Seeing the emptiness of all things is becoming Buddha.*
     If a name can be put to it, it is called Kanjizai
         Bodhisattva ('Seeing all Things').
     Truly seen into, the karmic bonds are originally empty.
     If not fully seen into, the karmic debts for all past deeds
         are fully exacted.

58   *If the starving refuse to eat of the banquet spread*
         before them,
     Or the sick spurn the help of the doctor, how can they
         be helped?
     Practising Zen while in the realm of desire becomes the
         power of Prajna.
     The lotus blooms unblemished amid the flames.

59   *Yuse (Bhikku) had committed a heinous crime, but with*
         genuine insight into No-birth
     He at once became Buddha (awakened), and now still exists.
     The lion's roar proclaims fearlessness.
     Alas, foolish and stubborn like old leather, people do not know it.

Commentary

Yoka Daishi continues, 'There are those who, foolish and childish, / Mistake the empty fist or pointing finger for the Truth.' We are all acquainted with the analogy of not mistaking the pointing finger for the truth, but nevertheless usually do. The finger pointing at the moon – is it the moon that the finger is pointing to, or do we fasten onto the finger? With regards to the empty fist, the Buddha himself often said, and certainly we have it in the Southern Scriptures, that he did not hold anything back. In the most simple utterance of the Buddha we find the whole of the truth, but if we just stick to the surface of it we are mistaken. 'Foolish and childish' – seeing a few autumn leaves and thinking that they are gold, getting one aspect and being convinced it is already the whole, or seeing but the pointing finger and not what it points to.

'But mistaking the pointing finger for the moon dissolves all their merit.' The moment that I think 'I know' I have already lost all the merit of the training, and have joined the foolish and childish. Not only that – actually, with the belief that I know, I have put a concrete ceiling right over my head. I think that now I know, and do not need to enquire any further because I already know. But when we really look, even from our limited understanding, we do not and cannot know all. Every so often something new comes up and we struggle against it, but then it slowly takes over. Then something else unexpectedly appears, and we struggle against that until it too becomes accepted. What can we know? Four hundred years ago we were deeply convinced that the sun moved round the

Earth, and that we were the centre of the universe here on our tiny planet. That is a totally different way of looking at things from how we look at them now, yet, in spite of hundreds of years having passed, we still say that the sun rises and that the sun sets. We do not feel as though we are stuck with our feet on a spinning surface that races round, do we?

Truly, 'mistaking the pointing finger for the moon dissolves all their merit / And, like phantoms, they bob about in the sense fields of objectivity.' Bobbing up and down like phantoms or ghosts – not just in the sea of birth and death, but in the sense fields of objectivity. In Buddhism it is held that we have six senses, and one of the sense fields of objectivity is also our mind, our thoughts. All fancies that are there, and those which come up are delusory ghosts which we take for real. They can become remarkably real, and the more I believe in them the more I give them substance. Then, like phantoms, they lead astray in the most unbelievable ways. The more I cling to something, the more I believe in something, or the more I refuse something, the more that begins to gain power over me. True faith can move mountains, but there is also impassioned conviction which is the opposite of true faith, and which distorts and blinds sense perception.

So, rather than being deceived and deceiving ourselves, Yoka Daishi says, 'Seeing the emptiness of all things is becoming Buddha.' Not seeing the shifting shapes as they bob up and down, and certainly not taking them for real, but just seeing the emptiness of all things, that is the Buddha-seeing. That is seeing all things as they really are.

He continues, 'If a name can be put to it, it is called Kanjizai Bosatsu.' We chant the *Heart Sutra* every day, which talks of Kanjizai, who is the Bodhisattva Avalokitesvara, the Bodhisattva who sees all things. Here we come across a new aspect of the Bodhisattva, for we have always considered him as the compassionate one because he is fearless. In a way, a name cannot be put to the Buddha-seeing, for it is empty but, 'if a name can be put to it', then it is to the function, the seeing. As the function, it is the Bodhisattva; that is what we need to realize. As that, it is functioning in clear seeing. In the emptiness of all things, a name is put to the functioning amongst these shadowy ghosts. The Bodhisattva, as this functioning, is there to show that it is possible to come to that state and to act in that state.

'Truly seen into, the karmic bonds are originally empty.' In seeing the emptiness of all things, in that Buddha-seeing, the karmic bonds are not there. That is why it is said in the texts that it is possible to spring free from the karmic fetters by truly seeing into them. When there is nothing, in that emptiness there are no karmic bonds or anything else. This is why the Sixth Patriarch said, 'When everything is empty, where can dust collect?' But, 'If not fully seen into, the karmic debts for all past deeds are fully exacted': as long as we are not fully in the state of clear seeing, the Buddha-seeing, we are subject to the law of Karma, of cause and effect.

Although we know the law of cause and effect, we often take Karma too narrowly. It is quite true that if I put my finger on a red-hot stove, then the finger will be burnt. You could say that this is the simplest and most natural example of Karma, but it is not so obvious that what I have done is already working, and not just in the one line but with ramifications. We have to be very careful, because the consequences of whatever I do do not just work in one line. Every act, every desire has not only one cause, but two or three main causes and a number of auxiliary ones. Our deeds spread out like ripples in a pond, they cross over and affect each other, and it becomes an intricate web. It is for that reason that the Buddha said that we should be very careful in our actions so as not to add further suffering to our world. We can bring about suffering not only when we actively want to do something nasty, but also by being heedless, by being bigoted or by being convinced of our ideas.

There is still another aspect to it. We usually think of karmic debts exacted for things we have done, but as we have just seen, there is an intricate web of interaction in which there are patterns that stretch forward into the future. Not that they are made by anybody; they stipple themselves in conformity with the inherent law. In order for a particular thing to come about in a way that fits the general pattern, all sorts of things have to happen that may not have much to do with the past, except that they come out of it meaningfully and roll forwards meaningfully. We are in that kind of tremendous and huge web which is not flat but is three-dimensional – Indra's Net – where everything reflects everything else. To be aware of that pattern and to go with it is to meaningfully play one's role in it. This is not in the way that I want to do it or how I understand it, because I cannot, but as the heart is geared to partake in this big game. The heart has the full wisdom and power of the Tathagata, the seeing of the emptiness of all things, which is becoming Buddha.

Kanjizai Bosatsu is the seeing of all things and willingly rolling with them. This willingly rolling with it is actually the obedience to life, and in that obedience is the partaking. That is what the heart really wants: only then can it feel fulfilled. This partaking sometimes can be painful and hurt, but underneath there is a meaningful going with it. The training helps us to approach the importance and the beauty of this until finally we fall into it. It can be put into all kinds of words, but one can also talk too much about things. It is much more important that we put our nose to the grindstone and go with our practice until there is not much left, or, as the Buddha said, until the eyes are only a little covered with dust. Then the seeing becomes clearer, and so does the hearing. As the hearing gets clearer, the Kanjizai Bosatsu is also the Kannon Bosatsu: not only does he see all things but, having come to his insight by means of sound, he also hears all things, and so really goes with all things.

Following that Way, we may think of ourselves as links in a long, long chain going back to all those who spent their lives walking the Buddha's Path, so that it is still clear and open for us today, so we can see it and are prevented from going astray. We ourselves, doing one or two steps on that Path, will keep it open for those who come after. That also ties us into a commonality that completely liberates us from that narrowness of 'I' -only, 'as I see it' and 'as I believe', etc., for it is truly 'for the sake of all beings'.

'If the starving refuse to eat of the banquet spread before them, / Or the sick spurn the help of the doctor, how can they be helped?' Much later Zen Master Hakuin put it into other words: 'In the midst of water pitifully crying from thirst.' The Buddha-dharma is always spread there. What is the Buddha-dharma? Seeing all things the way they really are – this is what the Buddha taught, and to that insight the Buddha's teaching is pointing the Way. But we, in the midst of all this, refuse to eat the banquet spread before us. We hang on to ourselves, cling to ourselves, moan about our difficulties, insist on our rights and wants, etc. We want to get out of this straitjacket, but when it comes right down to it, we would rather change the whole world according to how we think it should be than change ourselves. We complain that we are ill, that we have difficulties, that we do not have enough. You can lead a horse to water, but you cannot make him drink.

'If the starving refuse to eat of the banquet spread before them, / Or the sick spurn the help of the doctor, how can they be helped?' And so quite rightly Yoka Daishi says, 'Practising Zen whilst in the realm of desire [in Samsara] becomes the power of Prajna.' Whether it is desire for food or to have our ideal come true or our wishes fulfilled, it does not matter. And practising Zen means not bothering about our desires, but just getting on with the practice of giving ourselves into what at this moment is being done.

You remember the golden ball and how it led the monk astray (see Commentary on Verses 3 & 4)? Resisting and learning to resist the temptation of the seemingly overwhelming pull is due to the power of Prajna, the power of wisdom. This is genuine insight that makes it possible not to be swayed, even by a full eruption of the 'afflicting passions' (the Klesas), but to endure the onslaught and, realizing it is not an enemy, asking with folded hands, 'I am still here, please burn me away.' That is practising Zen, and that becomes the power of Prajna in which the 'afflicting passions' have been transformed. There is a quotation that 'the lotus blooms unblemished amid the flames'. That is the Buddha-lotus that is not burnt by the Fires in one of those hefty emotional eruptions. That is really what practising Zen means. Such power is in all of us.

'Yuse (Bhikku) had committed a heinous crime, but when he had genuine insight into No-birth / He at once became Buddha and now still exists.' That sounds very strange indeed. First he commits a serious fault, but then nevertheless has genuine insight and, thus awakened, still exists. There are a few other examples: perhaps the most famous one in the Buddha's teaching is that of Angulimala, who was a murderer. From each person that he killed, he cut a finger off. He strung the fingers into a necklace, and already had 999 fingers hanging around his neck. He decided that, as the crowning number of one thousand, he would have the Buddha's finger, so he stalked the Buddha. The Buddha was quite aware of being followed, and when Angulimala was practically upon him he turned and looked at him. Angulimala was so struck by that full power of the Prajna, the whole wisdom and power of the Tathagata manifested in front of him, that he had a complete change of heart. He prostrated himself and asked to be taken as a disciple.

In all religious traditions we find such stories. In the Christian tradition it is said that there is more joy over a converted sinner than over a good man. It is a question of the power of Prajna. If I always have been good, have never been tempted or tested, not much strength will have developed. But not always having been good, when something then suddenly happens and we have the strength to resist the temptation and really give ourselves into the training, even against seemingly overwhelming odds, then the power of Prajna unfolds. We must not forget or mistake such conversion stories when we hear them. They tell of the strength of the turning round, of the conversion.

So Yuse Bhikku, in spite of having been a sinner, had the strength and propensity to turn round and, eventually awakened, was delivered from the delusion of 'I'. Bodhidharma said of the Zen School that it was 'a special transmission outside the teachings, not relying on words or letters, pointing directly to the human heart, seeing into its nature and becoming Buddha.' So this awakening wipes out anything that was before, and, once this awakening has occurred, the state of 'No-thing', Sunyata – clear emptiness – prevails. It is from this state that in the Southern tradition, the Buddha told his monks, 'There is, O monks, an unborn, uncreated, unproduced.' And Yuse Bhikku, when awakened, became a Buddha – no longer Yuse Bhikku because he had gone, but awakened exists, just as Buddha still exists.

There is still another aspect to awakening. Since the other side of 'I' is fear, awakening from the delusion of 'I' spells fearlessness. 'The lion's roar proclaims fearlessness.' The lion does not fear anything. He is truly the King of the Beasts, as we think of him. So 'The lion's roar proclaims fearlessness' and a newly-fledged Bodhisattva's first gesture, or Mudra, is that of fearlessness. True fearlessness indicates that 'I' has dropped off. Awakening, having come into the power of the Tathagata as the lion's roar proclaims this fearlessness, of this Yoka Daishi says, 'Alas, foolish and stubborn like old leather, people do not know it.'

At that, something in me rears up. 'I want to go the Buddha's Path and I am certainly not foolish and stubborn like old leather.' Try digging down to your most ingrained conviction, to that one on which your whole life seems to be built – that is what has to be pulled out. Are we willing to do that? 'Foolish and stubborn like old leather, people do not know it.' In our delusion we think that we are doing the training, or we learn in order to get and become more and better, in the hopes of one day being secure. But it does not go like that because, in our training, if correctly done, we do not add to ourselves. We become less and less until we finally vanish like the grin of the Cheshire Cat. When truly gone, what remains?

When everything is dropped, like Master Joshu's monk who had to drop the plants he had nurtured for over twenty years (see Commentary on Verses 3 & 4), when all that is let go of, then that which cannot be dropped is what really is, and it cannot be taken away. That is where 'The lion's roar proclaims fearlessness' and 'The lotus blooms unblemished amid the flames.' But 'foolish and stubborn' we do not know it, will not do it, will not let go. This is what is learnt in Zen training. Then it becomes alive, and we find out and learn to outgrow our personal limitations. It is the first step. When that is accomplished, a door opens on the other side, and we realize what Master Hakuin meant when he said, 'in the midst of water pitifully crying from thirst.'

60   *All they know is that grave offences obstruct the*
        attainment of enlightenment,
     And so they do not see the door of the Tathagata's
        secret teachings.
     As to the monk who had committed a murder, and the
        other guilty of a carnal offence,
     Upali's understanding of their offence is shallow, only
        further tightening their bonds.

61   *But Vimalakirti instantly dissolved their doubts*
     Like frost and snow vanish in the radiance of the hot
        midday sun.
     The power of enlightenment is utterly incomprehensible,
     The wondrous functioning is as incalculable as the
        sands of the Ganges.

62   *Then the Four Necessities are gladly offered;*
     Ten thousand pieces of yellow gold are not enough,
     Even bones crushed and body broken do not pay
     For one phrase that obliterates the Karma of millions
        of Kalpas.

63   *Tathagatas as innumerable as the sands of the Ganges*
        confirm
     That the Dharma King is of unsurpassed splendour.
     Now that I truly understand this Mani Jewel, I know
     That all true believers are in accord with it.

Commentary

'All they know is that grave offences obstruct the attainment of enlightenment.' Certainly that is the teaching as we read it in the texts, but what we then fail to see is that if we stick to the letter we miss the message. Bodhidharma expressly warned against that, for then we 'do not see the door of the Tathagata's teachings.'

We read in the teachings that the Buddha said he had an open hand, that he did not hide anything in his teachings, but elsewhere we also read that, taking up a handful of leaves, the Buddha said, 'That is what I have revealed. What still could be said is as numerous as all the other leaves around, but', he carefully added, 'that is not conducive to awakening.' In other words, there is much more to be said, much more to be seen. But if we concern ourselves with that we will go round and round, and never find the way to awakening.

If we become distracted from the Buddha's Way we are bound to lose it, but we can also go astray if we think that we know the Way and its teachings, and that 'grave offences obstruct the attainment of enlightenment.' Then we may get very rigid, become sticklers for minutiae and be quick to judge, harsh not only about others, but also about ourselves. It is useful to be aware of that trend in ourselves. Hence the Buddha proclaimed the Middle Way. At word level, what it means to me is biased. It is true, but not immutable. The Buddha-eye, or the clear eye, is necessary to actually get the message. Deep repentance may shift the obstruction, and with sufficient training, dissolve it.

The text says, 'All they know is that grave offences obstruct the attainment of enlightenment / And so do not see the door to the Tathagata's secret teachings.' There is a medieval German legend about a grave sinner who made a pilgrimage to Rome to be absolved by the Pope, but the Pope said, 'Just as the pilgrim staff in your hand will never sprout fresh green again, so nothing can save you from hell's fires.' In those days people took such things seriously. He felt, and was, ostracized; he could no longer join the other pilgrims. Alone and dejected, he walked back, truly repenting all the way, but hardly had he returned home when new green shoots were sprouting from his staff, and he knew he had been shriven.

We too have always known the hidden secret teachings of the Tathagata. But when we are too 'I'-ridden, we can, and do, forget or mistake them, and instead we follow our own imagination which leads us astray. Again, we need to cultivate the eye of No-I. The more we look the more we see how deep the Buddha's teaching is, how far it reaches, and how it shows us our connection with everything that is – a live connection with all, instead of the alienation of 'I', where we feel cut off and separate from everything else.

Yoka Daishi continues, 'As to the monk who had committed a murder, and the other one guilty of a carnal offence, / Upali's understanding of their offence is shallow, only further tightening their bonds.' The story is from the Vimalakirti Sutra. Both monks bitterly repented their transgression and confessed it to the big assembly; but they also wanted to make a personal confession, to be understood by the superior and to beg him for advice. It sounds somewhat easy – you confess, you repent and are released – but what we do not realize is why a personal confessor is deemed necessary.

It was understood that if repenting sincerely, and also confessing to somebody personally, face-to-face, the causes of one's fault would be pointed out and then admonition would strengthen one's resolve. Moreover, the confessor would expound the Buddha-dharma, and this would give the strength never ever to repeat such a fault again. Pratimokha, public confession, is still the same nowadays as it was then, and the personal one is also still quietly done. Upali was considered the keeper of the Vinaya, the rules of discipline governing the Sangha, the monastic community. He could faultlessly recite all the rules, and was known as their receptacle and as the foremost arbiter of what those rules were. The two monks went to Upali, who listened to them and recognized their repentance.

So Upali was in the middle of giving the two monks an inspiring talk when Vimalakirti came along. Although a layman, he had attained the full stature of a Bodhisattva. He is a figure marking the beginning of the Mahayana teaching, proclaiming that not only a monk but a layman too can attain deliverance from the Wheel, provided he really bestirs himself. Vimalakirti is described as a wealthy householder with wife and children, a palatial mansion, etc., but there is the hint that he was a Bodhisattva who had especially come into this world at the time of the Buddha to be of use to him and to help his disciples. So Vimalakirti, hearing Upali delivering an edifying sermon, interrupted him firmly: 'What is all this lengthy, beautiful talking about? Just look at things, look at the simple teachings. There is no 'I', there is no 'other.'

There is nothing. In that nothing, what can actually go wrong? In that nothing, who can harm whom? In that nothing, there is room to move about freely; there is no guilt, there is no fault, there is not even nothing.' When the two monks heard that they prostrated themselves and, with tears in their eyes, realized that although there was the offence that they had bitterly regretted and repented of, that in reality there was actually also no consequence.

We find ourselves here in the Mahayana teaching of the Two Truths. Of course, there is consequence in the realm of cause and effect, but that consequence cancels out, is no more, when there is nothing. Then the consequence does not affect anymore. As principle, essence or law, it is in all of us – the Buddha-nature or the True Face, it does not matter what you call it. But it is definitely not mine, has nothing whatsoever to do with me and mine. It always has been, always will be. This is what the Sixth Patriarch tried to express, when he asked, 'Before thinking of good or bad, what at that moment is the True Face before father and mother were born?' It makes the snowdrop come out from frozen ground, makes the apple tree blossom in spring, and the dahlias flower in autumn, each according to its form, and it informs each form in ways that are appropriate to that form. It is only we who offend against it, because of our 'I'-delusion. The Buddha-nature can never produce an offence, only 'I' can. And only I will reap the consequence; the principle, in itself nothing, will not.

So 'Vimalakirti instantly dissolved their doubts' by telling them that there is nothing left, because their repentance has dissolved it 'Like frost and snow vanish in the radiance of the hot midday sun.' Frost and snow stiffen and make rigid, but the rays of the hot midday sun warm them up and melt them away, just as the Buddha's teachings have the power to melt our own rigid, frozen hearts, encrusted by all our fancies of 'I' and how 'I must have it' and how 'it should be.' That being melted away, the inherent warmth of the human heart can again flow freely. That is what awakening and becoming truly human means.

Yoka Daishi adds, 'The power of enlightenment is utterly incomprehensible, / The wondrous functioning is as incalculable as the sands of the Ganges.' The power of enlightenment, of genuine insight, is not only utterly incomprehensible to me, it just is incomprehensible. In a way, it can be said that it is not, and yet it functions. We try to make it two, the power and its functioning, but it is not so. The functioning is the power, and without the power there is no functioning. So 'The power of enlightenment is utterly incomprehensible, / The wondrous functioning is as incalculable as the sands of the Ganges.' And it also has as many ramifications as the grains of sand of the Ganges. Such insight makes us very humble and very careful about whatever we do, so that, without our being really aware of it, unwittingly, we do no harm. For even trying to do good may produce further harm. It is one of our particularly human traits, laying down the law (our law, of course), and rigidly sticking to the letter of it.

'Then the Four Necessities are gladly offered.' This refers to the previous verse where it is said that, 'The power of enlightenment is utterly incomprehensible, / The wondrous functioning is as incalculable as the sands of the Ganges.' If that is incorporated, truly incorporated, 'then the Four

Necessities are gladly offered.' The Four Necessities are shelter, food, clothing and medicine. That is what a monk needs for survival, but is, in effect, also all we really need. Not only are these gladly offered to one who incorporates this incomprehensible power, but 'Ten thousand pieces of yellow gold are not enough, / Even bones crushed and body broken do not pay / For one phrase that obliterates the Karma of millions of Kalpas.'

Since beginningless time we all carry our Karma with us. We have made it and we are the result of it – just as we are, with our problems and our difficulties, with our likes and dislikes. Round and round we go on the Wheel of Change, and for the Buddhist the greatest boon is to get off that Wheel, to end the continuous round of 'coming to be and ceasing to be' through the Six Realms without end, with all the concomitant suffering. This is what the Buddhist strives for, at least to begin with. But now Yoka Daishi says that even one sentence of an enlightened being obliterates the Karma of millions of Kalpas, causes all the karmic load to drop off! Well, naturally we would give everything for that, wouldn't we? But there is another side to it, which indicates what it entails.

'Even bones crushed and body broken do not pay / For one phrase...' With bones crushed and body broken, where am I then? So the awesome point is that as long as I am there, though I pay ten thousand pieces of yellow gold, it is not sufficient. I myself have to get out of the way, I myself prohibit my deliverance, I myself am the obstacle. And even 'bones crushed and body broken' is not enough because, although that gets rid of 'I', the Karma of millions of Kalpas still remains. So what more can be exacted? Crushing bones, 'storming heaven by force' (remember that is still intentional, producing Karma) – there is no such speedy way. But one sentence may stir up the aspiration towards enlightenment, which then becomes the driving power. Thus it is possible to willingly undergo the training needed, listening to the Dharma, to the Buddha's teaching which shows the Way. And if we walk it, the karmic load of millions of Kalpas drops off.

With 'I' being what I am, I tend to deceive myself. We may believe that generous giving will somehow help us, and in a way it will, producing good Karma, but not release from the Wheel. Or we undergo fierce asceticism, but even the Buddha found this ineffective, and the Buddha's life story is always a guide to us. But one sentence stirring up the aspiration towards enlightenment at the right moment – that happened to the young man who became the Sixth Patriarch. He heard a wandering monk reciting the Diamond Sutra. One sentence, and at that moment he understood. And he himself later also delivered such a sentence, a 'turning phrase', to his pursuer – 'Before thinking, what is your True Face?'

Genuine insight means having become it, and thus functioning and living out of it. If we really, truly believe in something, we not only act in accordance with it, we cannot but do so. If I only half believe it and doubt it at the same time, or only believe it because I think I should, that cuts no ice at all. To really believe it is not that I have to obey a commandment, but is a labour of love.

We are told in Zen training that three things are necessary. First there is the Great Root of Faith, which is exactly that real deep belief in the inherent Buddha-nature. Then there is the Great Ball of Doubt, that is to always doubt myself, my fancies, opinions, convictions, and to ruthlessly ignore them. And the third one is Passionate Courage, which goes through doubt and flows into true faith, from which the strength to act in accordance with it is derived. With that comes the insight that when 'I' get out of the way and open up, 'I' and the blinkers are off. And that then naturally 'obliterates the Karma of millions of Kalpas.'

'Tathagatas as innumerable as the sands of the Ganges confirm / That the Dharma King is of unsurpassed splendour.' Here we approach the depths of Mahayana, but also what lifts us above ourselves. 'Tathagatas as innumerable as the sands of the Ganges,' and suddenly all things are Buddha-things. Veneration of the historical Buddha helps us to begin with, but then slowly, as this opens up, all things are seen as Buddha-things, we are surrounded by nothing but Buddha-things and have become one with the flow. Then we put 'things' away and are supported and guided by Buddhas all around. In the midst of the Buddhas, that is what the Dharma King actually means, in his unsurpassed splendour, that is the miracle, isn't it? You can intellectually ponder it – Buddhas all around us, on top of us, underneath us and we are gently carried by a Buddha wave! It's a lovely thought, isn't it?

Yet, as long as I am being carried, I am still there. So, what is pointed at here is actually a becoming it. And so from this insight Yoka Daishi can say, 'Now that I truly understand this Mani Jewel, I know / That all the true believers are in accord with it.' The Mani Jewel is that wish-fulfilling gem, the Buddha-dharma which stills the heart's longing. 'All true believers are in accord with it.' Again, true believing, the Great Faith, is stressed, not just believing in the head, but acting in accordance with or out of that Faith. In our ordinary daily lives, do we really act as if we believed the Buddha's teaching? To what extent do we give ourselves into the Daily Life Practice so that we forget ourselves and are, therefore, 'carried'? To what extent am I still clinging on to 'I', quietly hoping underneath, that it will be to my advantage, my insight and my this and my that? That will not bring us any further. We need the old texts as supports, for as long as there is any notion of 'I' ghosting about, it is in the head only and not yet fully incorporated. The genuine insight is still lacking.

Therefore, it is said that the first insight is relatively easy, but long and hard practice is needed to live out of it. Only then is it also irreversible and works under all circumstances. Do we naturally, always, under all circumstances, act from the heart as human beings? Or do we sometimes act like raging demons, at other times like hungry ghosts? Occasionally we are almost divine, and then again suffer hellishly, or we behave like animals, and are only rarely truly human. We pass continuously through those six states on the Wheel of Change, on and on – which is what 'the Karma of millions of Kalpas' means.

Hence the Buddha's great teaching of change. We often dislike it, for it robs us of things we hold dear. But it is not so – it is the greatest consolation. It will not last, it cannot last, whether it is the dark or whether it is the pain in the legs, whatever it is, it cannot last. This too is the Mani Jewel which Yoka Daishi is talking about. Nothing lasts.

There is an Indian story of a renowned goldsmith, who was summoned by the Raja and asked to make him a jewel. He wanted it to be supremely beautiful, yet at the same time it should be able to console and support him in distress. But should he at any time become proud and swollen with success, the jewel should make him humble and appreciate the joys in ordinary life. The goldsmith accepted the order, and a year later he came back with what seemed a simple gold ring, rather like a narrow wedding ring. The Raja, who had expected a magnificent jewel, was furious and about to have the goldsmith beheaded, but the goldsmith just said, 'Look inside.' And inside on that small golden band was written in the most beautiful Sanskrit script, 'It will pass.' We, too, can hold on to this advice and remember, 'Yes, it will pass.'

But do we truly believe that? In the midst of calamity, or faced with something we utterly dislike, do we not feel as if it is going to last forever, as if we are saddled with it for good and simply cannot bear it? Then to remember that 'it will pass' has a very real effect. And from that we may also begin to understand that the Dharma King is unsurpassed, unsurpassed in a splendour that will carry under all circumstances, good, bad or indifferent, and will help us to remain human even in the worst situations. With that we have a first taste of what the Buddha-dharma actually is.

64 *Clearly seen, not a single thing exists,*
    And there is neither human being nor Buddha.
    A Great Chiliocosm is like spray blown on the ocean,
    And sages and saints are but flashes of lightning.

65 *Even though an iron wheel was turning on one's head,*
    Though the sun may turn cold and the moon red-hot,
    The clear radiance of Dhyana and Prajna can never be lost.
    Not even all the Maras combined can destroy the true
        Teachings.

66 *The elephant steadfastly pulls the carriage uphill;*
    How could the grasshopper in the rut ward it off?
    A big elephant does not play about in a hare's track.
    Great Satori is not hemmed in by little rules.

67 *So do not try to measure with your narrow views*
    The vast expanse of heaven.
    If you have not yet understood,
    I'll sort it out for you.

Commentary

We come to the end of Yoka Daishi's *Song on the Realization of the Way*, a very carefully considered and expounded summary that has the whole of the teaching in it. 'Clearly seen, not a single thing exists, / And there is neither human being nor Buddha.' We are right in the Madhyamaka teaching – Sunyata, total voidness, which to 'I' is terrifying. Seen into, however, that is where the beauty and the miracle and the splendour is: it is only 'I' who cannot bear it.

For an unprepared 'I' to suddenly plunge into Sunyata, into wide-open vastness, is shattering. Hence our training, our Daily Life Practice, where we give ourselves into what at this moment is being done, and continue always deeper, so that a little more of 'I' drops off. I am thus softened up and chipped away at until there is so little left that the final shift is an opening towards rather than a stunning shock. Yoka Daishi points to it: 'Clearly seen, not a single thing exists / And there is neither human being nor Buddha.'

If I hear such things, I may wonder, 'What am I doing the training for? What's the use of it? Bestirring myself for nothing! Instead of becoming something more, bigger, greater, better, everything vanishes!' That is not what I want, is it? But then perhaps something happens, and things go badly wrong and I wish I were dead. What I really mean is, I would like to be rid of the problem, but actually the perception is right. If I am out of the way, dead, the problem is gone too.

For good measure, Yoka Daishi then continues, 'A Great Chiliocosm is like spray blown on the ocean / And sages and saints are but flashes of lightning.' In Hindu cosmology the numerology gets very complex, but for us ordinary Zen students it suffices to say that a Great Chiliocosm is an unimaginable number of time cycles revolving through unimaginable aeons. And yet Yoka Daishi says it is as impermanent and insubstantial as spray blown on the ocean, and that sages and saints are but flashes of lightning, and as quickly come and go. I am inclined to take that as being out there and concrete, quite forgetting that it is I, we, who have thought it up, have made all the words, all the names, all the systems. But what happens to all these if there is no 'I' there?

Master Rinzai says, 'Behold the puppets prancing on the stage and look for him behind who pulls the strings.' We forget that we live by our own thought constructions. We believe we have discovered something, but it is not true. We have only set up yet another thought construction, and all of those thought constructions change like dreams, like clouds floating across the sky, like spray blown on the ocean. Sages and saints too are but flashes of lightning; as the Buddha says, 'coming to be and ceasing to be', an unreal, swirling, ever-changing cloud or torrent which, in itself, is not, is only a dream. But a dream, whilst we are dreaming, seems extremely real. And we take things for real because we will not take in what at this moment is really given. And what is given at this moment only lasts for this moment, in the moment after it is gone, does not exist anymore. We hold on to these dead and gone moments as a memory, out of which we build all sorts of mental concepts, and believe them to be true. Moreover, they always have 'I' – my likes, concepts and opinions – as their central point, even if I try to avoid it.

Yoka Daishi continues, 'Even though an iron wheel was turning on one's head, / Though the sun may turn cold and the moon red-hot, / The clear radiance of Dhyana and Prajna can never be lost.' This iron wheel refers to an Indian story. A man walking through the jungle comes upon a man sitting in great pain with a heavy iron wheel turning on his head.

Full of compassion, he asks, 'What is that, why do you have that?' Suddenly the wheel is on his own head! The man freed of the wheel says, 'Thank you, thank you, I am so relieved. For thirty years I've been waiting for somebody to come and ask me that. Now the wheel is yours.' 'Take it away, take it away', wails the man. 'No!' says the erstwhile sufferer. 'I am glad I am rid of it', and walks away. And so the poor man sits there perhaps ten, twenty or thirty years until the next one comes and asks, and with that the wheel is on his head. And so it goes, from one to the other. It does not cease. That is the load that we all carry. In the story, the man, you and me, we all carry it, because we are all connected with each other, which we so easily forget. So forgetting the shared load, we ask, 'What is the matter with you?' Whoops, we have got it!

We are open towards each other, but not completely, because we are also selfish. Therefore, the one who just got rid of that wheel has no intention of taking it back again. As a matter of fact, come to think of it, one wonders whether he could take it back again. Rolling on, you cannot make a moment that has gone come back again. It is only this moment, now, and this moment has to be taken and lived as it is.

What I did five minutes ago or yesterday... oh, I wish I could make it different, wish I could change it! It is not possible. If we are clear on that, then we might perhaps also be more careful, not only with what we actually do and say, but we might even realize that what we do and say affects both ourselves and others and sends out wide ripples. But in a way it is all a shadow play that in itself has no substance. 'Though the sun may turn cold and the moon red-hot' –

in other words, in the most unbelievable circumstances – 'The clear radiance of Dhyana and Prajna can never be lost.'

There is that principle or law that gives rise to things or does not give rise to things. As a principle, a law, it is in itself nothing. It is not a thing, not a phenomenon. We call it law and make it a mental 'thing', but it is not that either, just a name that we give to it. That is where we truly go into the void and, floating about in that void, are not different from it, and not the same either. All the Chiliocosms and all the sages and saints are insubstantial, like blown spray and flashes of light-ning. In this multiplicity of constant change, whatever it is or is not, in whatever convolution it distorts itself or smoothly flows, 'Even though an iron wheel was turning on one's head, / Though the sun may turn cold and the moon red-hot, / The clear radiance of Dhyana and Prajna can never be lost.'

The clear radiance of that principle, of insight into and certainty of the principle, can never vanish, neither can the oneness with it be lost if once forged by thorough train-ing. 'Not even all the Maras combined can destroy the true Teachings', and however much we may bemoan the fact that there is so much misunderstanding, so much short-cutting of the real values, the principle is, and cannot be lost. So all the Maras, Mara's daughters and Mara's demons, cannot destroy the working principle, because it is not a 'thing' that can be destroyed. It just is, irrespective of what is tried or is not tried. Mara has lost his power and, having lost it, Mara himself also turns into this principle.

Something else that is important for us needs to be said about Mara. In the Western view, from the old Persians onwards and in us too, we have split this principle into two opposing halves, of good and bad, of right and wrong. These oppose and fight with each other and we hope will end with the good, the right, winning, and with the wrong, the bad, vanquished and extirpated, completely and forever. Because of our judgements, we see them as irreconcilably split, split as two opposites at war with each other. This split is in us too, and has made us Westerners remarkably aggressive, always willing and ready to rid the world of what we call 'wrong'.

Carried by his insight and compassion, Yoka Daishi composed this very long and beautiful poem to help others. At the very end, in the last few lines, he sums it all up. The poem is full of allusions yet gives clear indications. The Chinese have a knack for using concrete, earthy analogies for things which otherwise are extremely difficult to encompass. If we take these analogies at their face value, we go wrong. If we can see where they point to, then we see the moon rather than the pointing finger.

'The elephant steadfastly pulls the carriage uphill.' An elephant does not prance about, it is too big an animal. He does not even run very often, but has tremendous stamina and just keeps on walking, step by step, and 'steadfastly pulls the carriage uphill'. This is what we need to do in our training. If we only rely on 'I', we will soon give up. We all know how it goes: 'Oh, this is too difficult, I can't do that.' 'I would like to, but I can't bring it off.' 'I don't feel very well today.' 'I have no time today.' 'It's a busy day at the office, I can't bother with the practice.' We use every possible excuse, and then are surprised that nothing happens. But 'the elephant steadfastly pulls the carriage uphill.'

Yoka Daishi asks, 'How could the grasshopper in the rut ward it off?' All those millions of grasshoppers out there are the various delusions of myself, of 'I', who thinks that this might be the right way, or that that might be a better way, who is full of my ideas, notions and convictions. But the 'heart inclines towards Nirvana, slides towards Nirvana, tends to Nirvana.' My little bits of this and that will not ward off a heart aware of its inclination.

Still another important analogy is contained in it. 'The elephant steadfastly pulls the carriage uphill; / How could the grasshopper in the rut ward it off?' If we take the elephant as the karmic linkage that rolls steadily on, how could I possibly think that I could stop it or ward it off? There is only one way, and that is through the Buddha's great lion's roar that can wear it out. Following the Buddha's Way, little by little the karmic linkage begins to drop off. Karma cannot be warded off, that is silly, but it can be worn out. We need to be clear about that and, like the elephant, willingly and steadfastly pull that carriage uphill until it gets lighter and lighter, and then ceases to be a carriage.

For good measure, Yoka Daishi adds, 'A big elephant does not play about in a hare's track.' A big elephant cannot play about in a hare's track! In our deluded littleness, we do not know what a 'big elephant' stands for. The human heart is not a little thing. Like everything else, it contains the whole principle, is informed by it. When that really opens, then 'I', with my silly little ideas, am just blown away. The more usual phrase for this is, 'A big fish does not flit about in a valley brook.'

If you really want to see what is within, what 'big elephants', you only need to spend a night alone in some remote place. Or when awakened in the small hours of the morning by a board creaking or some such thing, we easily get frightened. There is, moreover, an irrational fear in us which leads back to what we actually are, but which is too big for our little 'I' to realize. So we hang between two poles, and to be able to realize it we need training. To try to rush at it is, at best, counterproductive. And if we try to avoid it, it will not leave us alone, for it is our own ground of being. So 'A big elephant does not play about in a hare's track.' It is far too big for it. To realize that, and to be able to bow in front of it – that is when we find our own roots.

'Great Satori is not hemmed in by little rules.' We have imaginary notions of what it is, or we would not attempt a training. However misinterpreted, there is an undeniable urge within us – the heart pulling, inclining towards its own roots, and it will give no peace. But it 'is not hemmed in by little rules', by 'my' understanding. 'Of course it is not hemmed in by little rules, a liberated man can do whatever he wants,' I say, and act accordingly. But as long as there is an 'I', there can be no deliverance. And a liberated being no longer has any wants, but just is; truly is in the situation, working and responding to the situation. We mistake it only too easily or, getting too close too quickly, become frightened. So we need careful preparation – hence the training – in order to be able to open up towards that which is the 'big elephant'. He is also inside.

'So do not try to measure with your narrow views / The vast expanse of heaven.' What we know, or what we think we know, is only what comes in through our sense organs. What is outside, the object itself or the thing, we cannot know, we only imagine it. In our foolishness we imagine that we can understand somebody else, which we can't. We sentimentalize about animals and give them human traits, which is simply silly. We imagine things that we know do not exist. Our present spiritually impoverished age is full of fantasies, New Age and otherwise. It is all in our head, and it obscures even what we perceive with our sense organs, but, with our little views, we do not realize that. 'Great Satori is not hemmed in by little rules. / So do not try to measure with your narrow views / The vast expanse of heaven.'

At the end of the Bull-herding analogy the Great Being returns to the marketplace with bliss-bestowing hands. He is not large by stature, he only seems large because he no longer has any fear, and so is no longer an 'I'. Somebody who has that stature strikes us as great, as having a special ambience, and he is portrayed carrying a big bundle on the end of his staff and a little calabash on his arm. The bundle contains goodies to help people go further when they have lost their courage or their energy, but in that little calabash is the mystery of what is. We, with our little views, want to look, want to understand mysteries, see what is in them, 'then I will know', but a mystery cannot be known. As far as I am concerned, the only way to confront a mystery is to bow down before it and revere it. In so bowing reverently, the heart can open and partake, but this transcends thought, is incommunicable.

And that is precisely what the heart needs and longs for because, in that moment, it has become at one with that Presence, is liberated from the narrow limits of 'I', and is taking part in the great game of life. And it is a game, however terrible or painful it sometimes is. That 'vast expanse of heaven' cannot be caught and encompassed within our little views.

Yoka Daishi, having tried his best to explain it to us, finishes, 'If you have not yet understood, / I'll sort it out for you.' In other words, if you have not yet understood, come and undertake some real training if you wish, and in that real training you will find the Way and be able to walk it too. There is a long-standing Zen saying that 'the old masters had ways of making men (women too) whole human beings'. That is the Great Being at the end of the Bull-herding analogy who is liberated from the bonds on the Wheel but voluntarily remains to be of use to the beings suffering in their bondage. That is the Buddha's lion's roar and Yoka Daishi's message – there is a Way out. Whether we want to follow it or not is up to us. The Way is open.